REGENCY PROFESSIONAL EDITION

spdri srlhn dcly + TS1*

Joe M. Pullis, Ed.D.

Professor, Department of Office Administration and Business Communication
College of Administration and Business
Louisiana Tech University

GLENCOE/McGRAW-HILL
A Macmillan/McGraw-Hill Company
Mission Hills, California

****Speedwriting* SHORTHAND DICTATION AND TRANSCRIPTION**

Cheryl D. Pullis, M.Ed.
System Consultant

Peggy Runnels
Contributor

Send all inquiries to:
Glencoe/McGraw-Hill
15319 Chatsworth Street
P.O. Box 9609
Mission Hills, CA 91346-9609
Printed in the United States of America

ISBN 0-02-685130-X (Student Text)
ISBN 0-02-685140-7 (Student Transcript)
ISBN 0-02-685150-4 (Instructor's Guide)

3 4 5 6 7 8 9   92 91 90

CONTENTS

Setting Your Goals

Now that you have completed your study of the *Principles of Speedwriting Shorthand, Regency Professional Edition*, you are ready to continue developing your shorthand skills. Before beginning the study of *Speedwriting Shorthand Dictation and Transcription*, ask yourself these questions. What do I expect from this course? How can I improve my skills?

You should set meaningful goals for yourself. Although speed building is excellent training, recording dictation is only one part of the shorthand process. Refining your English usage skills and knowing how to keyboard, spell, and punctuate correctly are also important. Remember that the primary purpose of dictation is to produce top-quality correspondence. Once a letter has been dictated to you, it is up to you to turn your notes into an impressive, mailable transcript that reflects well on you and your employer.

Guidelines for using the text are presented in this introduction. By using proper study habits from the beginning, you will be able to develop various skills simultaneously. This text is designed to help you

1. increase your shorthand writing speed
2. improve your transcribing efficiency
3. increase your shorthand vocabulary
4. increase your knowledge of business terms
5. improve your spelling ability
6. improve your punctuation skills

7. increase your knowledge of keyboarding and formatting techniques
8. increase your knowledge of office procedures

KNOWING THE TEXT'S STRUCTURE

The text is divided into 12 units. The dictation material in each unit relates to a specific field, such as "Information Processing" or "Real Estate." The subject matter will help broaden your knowledge of terms and procedures related to these 12 areas. The five lessons in each unit represent a combination of skill-building information and exercises.

Each unit begins with a review of one or more *Speedwriting Shorthand* principles. Shorthand vocabulary words that illustrate the principle or principles are selected from the letters and memos presented in the unit. Also, in the opening section of each unit, punctuation rules are given and are illustrated with example sentences. Punctuation usage is reinforced in the letters and memos that follow, and frequently used rules of punctuation are highlighted in the Reading and Writing Exercises.

Speedwriting Shorthand principles and specific applications of the system are reviewed in each lesson, as follows:

Theory Review. The first lesson of each unit contains a brief form and phrase review; the second lesson, an abbreviation review; the third and fourth lessons, a shorthand vocabulary review; and the fifth lesson, word development.

Transcription Aids. Transcription aids such as English usage and formatting procedures, similar words, and spelling are provided in the second, third, and fourth lessons, respectively, in each unit.

Your Business Vocabulary. Business terms that appear in the dictation material are defined and illustrated with example sentences.

Reading and Writing Exercises. A combination of five letters and memos is presented in each lesson. The fifth letter or memo of each lesson includes a punctuation exercise in which you will provide commas that have been omitted from the shorthand copy. Numbers indicating the typing words for each line of shorthand have been provided for determining your transcription speed.

Beginning in Lesson 52, the fourth letter in each lesson includes an exercise in supplying missing shorthand outlines. You will be asked to provide an acceptable word for each of the two outlines that have been omitted from the shorthand copy.

USING YOUR TEXT

Prepare for each lesson carefully:

1. Read and write the example outlines in the *Shorthand Vocabulary Review* sections.

2. Study the concepts presented in the *Transcription Aid* and *Your Business Vocabulary* sections.
3. Study the punctuation drills. Think about each rule and how it is applied in the letters and memos that follow.
4. Read all shorthand (aloud, if possible) before writing it. If you cannot identify a particular outline, sound-spell the outline. If the translation is not readily apparent, continue reading to the end of the sentence. If the context of the sentence does not help you to read the outline, use the Student Transcript.
5. Now write your shorthand copy as rapidly as possible, being careful to write correctly. Speed is important, but legibility is essential.
6. Read your notes aloud. If you are called upon later to read your notes in class, your reading fluency will be enhanced by your previous practice.

REVIEWING PUNCTUATION RULES

In *Principles of Speedwriting Shorthand, Regency Professional Edition*, you studied eight rules of punctuation commonly used in business correspondence. These rules are also highlighted in the Reading and Writing Exercises presented in *Speedwriting Shorthand Dictation and Transcription*. Review these rules thoroughly before proceeding.

Use commas between three or more words in a series. The last word in a series will be preceded by either of these two words: *and*, *or*. In this text, we will always place a comma before *and* and *or* in a series. Some offices, however, may prefer that this comma be omitted. Use the style preferred in your office.

- ☐ An agenda will be written, typed, *and* distributed in advance of the meeting.
- ☐ Would you prefer to pay the bill with cash, with a check, *or* with a credit card?

Use commas after introductory dependent clauses. An introductory dependent clause is a group of words containing a subject and a verb that occurs at the beginning of a sentence. However, this clause is not a complete thought and cannot stand alone. It requires a main (independent) clause to make the sentence complete.

Introductory dependent clauses usually begin with recognizable words. The most common words are *when*, *as*, and *if*. Other common examples are *although*, *though*, *unless*, *since*, *while*, *until*, *before*, *whether*, and *because*.

- ☐ *When* the contract arrives, I will sign and return your copy immediately.
- ☐ *As* Cynthia read the revised report, she noted the recent modifications.
- ☐ *If* you mail the forms today, Mr. Harris should receive them by Friday.

Use commas with nouns of direct address. A direct address is a specific reference to a person's name, title, and/or other designation. When the direct address occurs in the middle of the sentence, place a comma before and after it. If the direct address occurs at the beginning or at the end of the sentence, use only one comma.

- ☐ I would be delighted, Senator Walker, to join your committee.
- ☐ We would greatly appreciate your help, Mrs. Cunningham.

Use commas with appositives. An appositive is a word or group of words that explains, renames, or identifies someone or something that immediately precedes it in the sentence. Appositives usually are set off by commas from the rest of the sentence.

- ☐ My assistant, Allen Colvin, will meet you at the airport.
- ☐ I enjoyed reading Mrs. Cooper's new book, *Today's Office*.

Use commas with parenthetical expressions. A parenthetical expression is a word or group of words that interrupts the natural flow of the sentence. These expressions are often used to add emphasis or show contrast, but when removed from the sentence, they do not change the meaning of the sentence.

When a parenthetical expression occurs in the middle of the sentence, place a comma before and after it. If the expression occurs at the beginning or the end of the sentence, use only one comma. Some common examples of parenthetical expressions are *for example, therefore, however, furthermore, of course*, and *in fact*.

- ☐ We did, in fact, ship the order as requested.
- ☐ Furthermore, Mr. Morrison did not indicate the time of his arrival.

Use commas to set off dates in sentences. When naming a day of the week, followed by the date, place a comma after the day of the week and the date. If the date falls at the end of the sentence, place a comma only after the day of the week.

- ☐ I will arrive on Tuesday, March 7, at approximately 10 a.m.
- ☐ Please return the enclosed form by Friday, July 1.

Use a comma before coordinate conjunctions. When two complete thoughts are connected by the conjunctions *and, or, but, for, nor,* place a comma before the conjunction. Make certain that the conjunction is connecting two complete thoughts—that is, either thought can stand alone without the rest of the sentence.

- □ The order was placed on Thursday afternoon, *and* the shipment left our warehouse on the following afternoon.
- □ We received your check, *but* the order form was not enclosed in your letter.

Use commas with introductory phrases. Place a comma after an introductory infinitive phrase (a verb preceded by *to*).

- □ *To* ensure completion of the project, we are reassigning responsibilities.

Place a comma after an introductory participial phrase (a verb form used as an adjective).

- □ *Taking* care to avoid errors, we will produce the report as quickly as possible.

Place a comma after an introductory prepositional phrase or phrases consisting of five or more words, or after an introductory prepositional phrase containing a verb form.

- □ In agreement with the terms of the contract, we will deliver the first shipment at no additional charge.
- □ After talking with Mrs. Irwin, I am convinced that we should proceed with our plan.

UNIT ONE

EMPLOYMENT

SHORTHAND VOCABULARY REVIEW

The following words will occur in the letters and memos in this unit. Read the principles and practice the words before beginning your study of this unit.

1. Write *ℬ* for the word endings *bil*, *ble* (*bul*), or *bly*.

capable	*cpℬ*	comfortable	*kflℬ*
available	*avlℬ*	dependable	*dpnℬ*
possible	*psℬ*	eligible	*eljℬ*
responsible	*rspℬ*	favorable	*fvrℬ*
responsibility	*rspℬ*	reliable	*rliℬ*

aso ndn alo sln frn vpn

Dcs parl Dapr llg ra X

plzr cn' vpln psℬ ac asr

2. Write [shorthand symbol] for the sound of *st* (pronounced *est*).

best [shorthand]

justify [shorthand]

outstanding [shorthand]

Boston [shorthand]

staff [shorthand]

understand [shorthand]

tests [shorthand]

store [shorthand]

assistance [shorthand]

finest [shorthand]

request [shorthand]

system [shorthand]

LESSON 1

BRIEF FORMS AND DERIVATIVES

Brief forms and abbreviations are used to develop hundreds of new words called **derivatives**. Review the examples below before beginning the Reading and Writing Exercises.

1. *v* *d* *·* *ʒ* *ℓ* *u* *p* *bs*

2. *O* *ℓ* *du̱* *la* *f* *ɔ* *kp* *ks*

3. *apo* *δ̓* *ap-* *prs* *rfɴ* *ogʃ*

Key

1. of/have/very, would, a/an, as/was, will/well, your, please/up, business

2. over, letter, during, that, from, work/world, complete, consider

3. appropriate, ability, appreciated, employers, reference, organizational

PHRASE REVIEW

1. *ɪd* *ɪvh* *ɪ* *ɪhp* *ɪblv* *ɪcb*

2. *er* *ev* *edlc* *el* *ec*

3. *uʒ* *uc* *ul* *ʟc* *f* *ʌ*

Key

1. I would, I have had, I am, I hope, I believe, I can be

2. we are, we have, we would like, we will, we can

3. you are, you can, you will, to make, for the, it is

■ **READING AND WRITING EXERCISES** ■

The following letters contain many brief forms and commonly used business words. Before beginning each letter, practice the preview words. Then see how quickly you can read and write the letter.

PREVIEW WORDS

1. resumé *(shorthand)*
 helpful *(shorthand)*
 guidance *(shorthand)*
 justify *(shorthand)*

 career *(shorthand)*
 interest *(shorthand)*
 education *(shorthand)*
 forward *(shorthand)*

2. West *(shorthand)*
 routine *(shorthand)*
 answers *(shorthand)*
 Jennifer *(shorthand)*

 inquiry *(shorthand)*
 interview *(shorthand)*
 therefore *(shorthand)*
 willingness *(shorthand)*

3. result *(shorthand)*
 data *(shorthand)*
 described *(shorthand)*
 placement *(shorthand)*

 accounting *(shorthand)*
 appointment *(shorthand)*
 expansion *(shorthand)*
 extensive *(shorthand)*

4. minds *(shorthand)*
 reward *(shorthand)*
 Fields *(shorthand)*
 quickly *(shorthand)*

 Jerry *(shorthand)*
 pleasure *(shorthand)*
 exceptional *(shorthand)*
 independently *(shorthand)*

5. image *(shorthand)*
 things *(shorthand)*
 succeed *(shorthand)*
 logical *(shorthand)*

 document *(shorthand)*
 academic *(shorthand)*
 attractive *(shorthand)*
 dependability *(shorthand)*

1

Mrs. Jane Rogers, Department of Business Education, Pierpoint High School, 166 Winthrop Avenue, Portland, ME 04101

Conj

Intro DC

Conj

2

Mrs. Jane Rogers, Department of Business Education, Pierpoint High School, 166 Winthrop Avenue, Portland, ME 04101

Ap

Ap

Conj

Paren

Paren

Series

Series

3

Mr. Nathaniel Watson, Campus View Residence Hall, Room 314, 711 West Kingsport Road, St. Louis, MO 36131

Paren

Intro P

Intro P

Intro DC

4

Ms. Carolyn S. White, Personnel Director, McCormick Allied Corporation, 4300 South Woodburn Avenue, Charlotte, NC 28210

Intro DC

Intro DC

Series

Series

Series

Series

5

Four commas are missing from the following letter. Read the letter for meaning, then place a comma after the two introductory dependent clauses and after the words in a series.

Ms. Barbara Conners, 10073 Red Rock Drive, Denver, CO 80237

5

12

17

22

27

33

38

43

49

54

60

66

a v lgs lS- abv, 72
dmSra ogjl scls 79
b lS inf n . ljcl 87
od, dmSra lp + 93
spl scls b P . 99
fnl cpe la , alrcv 105
+ fre v errs, rmbr 111
laur l lrn- f pzl 120
ur sc, if u -pv 127
c -y vu Pdc ul 134
v . dcm la spcs 140
hl vu qlffs, ul 149

LESSON

ABBREVIATIONS AND DERIVATIVES

1. co q dpt mo att
2. rec enc inf + av

Key

1. company, question, department, month, attention
2. record, enclose/enclosure, information, and, advertising

TRANSCRIPTION AID

Typing/Keyboarding Materials. The following items are essential for good transcription practices:

1. Dictionary: Use it for correct spellings, definitions, and pronunciations.
2. Zip code directory: Use correct zip codes to speed mail delivery.
3. Address file: Keep a file for frequently used addresses and phone numbers.
4. Secretarial handbook: Use it to prepare written communications; to supply postal, telephone, and telegraphic information; and to assist in other office activities.
5. English usage manual: Use it for punctuation, grammar, and other related information.
6. Supplies: Use items such as paper clips, staplers, rubber bands, and colored pens to organize your materials for transcription.

YOUR BUSINESS VOCABULARY

confirm kfr — To verify or make certain of.

□ This letter is to confirm your reservations for September 23.

public relations — pb rlys — Methods used to build goodwill with the public.

□ We are interviewing applicants who have a strong background in public relations.

READING AND WRITING EXERCISES

PREVIEW WORDS

1 useful usf, public pb, overlook Olc, unusual uuz, creative crav, impression pry, frequently frqNl, intelligent nlyN

2 Jordan jrdn, computer kpur, automation aty, language lgy, subscribe sS, ordinary ord, appreciation apy, relationship rlys

3 Webb wb, Janet jnt, further frtr, fashion fy, firm fr, graduating gry, advancement avNm, outstanding olSN

4 assume asm, contract kc, excellent xlN, comfortable kftB

Boston *bSn*

brochure *brsr*

relocating *rlca*

transportation *Tpl*

5 extra *X*

Thursday *Th*

confirm *kfr*

register *rjSr*

direct *dr*

understand *USM*

middle *dl*

supervisor *Svzr*

1

Mr. Ray Ottmier, Manager, Appleton Manufacturing Company, 4300 Arlington Avenue, Trenton, NJ 08690

d ra ι rsv- ⌐ alC- L v aplcy f . yq cly SdM, bcz ⸣ uuz⸒ ⌐ brq_ / lu all, if u cM suq . pzy f h⸒ Ph ucd sM cpes v L l r ol Srs⸒ ⌐ yq m aprs lb crav⸒ nlyM⸒ + egr l c . q pry, h hs uz-⸒ L l dmSra

(Intro DC)
(Intro DC)
(Series)
(Series)

, Bl l sl Pdcs, n ls cs⸒ (Pdc) hsf⸒ ⸒ nly vr eqpm l b usf n ol as, f ex⸒ du ev . opn_ n r Av_ dpl x pt rlys dl aol psBl⸒ + e frqMl nd adyl hlp n Ppr_ r sls cal⸒ qlf- ppl r dfc l fM, id n M l Olc ls ι, s

(Paren)
(Paren)
(Conj)

2

Mr. James H. Jordan, New Century Computerworld Stores, 7401 Executive Park, Akron, OH 44313

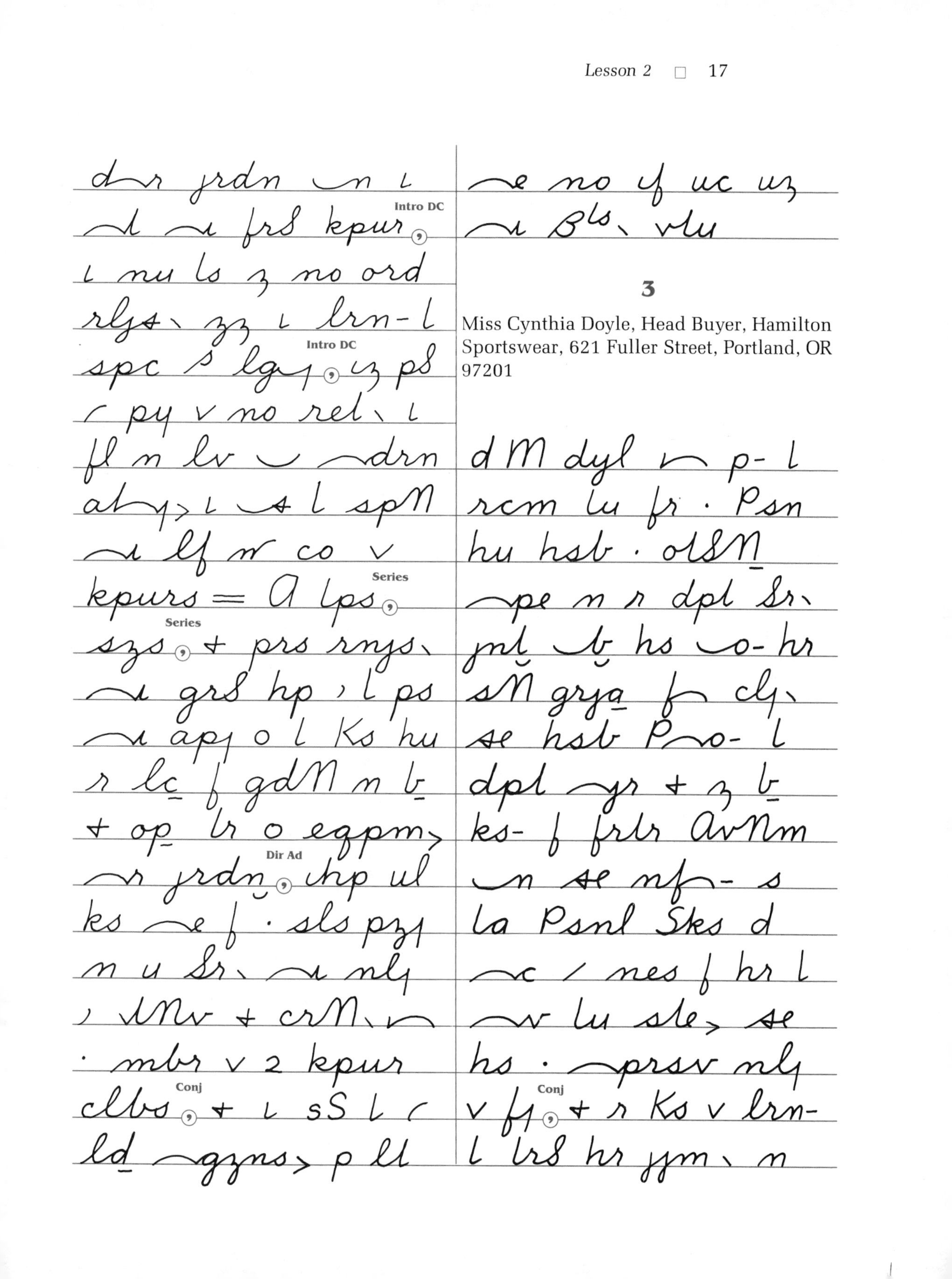

3

Miss Cynthia Doyle, Head Buyer, Hamilton Sportswear, 621 Fuller Street, Portland, OR 97201

ady l hr rglr
dles, *Intro P* se hs oq- lrn
sys f nu pes +
hlp- pln sv sls
P js, ublv la jnl
, . cpB Psn f
pzj u dS- + l kb
grl l (suc vu
rll bo. p ll e
no f ucb v frlr
assN. su

4

Mr. Wayne Dobson, 43154 Cardinal Lane, Cincinnati, OH 45214

dr dbsn er dli-
la uv jyn- r fr +
lb w u fl l
bSn nx o. p alo
s l hlp n ne a
ec, ze Dcs- erlr, *Intro DC*
r co l as kp
rspSl fu w. ev

. kc . lcl w
fr C Prds A Tply
Svss f nu pes. ls
co hs . lM rec +
cb lrS- l hMl u
fnS uhs, n enc
. brsr f (w
ajM. ls inf l asr
me vu qs + hlp
u pln u w. zz
uv dsd- o . apx
da fu w, *Intro DC* p fn
r ofs lc sp
plns, bcz eno la
rlca cb dfc, *Intro DC* el
du A ec lc u fl
kflS hr. ul

5

Five commas are missing from the following letter. Place one after each of the three introductory dependent clauses, after the parenthetical expression, and before the conjunction.

Mr. C. David Moore, 5202 Willow Cove Drive, Apartment 2A, Tampa, FL 33617

dr — ls L , l 7
kfr u apym f Th 14
afnn, ze Dcs- b 21
Ulfn i rsv- u L 27
+ rz a, hoE s 33
a · q ida l brq 39
· X cpe —n u k 44
f Nvu, yf s psB 52
el fl ls pzy b r 59
—dl v nx —c, 63
s crN Svzs , lv 70
S N v —o + 76
edlc hr rplsm 82

lv r bnfl v —o 88
— hr, ul —e — 94
sv ppl —l ur hr, 101
eblv la · q Ndcj 108
l r fsl + Sf 114
hlps · aplcN l 118
USN s opjs + 124
dsd yf h or se 128
—so l bk · —pe, 134
—n u arv p rySr 141
S frN dsc, s—i 146
l ln dr u l —u 152
ofs, uvl 157

LESSON 3

SHORTHAND VOCABULARY REVIEW

Write the months of the year as follows:

January	Ja	July	Jl
February	Fb	August	Ag
March	Mr	September	Sp
April	Ap	October	Oc
May	Ma	November	Nv
June	Jn	December	Dc

TRANSCRIPTION AID

Similar Words

weather *ltr* The condition of our atmosphere.

□ The weather today is mild and sunny.

whether *ltr* Used in an indirect question to indicate an alternative.

□ Please let me know whether or not you plan to attend.

YOUR BUSINESS VOCABULARY

priority *prirl* Precedence; having a high ranking in order of importance.

□ Answering the telephone should take priority over all other duties.

anticipate *alspa* Expect to happen.

□ We anticipate having the report finished ahead of time.

READING AND WRITING EXERCISES

PREVIEW WORDS

1 claims *chs*

contact *klc*

previous *Pves*

expansion *ypny*

priority *prvr*

inquiring *nq*

notation *nly*

performance *Pfm*

2 weather *hr*

transfer *Tfr*

thought *U*

positive *pzv*

Denver *dnvr*

materials *trels*

physician *fzr*

controlling *kl*

3 resign *rzn*

exciting *vl*

refuse *rfz*

include *l*

National *nyl*

Publications *pbys*

departure *dplr*

conventions *kvnys*

4 second *sec*

network *nlo*

directly *drl*

whether *hr*

specific *sp*

assistant *assln*

international *Nnyl*

immediately *ml*

5 branch *brnc*

select *slc*

yesterday *ysrd*

candidate *cddl*

equally	eqll	anticipate	alspa
excellent	xln	continuing	ku

1

Miss Charlotte Marie Robinson, 535 Latigo Circle, Salt Lake City, UT 84120

Intro DC

Intro P

Conj

Intro DC

2

Memo to Eric Hunter from Kyle Anderson, SUBJECT: Request for Transfer

Intro P

Paren

dnvr d v . pzv
efc o ~ hll,
chp (co l ks ~
Pves rec n ~c s
dsp, rsM akms
l dv nu drels
f Pss f lS ~ans,
c Aso dzn- . ~
efsM ss f kl
yl flo, clc fw l
~ f (r ~ ls co,
cd no lc (opl
Lvc lz s ~ cMs
v kbzs N dnvr
ofs,

3

Mr. Fred Evanston, Vice President for Administration, Freepont Company, 19 Industrial Park, Milwaukee, WI 53217

d frd af q yrs ~
ls co, iv ~d (
Intro P
dfc dsy l rzn

f ~ dles z yr
v ~r + slo, nyl
pbzs hs asc- ~e
l bk s jn ~ yr, +
Conj
ls , . pzy c fM l
u l rfz, n ~
nu ofs clb pln +
dr . pny Pq ~c
l l sv nu Pdc
lns, cl A b NS-
n u fr, + c ~
Conj
u ku- suc, ~ k
o se me v ~
frMs (bs kvnys,
ec A cl p o nz
+ ~Cny cdas, ~
dplr da lb Aq 18,
ull c lv, cl du
Intro DC
A u l ad (Tfr
v rsp8 ls l ~
rplsm, uvl

4

Ms. Michelle Gregory, 5443 Amherst, Brooklyn, NY 11235

Intro DC

Intro DC

5

Six commas are missing from the following letter. Use commas to set off the two conjunctions, the introductory dependent clause, the parenthetical expression, and the introductory phrase.

Mr. Walter G. Richards, Tyler Personnel Specialists, 219 Alpine Avenue, Grand Rapids, MI 49503

5
13
19
25
32
39
47
53
61
67
73
79

n usu kcs / n 86
nes, r fMl n u 92
dS- ySrd hs lN 99
qlfjs + h hs agre- 105
l e s o Fb3, 112
edu n hoE alspa 118

c · dsj f sv 124
cs, bcz v nCr 130
v ls pzj el Nvu 137
z me aplcNs z 142
nes l fN r S 147
cpB Psn, su 154

LESSON

SHORTHAND VOCABULARY REVIEW

Write O for the sound of *ow* (ou). Always write the sound of *ow* in an outline.

background bcgroN | proud prod
now no | out ol
however hoE | sound soN

TRANSCRIPTION AID

Spelling. Many words contain similar sounds. The word endings *able* and *ible* sound alike. Learn the correct spelling of the following words that commonly occur in business correspondence. When you are in doubt about the spelling of a word, **look it up in the dictionary.** Your employer will count on you to spell correctly.

Words ending in *able*	**Words ending in *ible***
dependable dpNB	responsible rspB
capable cpB	possible psB
valuable vluB	flexible flxB
payable paB	eligible eljB
available avlB	deductible ddcB

YOUR BUSINESS VOCABULARY

data dla — Information that has been sequenced and organized for analysis.

□ We will make our decision based upon the data that we have available.

supportive *splv* To provide strength or assistance for; to boost morale.

□ The employees have indicated that they will be supportive of company policy.

READING AND WRITING EXERCISES

PREVIEW WORDS

1	science	*siN*	reports	*rpts*
	projects	*Pjcs*	electronics	*elncs*
	shortly	*srtl*	settled	*stl-*
	worthwhile	*rtl*	contributions	*kbjs*
2	data	*dta*	reliable	*rliB*
	thorough	*tro*	bookkeeping	*bccp*
	once	*oN*	resource	*rsrs*
	possible	*psB*	qualifications	*qlfjs*
3	staff	*Sf*	college	*clj*
	advantage	*avj*	confidence	*kfdN*
	educational	*ejcjl*	generous	*jnrs*
	situation	*sij*	scholarship	*sclrs*
4	Olson	*olsn*	answer	*asr*
	American	*a*	dedication	*ddcj*

regard re	apparent aprN
conditions kdjs	supportive splv
5 rarely rrl	effective efcv
someday s-d	commented kN-
varied vre-	demanding dm
favorable fvrB	workload old

1

Dr. Emerson Harper, 3001 Sherbrooke, Montreal, PQ H3C 3A4

ddr hrpr u acN v ls pzj k z Nrf nz, u p n elncs + kpur siN lb v gr vlu l s, lr r 2 v pl Pjcs C l bgn srll af u arv, n od lgv u bcgroN inf o

Intro P

, enc 2 rpls fu l rd no, ino laur v bze v prprys

Conj

, b ifl Sln la r spN o lz rpls l pv v rll n u bgn u o hr, er lc fu l r kbjs ul c l r Pq, if lr , ne i ofs c du l asS u n gl sll-

Intro DC

hr, p ll e no, vlu

2

Miss Mary Elizabeth Thomason, Business Education Department, Clarence Downing High School, 1010 Brandstater Avenue, Riverside, CA 92325

[shorthand] d ⌒re er pM r
opjs n dla Pss_ *[Conj]*
+ ⌒ ru l asc u
l rcm . SdM hu
⸴ scl-n ak_ or
bccp⸴ ls Psn ⌒S
b rluβ + rde l
as⌒ . f lvl v
rspβˡ⸴ c u suq
s⌒l hu ⌒es lᵧ
qlfjs× yf ⌒ asr⸴
ys *[Intro DC]* p v ⌒ eljβ
cddl cl ⌒e ᵧᵧ
psβ⸴ ev · lro lrn_
Pq f nu ⌒pes *[Conj]* +
edlc l nrl u
SdM ru a a⸴ uv
a b · lM rsrs
f s *[Dir Ad]* ⌒re⸴ e vlu
u yym⸴ ihp uc
hlp s oM aq⸴ su

3

Mrs. Susan Miller, Personnel Manager, Prescott Corporation, 103 Valley Vista Way, Nashville, TN 37214

[shorthand] d rs ⌒lr lqf
nvⁱ ⌒e l bk ·
mlⁱ vu Sf⸴ ⌒
p- la uv An kfdM
n ⌒ι βˡᵧ ⌒n e
lc- lβ ⌒c *[Intro DC]* ι dd
n blv la ιdb
β l ku ⌒ι cl ᵧ
eᵧcp⸴ hoⱸ *[Paren]* la suᵧ
sdnl Cnᵧ- ⌒n ιᵧ
ofr- · f sclⱼ⸴ Alo
⟋ ⌒ms la ιcn
ac u ynrs ofr *[Intro DC]*
yfl lai ⌒S lc
avᵧ v ls eᵧcᵧl
opl⸴ ⟋ d vⁱ ·
plᵧr ⌒o ⌣ u⸴
f ⌒ dSᵧ u gv *[Intro P]*
⌒e ⸴ ιᵧ Sln la ls

Intro DC

Dir Ad

Intro DC

4

Mr. Carlyle Olson, American Electronics, 2201 West 54 Street, Baltimore, MD 21228

Conj

5

Place commas in the letter below. Use commas to set off the introductory phrase, two conjunctions, and two parenthetical expressions.

Mr. Edward A. Cox, Rural Route 7, Box 553, Lincoln, NE 68502

8

17

23

28

34

39

45

ho lq / lcs c 50
r arms llb v 57
l i nu h v 61
sn, l alspa me 66
ol Cnys ahd, i 71
dles lb vre- + 78
old lb qi dm, 84
ndls lsa ls , r 90
opl w lq a- 97

f + Sln la 102
llb uz A v scls 109
w o- so hrd 113
l dv, u spl hs 119
m . gr dl l e, 124
chp la s d llb 130
B l hlp s l z 135
uv hlp- e, cu 143

LESSON 5

WORD DEVELOPMENT

Build new words using the following brief forms:

after

aftermath af-l

afternoon afnn

afterward afw

hereafter hraf

by

bylaws blas

bypass bps

thereby lrb

nearby nrb

be

becoming bk_

before bf

maybe -ab

became bk

can

candy cde

cancellation csly

cannot cn

candid cdd

business

businessman bs-n

businessmen bsm

businesswomen bs-m

businesslike bslc

come

income nk

welcome lk

unwelcome ulk

forthcoming flk_

READING AND WRITING EXERCISES

PREVIEW WORDS

1 later *lar* — candidates *cddts*
remaining *rmn* — references *rfNs*
schedule *scjl* — assistant *asSN*
standards *Sds* — administrative *amv*

2 Tampa *Tpa* — relocate *rlca*
permanent *PmN* — headquarters *hdqtrs*
exactly *vcl* — always *a*
leadership *ldr+* — establishment *eslm*

3 Best *bS* — layout *laol*
welcome *lk* — Industries *Ns*
option *opj* — initial *in+l*
carefully *crfl* — hospitalization *hspzj*

4 world *o* — abroad *abrd*
overseas *Oses* — procedures *Psjrs*
travel *trvl* — although *alo*
languages *lgjs* — communications *kncjs*

5 comfortable *kftB* — already *ar*
situated *sit-* — associates *asos*

introduction · paperwork · facility · conversation

1

Mrs. Shelley Davis, Bradbury Corporation, P.O. Box 136, Columbus, OH 43224

2

Miss Jill Reynolds, 2214 Clairmont, Apartment 4B, Chicago, IL 60653

Intro DC

Intro DC

3

Form letter to employees from J. Alan Steele, Director of Personnel

Intro DC

Intro DC

4

Mr. Joseph Lee, Association of American Investors, 179 Avenue of the Americas, New York, NY 10013

dr le u sug-
t e z s l hu
d v inf o aplī f .
apym Oses. r
alC . Psnl dla
se dS u acd c
lrn + o p. z
uc se f u rec, Intro DC
w Sde- 2 ol lgys.
id Slnl b l l lrn
adjl 1s, n adj l
lp + srlhN, Intro P w
scls n ofs Psyrs
+ rd Pss. alo
w a b NS- n
pb rlys + kncjs, Intro DC
id n M l h
Cyss l loz
aras ol, l nyy
o lrvl + d lk
p v lv abrd.
cu

5

Punctuate the following letter by adding commas to three introductory dependent clauses and one parenthetical expression.

Ms. Ruth A. Martin, Wescott Industries, 1649 Georgetown Road, Macon, GA 31201

ds rln r 4
p- l ac lr s 10
e Dcs- ySrd. 15
ze agre- n r fn 20
kvrsj l bgn 26
nu dles o Oc 5. 31
if s kv fu l arv 40
erl la rn l kp 46
ppr o und, iap 54
u l' l alo e ls 60
adjl h z . rzll 67
lb S l kp me 73
lgs la ch ar Srt- 80
n u P jb. oN 85
r sil- n u olSN 92
nu fsl' l lc fw 98
l bgn nu rSC 104
Pjcs, lqu aq f c 111

⌒e kflB du_ ⌒i 116

vzl, p ll u asos 123

lai nyy- lr plzN 129

Ndcj l (sle, 135

vlu 138

UNIT
TWO

PERSONNEL

SHORTHAND VOCABULARY REVIEW

Study the following principles and the words that illustrate them. Each word will occur in the letters and memos in this unit.

1. Write ＼ for words beginning with the sound of any vowel + x (aks, eks, iks, oks, uks, or eggs). Write ⤫ for the medial and final sound of x.

exact	*vc*	exciting	*vᴸ*
expect	*vpc*	expansion	*vpnʳ*
explains	*vplns*	exercise	*vrsʒ*
flexible	*flxB*	accidents	*vdᴺs*

ra asr bq Svʒ elnc Aso

bcw byh vcʲ la qc frᴺ ndr

fsʒ P⌐⌐ kn r8 rq Slᴺ

2. When a word contains two medial (middle) vowels that are pronounced consecutively, write the first vowel.

dial	dil	science	siN
radius	rdes	Miami	—me
period	pred	material	—trel
various	vres	manual	—nul
annual	aul	tuition	tuj
realize	relz	Seattle	setl

3. When a word ends in two vowel sounds that are pronounced consecutively, write only the last vowel.

idea	ida	create	cra
area	ara	media	—da
radio	rdo	evaluate	evla
Gloria	glra	cafeteria	cftra

LESSON

BRIEF FORMS AND DERIVATIVES

1. plc Avj ku pl sug
2. sal sv bo k nkv arms

Key

1. particular, advantage, continue, part/port, suggest
2. satisfy/satisfactory, several, both, come/came/committee, inconvenience, arrangements

---

PHRASE REVIEW

1. il iv ivb eblv ehp
2. uv ulb udb lb lgv
3. / cb vr ✓ lb db

Key

1. I will, I have, I have been, we believe, we hope
2. you have, you will be, you would be, to be, to give
3. at the, can be, of our, of the, will be, would be

READING AND WRITING EXERCISES

PREVIEW WORDS

1 space sps

entire ntr

cafeteria cftra

flexible flxB

larger *lrjr*

Christmas *Xs*

2 careers *crrs*

science *siN*

entrance *NrN*

9 o'clock *9°*

3 Miami *me*

sponsor *spNr*

thought *u*

Florida *FL*

4 limit *ll*

courtesy *crlse*

confine *kfn*

patience *psN*

5 exact *Vc*

consult *ksll*

agency *ajNe*

contacts *klcs*

schedule *scjl*

satisfactory *sal*

technical *lcncl*

particular *plc*

definitely *dfnll*

engineering *njnr*

charter *Crlr*

reduced *rds-*

weekend *cN*

practical *prclcl*

sections *scjs*

unavailable *uavlB*

painters *pNrs*

inconvenience *nkv*

outside *olsd*

accordance *acrdN*

specified *sp-*

representatives *reps*

1

Mr. W. L. Howard, Stanton Catering and Food Services, 1903 Riverfront Drive, Charleston, SC 29407

dr hord r aul Xs ple , no b

pln-、 �like ⌣ ru̲ l asc
fu hlp n ⌣c ⌣ (
arms、 l8 yr u co
Pvd- a √ fd ⸝ ^{Series} lBs ⸝ ^{Series}
+ lB sl̲、 u ⌣pes
dd sc̲ · fn jb la
edlc ⌐ l hNl
(nlr evN aq
ls yr⸒ er lq̲ v ⌣w̲
(ple l r co cflra
n od lv · lryr ara、
/ db hlpf if u + l
cd lc ⸝ sps bf
dsd o sp arms、
y d̄N u cl ⌣ ofs
l sl · ⌐ f s lgl
lglr× ⌣ sgl ⸒
v flxB nx ⌣c ⸝ ^{Conj}
+ ⌐ Sln la ec
fN · ⌐ la ⸒
sal f bo v s、
su

2

Mr. Everett Clay, Math Department, Northside High School, 1117 Hastings Road, Spokane, WA 99218

d⌣r cla ilb hpe
l sl asd · d f
Dcs̲ ofs crrs ⌣
u cls、 nynr̲ frs
r lc̲ f plc scls
n ofs ⌣pes、 r
⌣o ⸒ so lcncl
la · nly v siN ⸒
⌣pl evn f bgn̲
pzjs、 SdNs hu
v Sde- siN +
⌣l dfnll v · Avn
O loz hu vn、 ⌣n
ev opn o r Sf ⸝ ^{Intro DC}
e lc f ŪN̄- ppl
hu r l l ku lrn⸒
z uno ⸝ ^{Intro DC} ev ⌣p-
me ppl f⌐ u
scl、 ly v Sn

Intro DC

Intro DC

3

Mr. Charles H. Michael, Global Travel Agency, 4252 Cypress Street, Pensacola, FL 32501

Intro DC

Intro P

4

Memo to All Employees from Keith Logan, SUBJECT: Parking Lot Repairs

Intro DC

Intro P

Intro DC

Intro DC

5

Punctuate the following memo. Add commas to set off one introductory phrase, two conjunctions, and one introductory dependent clause.

Memo to Richard Mitchell from Valerie M. Ferguson, SUBJECT: Vacancy for Department Supervisor

5

10

16

21

27

34

40

46

53

60

66

71

76

82

89

96

102

109

115

⌒c (SC f s, uf 120
u agre lae nd l 125
lc olsd r co f · 132
Svzr idb gld l 138

es · rlys ⌣ ls 145
ajNe, p ll ⌒e 149
no ⌣l u ⌣s ldu. 155

LESSON 7

ABBREVIATIONS AND DERIVATIVES

1. % ex U sq ft d
2. ins Xms ¢ mdse re ecol

Key

1. percent, example/executive, university, square, feet, day
2. insurance, Christmas, cent/cents, merchandise, regarding, economical

---

TRANSCRIPTION AID

Typing Numbers

1. In your transcribed copy, spell out numbers from one through ten in regular prose material. Use figures for 11 and higher.

□ We have *three* new branch offices.
□ Please send me *15* copies of your report.

2. When numbers below ten appear in the same sentence with related numbers above ten, use figures for both.

□ Jane ordered *6* copies for Bill, *12* copies for Mark, and *16* copies for me.

3. Always use figures to show percentages. Spell out the word *percent* in contextual material.

□ You will receive a discount of *10 percent* on all merchandise.

YOUR BUSINESS VOCABULARY

guidelines gdlns A statement of policy or specific instructions regarding an activity.

□ Please follow the guidelines presented in the company manual.

timely ⟿ Well timed; of current interest or an appropriate occurrence.

□ I enjoyed hearing your timely remarks.

READING AND WRITING EXERCISES

PREVIEW WORDS

1. timely *Lel*
 - extremely *Xel*
 - update *pda*
 - workload *old*

 - handbook *hNbc*
 - adjustments *ajSms*
 - participants *ppNs*
 - secretarial *secl*

2. Davis *dvs*
 - health *hll*
 - total *lol*
 - earliest *erls*

 - retirement *rlrm*
 - dedicated *ddca-*
 - guidelines *gdlns*
 - Electronics *elncs*

3. toy *ly*
 - retail *rll*
 - small *sl*
 - feature *fCr*

 - holiday *hld*
 - merchandise *dse*
 - appliances *aplNs*
 - possibilities *ps8ls*

4. ours *rs*
 - hire *hr*
 - edit *edl*

 - artwork *arlo*
 - newsletter *nzL*
 - periodical *predcl*

pages	pjs	photographs	flogrfs

5

a.m.	am	clarify	clrf
cancel	csl	differently	dfrNl
weather	wtr	snowstorm	snoStrm
station	Sj	accumulation	aclj

1

Memo to Helen Marshall from Andy Fairchild, SUBJECT: Update of the Secretarial Handbook

mo l hln rsl
me vr ofs Psnl
r sa la r secl
hNbc , ol v da.
d ub f l Cr . k
l pda r hNbc x
u vp z . ex sec
db Xl vluB. l
Aso no laur .
mbr v sv ogjs
f secs. Ph lz ogjs
cd kb l inf lb
l- n r plys , relz
la ls rspB l , . bq
adj lu old , b
e l b B hc
s ajSms lgv
u h. l pln
l rcm 10 or 12
ol ppNs f k.
cd e gl lglr hc
s fnl dsjs x

2

Form letter to new employees from Barbara Bainbridge, Personnel Manager

d pe lk l dvs
elncs. ur no pl
v . fr la hs sl hi
Sds v lN n elnc

Pdcs\ eblv la r
suc , (rzlt v
ddca- ppl ⌣o
lglr> ls ⌒nul l
Pvd u ⌣ gdlns
esl- b r ⌒pes\
/ vplns u ins +
rlrm Pgs\ / l
hlp u lse ho u
dpl fls nl (
lol ogj v co\
ulfN s⌒ bnfls
⌣C ⌒a Sprz
u\ f nSN, Paren a vr
⌒pes rsv Dk
ras ∠ hll clb
nx l r plN\ e
aso v ⌒ve pss
avlB / rds-ras>
b Ar l rd ls hNbc
/ u erlB opl\ ehp
/ reps (bgn v ·

sal crr ⌣ r
fr\ cu

3

Memo to All Employees from Janice Barry, SUBJECT: Christmas Discounts

mo l A ⌒pes oN
aq erp- l anoN
la el fCr spsl
Dks f A ⌒pes du
r X⌒s szn\ Pdcs
f⌒ r ln v s⌒l
apliNs lb A- lu
lB v psBls ls yr\
u ⌒a aso apli
(Dk l PCss n r
ly dpl> (⌒s
u Cz lb sld lu
/ · Dk v 40%
of (rll prs\ lz
sl prss lb avlB
p l Dc 11, Conj + u ⌒a
PCs p l · lol v

150$ n dse, ehp r Dk pln cs Ap . ltl ezer fu ls yr. ^ r a v A u . hpe hld szn.

4

Ms. Vivian Stevens, Editorial Manager, Arrowhead Press, 1230 Brooks Avenue, Lexington, KY 40508

d-s Svns wb Ud lau fr Pdss pbjs f cos lc rs. er lq v -l . -ol nzL l eC vr 4H -pes. / P h edu n v nel avlB l ru + edl sC . nzL, [Conj] + / d n b ecol l hr adjl Sf f la Pps, ev n m . pbj la , 3 l 4 pjs lq. / d kln . fu flogrfs + pss v arlo. edlc lse arlcls ab Nv -pes, [Series] anoNms v k evNs, [Series] + s-n nyl nz rla- l bs + N. r byl alos s l spN p l 50¢ P cpe n Pdc cSs, , ls r cN v predcl udb NS- n Pds f s, idap v u rsp zz psB. uvl

5

Add commas to show one introductory phrase and four introductory dependent clauses.

Memo to All Staff from Cynthia B. Alford, SUBJECT: Policy for Office Closings

mo l A Sf ls mo , l clrf r

plse re ofs hrs 16
du bd lr, w evN 22
v . hve snoLn p 28
lrn r dil ou rdo 34
l r U Sp. if lr hsb 43
. dsy l clz r ofss 49
or dla opn r ofss 55
la anoNm lb d 62
b 7a, s n r Sd 69
prcls v ls U l csl 77

clss bcz v . hve 82
acly v sno. n 88
clss r hld e vpc 93
r ofss l ku s 100
lvl v ops, if ur 107
ksrn- ab r kdy v 114
lr p lsn l r 120
rdo. uls u hr 125
dfrNl ulb vpc- 132
lk Lo la d. 137

LESSON

THEORY REVIEW

two o'clock 2°

7:30 a.m. 7 30 a

12 noon 12 nn

11:45 p.m. 11 45 p

TRANSCRIPTION AID

Similar Words

adapt adpl To adjust to a situation.

□ You can adapt this software program for your business use.

adopt adpl To take a course of action.

□ Our personnel division will adopt a new policy.

YOUR BUSINESS VOCABULARY

fiscal year fscl yr A 12-month period used by organizations for financial planning.

□ The fiscal year for our corporation begins July 1.

workshop osp A scheduled educational meeting or training session for a group of people in a specialized field.

□ The conference will include many workshops and lectures.

READING AND WRITING EXERCISES

PREVIEW WORDS

1 fiscal fscl

taught U

quality gl

understaff USf

growth *grl*

promised *P⌐s-*

2 adults *adlls*

Miami *⌐e*

outing *ol*

positive *pzv*

3 adopt *adpl*

flexible *flxB*

permit *P⌐l*

decreased *dcrs-*

4 1:30 p.m. *1 ³⁰p⌐*

sessions *sjs*

workshops *osps*

evaluations *evlujs*

5 maximum *⌐xm*

adapt *adpl*

unless *uls*

workday *od*

mistake *Mlc*

substitute *sSlu*

length *lql*

pleasure *plzr*

coupon *cpn*

children *Cldrn*

already *Ar*

efficiency *efsNe*

concept *kspl*

encountered *nkr-*

exercise *vrsz*

promotion *P⌐y*

evaluate *evla*

performance *PfM*

active *acv*

obligation *oblgy*

volunteer *vlnlr*

involvement *nvlvm*

1

Memo to Jessica Nelson from Robert J. Hopkins, SUBJECT: Staff Additions

Intro DC

Conj

Paren

2

Memo to All Staff from Annabelle Moffett, SUBJECT: Employee Trips

Intro DC

Intro DC

p se ⌐ enc- lS
v hlls + prss⸴ if
us NS- n ∿M-
Intro DC
lsp⸴ p rel ⌐ cpn⸴
e Sl nd ldl if ls
of̲ sdb ar-f adlls
of or if Cldrn r
Ub I-⸴ ehp u fM
ls plns ⸴ v̲ ⸴ edu⸴

3

Mr. Benjamin Thomas, Sandbar Manufacturing Company, 822 Whitman Street, Tuc-
son, AZ 85711

d⌐ Ls f me yrs
s ⌐pes v Srt- Lo
f hr v 8 a⌐⸴ no
er ks̲ · nu sS⸴
us_ ⌐ rzlts v ·
rsM Sde⸴ er pln̲
Intro P
L adpl · flxB L
scyl⸴ ls sS d
P∿l eC ⌐pe L C⸴
⸴ or hs o Srt̲ L⸴

sM u fr ⸴ Az uz_
Intro DC
ls lp v arm⸴ c u
asr s⌐ qs f s⨯
edlc Lno ho u
Nds- ls Psyr⸴ du u
lq s ⌐ bS pln⨯
∿l dfces v u nkr-⨯
hs u lvl v efsMe
ncrs- or dcrs-⸴
· rzll⨯⸴ e alspa
Nds̲ ls kspl n
nr fCr⸴ ne Avs
uv db ap-⸴ vlu

4

Memo to All Managers from Gloria
Stanislaw, SUBJECT: Performance Evaluations

mo L A ⌐yrs n ·
fu ⌐cs ulb asc-
L evla ⌐ Pf∿M
vu ⌐pes⸴ ⸴ prpry
f ls ⌐pl evM⸴ el
Intro P
kdc 2 ⌐osps o

ho ᒪ-c sucf
evlujs. ev Aso
rvz- (ᒪ ℓ ᒪℓ uz-
ℓ eℓ ⟋pe⟍ evℓuy
ᒪℓe cℓ · rᵤᵤ vrsz
ℓ ᵬᵒ u + u Sℓ edℓc
ℓ hℓp u ᵔ-c (ᵔℓ
v ℓs opℓ⟍ ⟋oⴵps
ℓℓ ofᵣ- ⟋ ⎮p⟍ᵔ o
Oc 6 + aq ⟋9ᵃ°
ᵟ fℓᵒ d⟍ ᵬ Ꙥℓ ℓ
aℓᴍ ⎮ v ℓz sjs⟍
ℓy ℓ gᴠ u nu �device
ᵟ gℓs + objcᴠs
v ⟋ym⟍ + ℓy ℓ

Conj

vpℓn ᴚ Sds ℓ Pᴚⴵ⟍
e ℓz uℓ agre ℓa ⟋
z ᒪ ℓ spᴍ⟍

5

Add commas to the following letter to show
two conjunctions, two introductory dependent clauses, and one introductory phrase.

Mrs. Allison Foster, Director of Volunteer
Services, Wintergreen Memorial Hospital,
1000 Breckenridge Boulevard, Buffalo, NY
14213

dᴚs fᵴr ᴚ co hs *(7)*
· acᴠ Sᴠs cℓℓ + *(12)*
er ℓc ℓ · nu Pⴵc *(19)*
ℓ spᴍᴚ⟍ ᴡ hᴚd *(24)*
me q ℓqs aℓ ⟋ *(30)*
vℓnℓᴚ Pᴵq n u hsp⟍ *(37)*
cd u ℓℓ s ho ⟋ *(42)*
ⴵoⴵ⟍⟍ sᴍ e Sᴚℓ- *(47)*
ᴚ Sᴠs cℓℓ ppⴵ hs *(54)*
grn ⟋ · Sde ᴚa⟍ *(59)*
e ofᴚ sᴠ opℓs ℓ *(66)*
⟋pes hu ⟋ ⴵ ℓ *(71)*
vℓnℓᴚ ᴚ knᴸ⟍ n *(77)*
od ℓ ncᴚⴵ ℓs cᴍ *(83)*
v nᴠℓᴠm e aℓo *(88)*
⟋ ⟋pes ℓ kp ℓᴚ *(94)*
vℓnℓᴚ obℓqⴵ du *(100)*
⟋ ⟋od⟍ uℓs ℓᴚ ᴚ *(106)*

spsl Sks (~xm 113
h alo- eC ~c, 118
2 hrs, edlc u l 125
pln u Pq l r Psnl, 133
(~u b nes f s l 139

adpl r pln l fl u 145
scjl b ~ Ar la 150
ec fM · ~a l asS 156
u / hsp, vlu 164

LESSON

SHORTHAND VOCABULARY REVIEW

Write for the word ending *tion* (pronounced *shun, zhun,* or *chun*: sion, cian, shion, cean, cion) or for a vowel + *tion* (a-tion, e-tion, i-tion or ish-un, o-tion, u-tion).

national

invitation

conservation

transition

construction

occasion

reception

reservation

possession

traditional

TRANSCRIPTION AID

Spelling. Omit the final *e* when adding *ing* to most words:

handle, handl*ing*
move, mov*ing*
leave, leav*ing*
have, hav*ing*
retire, retir*ing*
solve, solv*ing*
schedule, schedul*ing*
stimulate, stimulat*ing*
congratulate, congratulat*ing*
distribute, distribut*ing*
issue, issu*ing*
make, mak*ing*

YOUR BUSINESS VOCABULARY

radius — A measure of a circular area.

□ The broadcast will be carried within a radius of 42 miles.

evaluate — To examine and judge.

□ A committee was appointed to evaluate the findings.

READING AND WRITING EXERCISES

PREVIEW WORDS

1 bring, awards, banquet, conference, extremely, invitation, stimulating, reservation

2 radius, separate, energy, analysis, evaluate, excessive, electricity, superintendent

3 create, expense, badges, supervise, Debbie, collecting, security, identification

4 Gloria, generous, along, occasion, gather, luncheon, Hastings, fortunately

5 site, install, evidently, transition

doubts

wiring

possession

construction

1

Ms. Diana S. Fields, 701 West Georgia, Vancouver, BC V7Y 1K5

Intro DC

Conj

2

Mr. Stanley Clark, Diagnostic Research Corporation, 5912 Applewood Road, Little Rock, AR 72118

r plN 9 yrs ag , Intro P
ev rpls- r he +
cl sS ~ 2 sprl
unls, eC z dzn-
l akda · rdes v
6T sq fl, no er
ksrn- lae ~a b
uz · vsv a~l v
els, ublv la · kp
anlss , n od, p
cl ~u ofs l ar ·
d fu vzl, ul asc
r S vr bld l sl
asd r ntr d fu, cu

3

Memo to Debbie Leonard from Jim Wilkerson, SUBJECT: Visitor Identification Badges

mo l dbe lnrd
er w Pss v dzn
nu idNf bjs f
vzlrs n r bld, ul
sn rsv · bx v
idNf bjs lb uz- n
pls v m lgs la
ev uz- w pS, p
gv X all l D +
clc r bjs, lz ths
r f PmN us , + Conj
edu n ~+ l cra
· unes vpN b v l
rpls lS bjs, ino
lau Svz sv ppl
hu lc O r rspf
dsc ~n ur a a,
d u p se la eC
vu asSNs USNs r
Psyr f isu bjs x,
Ppr idNf , ~pl l
r scr vr co, ino
la ec k ou spl , dbe, Dir Ad

4

Memo to Customer Service Representatives from June Milton, Assistant Personnel Manager, SUBJECT: Retirement Luncheon for Gloria Hastings

mo l K Svo reps
me vu Ar no la
glra hs lb rlz
N v lo ᴏ p jyn
s o Jn 30 f · lnCn
n onr v hr rlrm
⌐ lnCn l bgn ⌐
11³⁰ᵃⁿ nr brd r
ndls lsa **Paren** lo frN
+ aso lb M— b E1
n r dpl. loz v s
hu vh ⌐ plzr v ᴏ
ᴗ hr no la se hs
· spsl scl f slv
dfc Pbl ᴏ. fCnll **Paren**
se hsb v jnrs n ps
hr nly alg l ⌐ ppl
ᴗᴏ ᴗ hr, if u ᴗ
l alN ⌐ lnCn **Intro DC** p
kp + rel ⌐ enc—
f. ehp laul glr

ᴗ s f lo v spsl
ocy

5

Add commas to show two conjunctions, one introductory phrase, and two parenthetical expressions.

Mr. Ronald S. Mason, Mason Construction, Inc., 2119 Jackson Street, Kansas City, KS 67501

dr r ᴗsn er pln_ — 6
l ᴗr nl r nu — 11
ofss nx ᴗo b w — 17
sr dols ab ᴗn — 21
ly lb rde f s. l — 27
vzl— ⌐ su lo ᴗrn — 34
+ ᴗ ksrn—,) u — 39
ᴗpvm Pq o scyl — 46
r agrem sps la ⌐ — 53
bld b kp— b Mr 3 — 60
acrd l ⌐ das ll— — 66
nr kc A ᴗ r sd — 73
vb jns— sv ds aq — 80

usd no b rde l 86
nsl (flr + bgn 92
pN, evdNl s⌒ 97
vluß ⌒ z ls du 103
l bd ⌣lr, du u 108
alspa ⌒c p ls ls 114
⌒x> er egr ⌒c (120

Ty l (nu fsl^L, 126
hoE edu n ⌣+ l 132
lc pzj ull a ksrq 140
hsb kp-, p avz⌒e 147
ru a a o ⌣n l 152
pln r ⌒v, su 158

LESSON

10

WORD DEVELOPMENT

Develop new words from the following brief forms:

with

withdraw *dra*

withstand *sn*

within *n*

without *ol*

withhold *hld*

work

workshop *osp*

paperwork *ppro*

overwork *Oo*

network *nlo*

framework *fro*

for

forbid *fbd*

foreign *fn*

foremost *fs*

forest *fs*

forever *fE*

forgive *fgv*

forget *fgl*

forgotten *fgln*

formula *fla*

forge *fy*

READING AND WRITING EXERCISES

PREVIEW WORDS

1 nearby *nrb*

 workday *od*

financial *fnnsl*

investigating *nvsga_*

formal *f~l*

trainees *trnes*

2 topic *tpc*

human *hm*

Coast *cs̩*

Seattle *sell*

3 vital *vll*

routine *rtn*

ensure *nsr*

strict *src*

4 Ward *w̩*

aspects *aspcs*

equally *eqll*

assembling *as~β*

5 endure *ndr*

overlook *Olc*

activity *acv^l*

confusion *kfj*

scholarships *sclrss*

representative *rep*

effective *efcv*

forthcoming *flk̲*

fundamental *fNml*

incorporated *inc*

minimal *m~l*

throughout *truol*

paperwork *ppr̲o*

approximately *apxl*

emphasize *~fsz*

traditional *trdjl*

secretarial *secl*

installing *nSl*

remodeling *r~dl*

construction *kSrcj*

concentrate *ksNra*

inconveniences *nkvo*

1

Mr. Kevin Brewer, Academic Services Director, Midwestern State University, 12 Lindwood Avenue, Davenport, IA 52804

d cvn ev ofn lc-
ab ofr̲ assN l

pes hu + l ku
lr ejcj, lr r vres
as ec q ab ak
ls, ec pa (luj
fes f loz ppl +
l nrl n · clj nrb,
ls fnnsl hlp u
b apli- l clss hld
n evn, uf (crs
, scjl- b r co z
pl v jb lrn, (Intro DC) hoE, (Paren)
db alo- du (
od, · osp n
rd Pss or bs ri
db · ex v ls cN
v lrn, nvSga
(psBl v ofr sclrss
f pes sc AvN-
dgres n lr plc aras
v Sde, njnrs +
jm lrnes r rep
v ls grp, p lq ab
lz idas, uf u lq (
, ri, (Intro DC) idlc l
Ppr · fl Ppzl
alq ls ln, su

2

Memo to All Department Heads from Gerald P. Cunningham, SUBJECT: Schedule for Training Sessions

mo l A dpl hds
ulb gld lno la er
rde l bgn (lrn
sjs uv rqS-, alC-
, · lS v Pgs la vb
scjl- so fr, lb
flk, ulfN (da +
f eC cls lS-
nx l (Ul v eC
Nv lpc, ev inc
S vu sugjs +
v A- · fu vr o,
a q loz lS- r 2
sjs lae Srgl rcm

Intro DC

Paren

Intro P

Intro DC

3

Memo to Office Supervisors from Bonnie Ashcraft, SUBJECT: Vacation Schedules

Intro P

Paren

Paren

Intro DC

4

Ms. Theresa Ward, Webster Consulting Agency, 444 Atlantic Avenue, Norfolk, VA 23517

5

Add six commas to the following letter to indicate one conjunction, two parenthetical expressions, one introductory dependent clause, and three words in a series.

Form letter to employees from Jason Allen

5

10

16

+ groNs, e aprC 21
ls acvl x- 26
fl, r dl l 32
rzlt n me bnfts 37
f E, b el v l 44
ndr s nkvs 49
n Pss, f ex el 57
PbB vp s dl 63
nyz + jn kff, 69
alo, , a 74
b dfc lri l ksNra 81

ou o + Olc r 87
acvl z C z 91
psB, edu asc 95
lau lc X cr l 101
PvN vdNs, C 106
r u c + lri 110
l avyd aras U 115
rpr, nCrlt el 120
du a ec l kp r 126
kSrcq qcl, lqf 134
hlp du ls , su 143

Developing a Professional Attitude

Many factors determine how successfully an office worker fits into the total office environment. Technical skills, such as typing, dictation and transcription, word processing, and data processing, are essential for performing certain duties. Knowing how to get along well with people is just as important. Because offices are centers for communication, people must be able to work effectively as a team.

In addition to these skills, another quality is important to advancement in office careers. This quality is best described as *a professional image*—an overall image that sets certain office workers apart from others. To project a professional image, you must first develop a professional *attitude*. Your attitude determines how you look, work, and interact with other people.

A professional attitude begins with these characteristics:

Enthusiasm. Be willing to accept new responsibilities. Approach each task with energy and seriousness. Be cheerful and courteous to others.

Maturity. Approach your work with dignified behavior. Take your responsibilities seriously and give full attention to your duties.

Competence. Learn your job well. Identify weaker skills and concentrate on improving them daily.

Confidence. When you are certain that you are giving your best effort to doing a job well, your behavior will reflect the confidence that you have gained from experience.

Cooperation. Office systems depend upon teams of people working together to process communications. Be a cooperative team member.

Reliability. Show that you are reliable by being on time, by completing your work on time, and by consistently producing high-quality work.

Positivism. A positive attitude should be evident in everything you say and do. Even when saying "no," learn to say it in a pleasant and positive way.

Unlike technical skills, *professionalism* is not usually taught as a subject in textbooks and classrooms. Yet, it is exhibited in everything you do—how you look, work, and behave. A professional attitude says to everyone around you, "I enjoy my work, I take pride in my work, and I plan to be successful in my career."

UNIT THREE

RETAILING

SHORTHAND VOCABULARY REVIEW

Study the following words and the principles they illustrate. You will find these words in the letters and memos in this unit.

1. Write a slightly raised and disjoined for the word ending *ity* (uh-tee).

quality	quantities
community	variety
quantity	dependability

2. Write for the word beginnings *extr* and *extra.*

extra X | extremely Xl
extreme X | extraordinary Xord

3. Write *el* for the word beginning *electr.*

electric elc | electronic elnc

MORE ABOUT PUNCTUATION

Use a comma to separate two independent adjectives that modify the same noun. The comma is being used in place of the word *and:*

□ Ellen is an intelligent, dedicated manager.

Do not use a comma if the first adjective modifies both the second adjective and the noun:

□ Ellen is an intelligent general manager.

If you are in doubt about whether or not to use a comma, consider these two questions.

1. Does the sentence still have the same meaning if you replace the comma with the word *and*?

□ Ellen is an intelligent and dedicated manager.

2. Does the sentence still have the same meaning if you reverse the order of the adjectives?

□ Ellen is a dedicated and intelligent manager.

If the adjectives meet these tests, they are independent adjectives and should be separated by a comma. Commas used between independent adjectives, where *and* has been omitted, will be identified in the Reading and Writing Exercises as **And O.**

LESSON 11

BRIEF FORMS AND DERIVATIVES

1. [illegible] ol Ph Nv pb E
2. [illegible] f crc spl sucf P,

Key

1. were/with, other, perhaps, individual, public, ever/every
2. include, for/full, character/characteristic, specifically, successful, presentation

PHRASE REVIEW

1. id idlc ecd e[illegible] usd udlc
2. lcl lk [illegible] s ou laul

Key

1. I would, I would like, we could, we were, you should, you would like
2. to call, to come, and the, it is, on you/on your, that you will

READING AND WRITING EXERCISES

PREVIEW WORDS

1 hours hrs
outfits olfls
appeal apl
fashions fjs
customers Ks
entertainment Nlnm
profitable PflB
establishments eslms

2 image _(shorthand)_

selecting _(shorthand)_ slc

clothing _(shorthand)_ clt

patronage _(shorthand)_ plrny

compliment _(shorthand)_ kplm

distinction _(shorthand)_ Dlq

acquainted _(shorthand)_ aqN-

professional _(shorthand)_ Pfyl

3 notes _(shorthand)_ nls

bulletins _(shorthand)_ bllns

Janet _(shorthand)_ jnl

brochures _(shorthand)_ brsrs

stationery _(shorthand)_ Syre

attraction _(shorthand)_ alrcy

handwritten _(shorthand)_ hNrln

typewritten _(shorthand)_ lprln

4 single _(shorthand)_ sgl

Williams _(shorthand)_ lyms

instance _(shorthand)_ nSN

satisfied _(shorthand)_ sal-

designers _(shorthand)_ dznrs

economizing _(shorthand)_ ecoz-

defining _(shorthand)_ dfn-

unfurnished _(shorthand)_ ufrns-

5 dress _(shorthand)_ drs

credited _(shorthand)_ cr-

smart _(shorthand)_ smrl

shoppers _(shorthand)_ sprs

amount _(shorthand)_ a-l

reliable _(shorthand)_ rliB

account _(shorthand)_ ak

prospered _(shorthand)_ Pspr-

1

Mrs. Virginia Moore, Upper Deck Restaurant, 514 Belmont Plaza, Fort Worth, TX 76110

Intro DC

2

Miss Andrea Grant, Penelope's Treasure Chest, 1993 West Sagecrest Avenue, Fort Worth, TX 76109

Conj

Conj

Conj

Paren

Intro DC

lcl ~ i ofs. Ph
ecd v lnC hr
ab 1 p~ + vzl
u Sp afws. uvl

3

Memo to Janet Masters from Adam Newlin, SUBJECT: October Sales Invitations

mo l jnl ~Srs
el hld . sl o
Oc 15 z . spSl
Svs l r G Ks.
d u p Su Psnl
nvlys l eC K ×
lr r sv aprCs
avlB lu. lS yr
e sN nls o s~l
Syre. lz crds gv
r efc v hNrln
nls, + e X~l (Conj)
p- ~ r rzlt, n
Pves yrs ev ~l-
Ls la ~ lprln.

ev Aso Su- brSrs
+ bllns. if uv s~
dfrN n m, id lk (Intro DC)
u idas, s ~pl
lau ~c r Ks fl
la ls alrcy, dzn-
spl f L. ls sl,
b clz- l r jn pb, (Conj)
+ er brg n spSl
~dse f sl, idb
gld l Dcs ls / u
kv, jnl. (Dir Ad)

4

Mr. Daniel H. Williams, Certified Public Accountant, 703 McCaw Street, Pittsburgh, PA 15204

dr ~lys me
bs exs k l s f
hlp n frnS lr
ofss. n E sgl
nSN w pS, ev (Intro P)
Pds- . Sprz- + sal-

Dir Ad

And O

Series

Series

Intro DC

5

Add commas to show one conjunction, two parenthetical expressions, one introductory dependent clause, and to show the omission of *and* between adjectives.

Mrs. Gary Marshall, 1660 Shore Acres Road, Tacoma, WA 98498

9

14

19

27

34

40

46

52

59

66

71

76

82

90

94

100

106

111

118

127

LESSON 12

ABBREVIATIONS AND DERIVATIVES

1. cal ave inv vol cr lit
2. No Hs eslms reps

Key

1. catalog, avenue, invoice, volume, credit, literature
2. number, hundreds, establishments, representatives

TRANSCRIPTION AID

Typing Numbers

1. When typing even sums of money in business letters, omit the decimal point and zeroes.

□ The stationery cost $62.
□ Our new desk cost nearly $800, but it is very handsome.

2. Type figures and decimal points for uneven sums of money.

□ If you order six cases at $24.95 each, the total will be $149.70.

3. When typing even numbers that are extremely large, spell out the numbers—million, billion, or trillion.

□ The budget will run a little over our $10 million estimate.
□ We may exceed our sales estimates by a quarter of a million dollars.

YOUR BUSINESS VOCABULARY

heir ar — One who inherits property.

□ Ownership of all stock will be transferred to his heirs.

wholesale hlsl — Sale of goods in large quantities, usually to a retailer.

□ We are ordering the merchandise from a wholesale distributor.

itemize *ᴜⱽᶻ* To make a list, item by item.

□ When doing inventory, please itemize the stock on every shelf.

READING AND WRITING EXERCISES

**PREVIEW
WORDS**

1 sports *spls*

formal *fml*

examine *vm*

inventory *nvnlre*

2 social *ssl*

promptly *Pʳᵗl*

behalf *bhf*

regularly *rglrl*

3 heirs *ars*

former *fᵐr*

doors *drs*

owner *oʳ*

4 itemize *ᴜⱽᶻ*

warranty *rⁿle*

colors *clrs*

common *kn*

coordinated *cordna-*

businesswoman *bs̶m*

Mitchell *Cl*

wholesale *hlsl*

character *crc*

distributor *Dr*

leather *llr*

superior *sprer*

manufacturer *fr*

Washington
Avenue *WA ave*

guarantee *grnle*

dealership *dlrs*

electric	elc	accordingly	acrdl
relatively	rlvl	commercials	krAls
5 simple	s—pl	beyond	beN
imported	—pl-	overhead	Ohd
samples	sa—s	entryway	Nre—a
beautiful	blef	affordable	afdB

1

Form letter to prospective customers from Betty Sanderson

dK ev q nz f
bs—m, er opn.
fy dpl jS fu> f
ur lc (rS v s, (Intro DC)
uv lc- lq + hrd
f apo clt f ofs,
me Srs —c (kn
Mlc v ofr Sc la,
elr l fl or n
fl enf, sC slcs
—i b fn f . spls
evN or . afnn
le, (Conj) b ly r n /
a apo f —m
ex> r nu Apl l
Cnj a la, dN
—a ull ur ps b,
—c . spAl lrp l
vm r nvnlre, ev
sus, (Series) drss, (Series) cos, (Series) +
Aus n dznr Sls
+ cordna- clrs, su

2

Mr. Timothy E. Clark, Central Bank and Trust, 222 Peabody Avenue, Toledo, OH 43614

dr clrc —p-
l ru ls L o bhf

(shorthand) **Intro P**

(shorthand) **Intro P**

(shorthand) **Intro P**

(shorthand) **Intro P**

3

Mr. Claude W. Lee, 4256 Sylvania Drive,
Belleville, IL 62223

(shorthand) **Paren**

(shorthand) **Conj**

(shorthand) **Intro DC**

(shorthand) **Intro DC**

4

Mr. Glen Jackson, American Supply, Inc., 1700 East 40 Street, Tulsa, OK 74106

5

Add commas to show two introductory dependent clauses, one conjunction, and two introductory phrases. Add commas also to show where *and* was omitted and to separate the words in a series.

Form letter to prospective customers from Sylvia Cole

dK me ppl asc s 7
ho ec sl blef gl^{L} 14
rgs / hf prs, / 19
asr , s-pl, e dN 24
kfz gl^{L} — pN, bcz 32
vr lry vol v sls n 39
-pl- rgs ev lor 44
Ohd cSs ln -S 49
kpe Srs, bcz e vlu 57
r plrns e ps la sv= 63
alq n f- v Dk- 70
prss, if u -N l 75
a nu lf lu h- 80

-ol q- beN u bgl 87
pa s · vzl, ev 92
ara rgs la l 96
drs p u Nre a u 101
dn r- or u frpls, 108
dN fgl lae Aso 113
cre / ld brNs v 119
crpl, r nuS Sm 125
v fl clrs , no o 130
Dpla + flr sa-s 136
-a b lcn ol o ln, 141
f gl^{L} + Svs / afdS 149
prss k o s, su 156

LESSON 13

THEORY REVIEW

Write money amounts in the following way:

$13.95	13 95	29 cents	29¢
$400	4H$	$8,425,000	8M425T$
$100,000	1HT$	$2,000,000,000	2B$

TRANSCRIPTION AID

Similar Words

great *gr* Extremely large; excellent.

□ The cost of purchasing that equipment is simply too great for our current budget.

□ Ms. Barnes, manager of the payroll department, is doing a great job in her new position.

grateful *grf* Thankful for benefits received.

□ We are grateful for the prompt and dependable service you have given us in the past.

YOUR BUSINESS VOCABULARY

eliminate *elma* To leave out or remove.

□ Please proofread the letter carefully to eliminate any possibility of error.

extensive *xnv* Large in amount or extent; having a wide range.

□ Professor Randolph has conducted extensive research in the field of genetics.

READING AND WRITING EXERCISES

PREVIEW WORDS

1 money *me*
seasonal *sznl*
cashier *cAr*
receipt *rse*

2 efforts *efls*
grateful *grf*
equally *eqll*
especially *esp*

3 once *oN*
truly *trul*
rare *rr*
beauty *ble*

4 sinks *sqs*
kitchen *cKn*
occupy *ocpi*
cabinets *cbnls*

5 spring *sprq*
presentation *P1*

eliminate *elma*
celebrate *slbra*
anniversary *avrsre*
exclusively *vclsvl*

encouraged *ncry-*
commending *kN-*
considerate *ksi*
acknowledge *acy*

collection *clcy*
entertainment *Nlnm*
invaluable *nvluB*
extraordinary *Xord*

island *lN*
appliances *apliNs*
imagine *yn*
photograph *flogrf*

consumer *ksr*
furnishings *frns=*

seating se_ superior spre>

extensive XNv informative nfv

1

Mr. John R. Flint, 202 Prince George Court, Indianapolis, IN 46217

dr flN l slbra
(avrsre vr grN
opn_, ev s_ spsl
n m fu> z . G K,
u Ar no lae ofr gl'
⌢dse / lo prss E
d, r rglr Dk
prss elma (nd f
sznl sls, b sp_ n
r Sr, u sv me
⌣ E PCs u ⌢c>
no er q_ lofr u
s_ evn blr ln r
Ed lo prss, er
nvi_ u l sr . sp_
vp la, b_ rzrv-
vclsvl f G Ks,
du_ (nlr ⌢o v
Nv, ulb nll- l .
adjl Dk v 20%
o E PCs, jS so u
crd, + csr l ⌢c
(ajSm ou rse,
su

2

Mrs. Peggy Sylvester, 3413 Parkland Place, Washington, DC 20032

drs slvSr lqfL
kN_ r Svs reps,
er grf la uv lcn (
⌊ l acq r Sf, u L
hsb fw- l (⌢pes
hu ⌣ o dle { ⌊
vu vzl> ev A ncrp-
r reps lb ksl lw
Ks, b erp- lhr ⌣n
s⌢ l hsb esp hlpf
+ USN_, s eqll rw_

l lrn la s Ks ap
lz X efls lgv q
Svo, ehp ul ku
l ll s no ab u
vps — r eslm.
lqu aq f ru uvl

3

Form letter to prospective customers from
Edwin Harrington Cooke, Vice President

dS oNn n .
gr l . **Intro P** . lrul
rr opl ks alq,
s r plzr l brq
u r flo anoNm,
f . lnl-l ol el c **Intro P**
avlB lu . olSN
clcy v bcs, lz
vols kln r fnS
slcys n lll f
a + aroN r
o, el v 12
vols , boN n .

hrd cvr v Xord
ble, r sl l bk
. nvluB srs v
nly + Nlnm fu
hl fl, bcz v ls **Intro P**
spsl ofr, r nlr
sl cb us f ol
129 95 , p rmbr
la r ofr vprs o
Ja 31, **Conj** so dN
dla, lz bcs r .
gfl la l mcrs
n vlu z r yrs
q b, cu

4

Mr. and Mrs. Leon Anderson, 341 Pine
Crest Lane, Birmingham, AL 35216

d r + rs adrsn
dd uno la uc v
. nu cln n u
h n 30 ds,
las ru, u dN v

Series

Series

Intro P

Intro DC

Series

Series

5

Add commas to show two conjunctions, one introductory dependent clause, and one parenthetical expression.

Form letter to members from Lynn Snyder

6
12
17
23
29
33
39
44
50
56
62
68
72
79
86
91

e lg ulfN (96
rzlts lb bo Sprz_ 102
+ nfw> if u ⌣+ 108
lvu dns Pvd-p 116
kp + rel (enc- 122

f⌢ , (f⌢ l Sv 128
z . rzrvq fu nv 134
evN la se , 138
bl- , ul 143

LESSON 14

SHORTHAND VOCABULARY REVIEW

Write *l* for the word ending *ly* (lee) or *ily* (uh-lee).

early	erl	lovely	lvl
carefully	crfl	rarely	rrl
closely	clsl	definitely	dfntl

TRANSCRIPTION AID

Spelling. Omit the final *e* when adding *ing* to most words.

dine	din*ing*
examine	examin*ing*
create	creat*ing*
excite	excit*ing*
trace	trac*ing*
confuse	confus*ing*
challenge	challeng*ing*
decorate	decorat*ing*

YOUR BUSINESS VOCABULARY

acknowledge *acq* To show recognition of.

□ This letter is to acknowledge your order of March 1.

merchandise *mdse* Goods that may be bought or sold.

□ That manufacturer produces an excellent quality of merchandise.

READING AND WRITING EXERCISES

PREVIEW WORDS

1 coat *co*

correct *crc*

jacket *jcl*

leather *llr*

material *trel*

reminding *rm*

situation *sily*

acknowledge *acy*

2 bowl *bl*

silver *slvr*

solid *sld*

leaves *lvs*

flowers *flors*

basically *bscl*

antique *alc*

decorating *dcra*

3 Susan *szn*

cooperate *cop*

Sanderson *sNrsn*

challenging *Clny*

effort *efl*

worthwhile *rll*

objective *objcv*

volunteers *vlnlrs*

4 owe *o*

sporting *spl*

brought *brl*

receipts *rses*

further *frlr*

unusual *uuz*

household *hoshld*

confusion *kfj*

5 yard *yd*

tracing *lrs*

later *lar*

loading *ld*

trees

touch

platform

evergreen

1

Mr. Paul Marvin, 3211 Albert Street, Regina, SK S4S 5W6

Intro P

Conj

Conj

2

Mrs. Ronald Hunter, 471 Mondalock Lane, Manchester, NH 03102

Intro DC

Conj

Conj

3

Mrs. Natalie Gregory, Public Relations Coordinator, Dos Hermanos Hospital, 1007 Palo Verde Boulevard, Albuquerque, NM 87114

h C vp n cra
lvl Dplas. se
, r Dpla yr, (Ap)
syn sNrsn. se
hs Pds- me v
idas f s, (Conj) + ino
se d re ls Pjc z
v rw + Clnj->
er hpe l pp n ls
rtl efl. cu

4

Mr. Jeffrey Sandifer, 9360 Camden Way, Apartment C, Rochester, NY 14610

dr sNfr af Cc
r recs crfl, (Intro P) ev
foN la / ad
sn ou 8 rsN
bl, crc. / lol
u no o, 76 89.
er enc cpes v
2 sls rses. /

fr8 PCs z d
n r spl gs dpl, (Conj)
+ sec z f hoshld
ids, du ls bze
h v yr, (Intro P) s n
uuz f Ks l Olc
. pam. no la ev
dl- / cz v kff, (Intro DC)
eno lau ak lb
brl pda, if uv
frlr qs ab r bl
Psyrs, (Intro DC) p cl e
Psnll / 613-2189.
su

5

Add commas to show two conjunctions, one direct address, and two introductory dependent clauses.

Ms. Robinette Jackson, 687 Cedarwood Circle, St. Paul, MN 55125

dr jcsn lqf ri 8
lsa lau od hs n 14

yl arv-, edu n 19
v . rzn f dla 25
b er crNl lc 31
nl (dr, (Egrn 37
lres s- o scyl, 43
ly lfl r ld plf 50
o s d lae rsv- 56
u rgl + ly sd v 63
rC- u rzdN / c 70
lar, Alo er lrs 76
la sm edu n 81

N u l a ne 85
lgr f lres, er 91
sN . nu od ld, 97
f uv n rsv- b 103
/ c f ld p cl 110
e l, ehp u 115
nyy u blef lres 121
s jcsn, ly l 126
a . lvl lC lu 131
yd, ul 135

LESSON 15

WORD DEVELOPMENT

Develop new words from the following brief forms:

on

only ol

onward ow

onset osl

upon po

firm

affirm afr

confirm kfr

confirmation kfrj

infirmary nfrre

over

moreover ᵔO

overall OA

overdue Odu

overhead Ohd

part

apartment aplm

counterpart krpl

depart dpl

partner plnr

READING AND WRITING EXERCISES

PREVIEW WORDS

1 before bf

reorder rod

bottom bl

catalog cal

remember rmbr

subtotal slol

figure fgr

quantity qNl

2 disks Dcs
manual mul
Boulevard blvd
prompt Pl

Lincoln lgn
processor Psss
electronic elnc
accustomed acS-

3 Elm el
Fifth 5l
parts pls
Street S

corner crnr
automotive atv
accessories ssres
neighborhood nbrh

4 water tr
section sc
notice nls
another aol

edition ed
original orynl
addition ad
recreation rcre

5 fashions fjs
private prvl
showroom sor
presence przN

American A
exclusive vclsv
favorite fvrl
refreshments rfrsms

1

Mr. Eric Davidson, Rural Route 2, Box 503, Racine, WI 53408

dr dvdsn lqf
rsN od f spl gs.

bf ec Pss u od, (Intro DC)
hoE, (Paren) el nd adyl
inf. r cpe v PCs
f sos lau dd n

I cal Nos f ne v
ths rqS-, p uz c
nu f la ev enc-
l rod c ndse,
rmbr l lS c qNl
f eC th, c unl (Series)
prs, & cal No, (Series)
E bh v pj, so (Intro P)
c tol No v ths
& tol cS v u PCss,
A c s fe l ls
stol & so c tol
a l o-, b sr u
Cc agres c fgr
f tol a l o-,
eap u psN n crc
ls od, el s c ndse
zz c kp-f & pam
r rsv-, ul

2

Ms. Karen Chase, Berghoff Container Corporation, P.O. Box 8215, Atlanta, GA 30317

ds Cs enc-, c
X lrn nul u
rqS- fu rd Pssr,
ev od- Dcs fu, (Conj)
& ly r Ub l-drl
lu ofs, usd v h
n 10 ds, er dli-
Uhr la A v unls
u rN- f s r Pf
l, c lprurs r aq
c nuS dls avlB
n elnc eqpm, so (Conj)
idu n alspa laul
nd rpr Svs l ur
rN h, hoE, lr, (Paren)
. Svs sNr lca-
nrb / 901 lqn
blvd, ly l gv u
Pd & rliB Svs, (Conj)
& ly r acS-l bl
s f sC cls, ehp ls
arm os l fu, su

3

Mr. and Mrs. Lawrence Walters, 180 Courtland Avenue, Bridgeport, CT 06604

Intro DC

4

Form letter to prospective customers from J. B. Hodges, Sales Manager

Conj

Paren

s orjnl sz, yx e
vlu r plrnj vr Ks, Conj
+ e M lofr b r
bl Cyss v dse,
avyd c unes
lrps l sp sMrs,
sv me r kv a
b od / hlsl prss,
uc k o s l olfl u
lu saly, vri +
dpMB v bk r
spslles, su

5

Add commas to show one appositive, one introductory dependent clause, and two introductory phrases.

Ms. Emily Evans, 1402 Little Creek Road, Bloomington, IN 47401

d s evns r ym 6
vr fr rgSs u przM 13
/ . prvl so v . u 20
clcj, / fCrs . fvrl 28
a Pdc dznr fjs, 35
jS n u lq uv sn 42
E . lrul r rcB 48
ida ks alq, l pv 54
ls py er nvl u l 61
vu orjnl fjs f r 67
S prsv dznrs 74
n a, hc r ocj 81
evn spsl ev 87
ar-f Mnm + rfrsms, 96
r enc- crd l Sv zu 103
nvlj, p so / zu 110
M r sor, / gvs 116
s plzr l hS ls 121
vclsv so, ehp 127
ulb r gS, uvl 135

UNIT FOUR

BANKING

SHORTHAND VOCABULARY REVIEW

Study the following words and the principles they illustrate. You will find these words in the letters and memos in this unit.

> **1.** Write a capital C for the sound of *ch*, *cha* (pronounced *chay*).

check *Cc*

mutual *Cul*

branch *brnC*

chairman *Crmn*

achieve *aCv*

change *Cny*

future *fCr*

structure *SrcCr*

approaching *aprC*

expenditure *pNCr*

P rel VP ⁓r corp E efcv

enc a l cr No% sv ida

lol dpl env ins inv re glfs

2. Write [shorthand] for the word ending *ful*.

grateful [shorthand] — carefully [shorthand]
helpful [shorthand] — successful [shorthand]
careful [shorthand] — successfully [shorthand]

3. Write [shorthand] for *self* and [shorthand] for *selves*.

yourself [shorthand] — themselves [shorthand]

MORE ABOUT PUNCTUATION

Compound adjectives are two or more words that are used as one thought to describe a noun. If these words come immediately before the noun, join them with a hyphen.

- ☐ Please place an order for a six-foot table.
- ☐ Where can we find an up-to-date book?
- ☐ She is a well-known expert.

If these words come after the noun, no hyphen is necessary.

- ☐ We already have a table that is six feet long.
- ☐ I believe that this book is up to date.
- ☐ Her skills are well known.

Do not use a hyphen if the first word ends in *ly*.

- ☐ Can you recommend a highly skilled craftsman?
- ☐ It was a closely guarded secret.

LESSON 16

BRIEF FORMS AND DERIVATIVES

1. sig y ty dr n
2. apxl dfce ac- ~jr or4

Key

1. signature/significant/significance, why, they, doctor/direct, in/not
2. approximately, difficulty, accepted, manager, ownership

PHRASE REVIEW

Easily recognized words are omitted from some phrases:

thank *you* for	tqf	as *soon* as	zz
thank *you* for *your*	tqf	time *to* time	tt
thank *you* for *your* letter	tqfL	up *to* date	pda
never*the*less	nvrls	none*the*less	nnls

1. und usd tv tsN tuz zu
2. fu hsb n zz pda

Key

1. you need, you should, to have, to send, to use, as you/as your
2. for you/for your, has been, in the, as soon as, up to date

READING AND WRITING EXERCISES

PREVIEW WORDS

1 honor *onr*

reject *ryc*

destroy *dSry*

difficulty *dfce*

identical *idNcl*

correctly *crcl*

automatic *atdc*

identification *idNfj*

2 today *ld*

goes *gs*

answer *asr*

into *nl*

wonder *Nr*

transfer *Tfr*

specified *sp-*

automatically *atdcl*

3 peace *ps*

stolen *Sln*

finances *fnNs*

vacation *vcq*

greater *grr*

financial *fnnsl*

arrangements *arms*

protection *Plcq*

4 assign *asn*

boxes *bxs*

period *pred*

assured *asr-*

therefore *lrf*

possessions *pzjs*

safe-deposit *sf = dpzl*

inexpensive *nxpNv*

5 dreams *drs*

burden *brdn*

country *cNre*

lending *lN*

yours	us	reasonable	rznB
corporation	corp	ownership	ors

1

Mr. Donald M. Jackson, 1033 Shadowdance Street, San Antonio, TX 78253

dr jcsn er enc
. nu idNfj crd
fu, p dSry u old
crd + rpls / ⌣
(nu crd, ze
Intro DC
agre- b llfn, r bq
l onr (Ccs uv rln
uz- u f m, w
Paren Paren
fCr, hoE, b Sln
la (sig u uz ou
Ccs , idNcl l la
sn ou nu idNfj
crd, e rgrt la 2
Conj
vu Ccs ⌣ rel-, b
r pes ryc Ccs
⌣C vn b sn-crcl,
Conj
ls , . ablc Psyr,
+ s dzn-l Plc u
ak, no la uv rsv-
Intro DC
u nu crd, usd v
no frlr dfce, uvl

2

Mr. and Mrs. Herbert Carlson, 217 Highland Place, Cheyenne, WY 82009

dr + rs crlsn
s ppl a s
lv (me ly nd,
dd u E Nr y, (
asr , gi spl f
r Ks, ly uz r me
ym Svs, b uz- r
Intro P
ym Svs, u pa
usf bf pa u bls,
hr , ho / os,
u bgn b dpzl u
f paCc w ak,
ln e abld Tfr (
sp- ad nl u sv

Intro DC

Intro DC

Intro P

3

Mr. and Mrs. Kenneth Webb, 4380 Magnolia Drive, Virginia Beach, VA 23464

Intro DC

Intro DC

4

Mr. Thomas Hastings, 3229 Prospect Boulevard, Boston, MA 02160

Intro DC

v · fre Svs、 u ⌒a
uz · sf=dpzl bx /
no cS f · pred v
4 ⌒cs, esl asn
(bxs w od la
rqSs r rsv-、
Paren
lrf , if uv · vcj
Intro DC
or lrp scjl- , usd
gv s u das zz
psB so la ucb
asr- v gl u Cys
v ⌒s, ehp u
njy ls Svs、 lz
dpzl bxs ofr (
ol sf ⌒a l Plc
⌒pl pprs + pzjs、
u ⌒a evn dsd l
rM 1 v lz dpzl
bxs o · yrl bss、
⌒n u ks (sl
Intro DC
cS , sC Plq , v
nxpNv、 su

5

Add commas to set off one series, two introductory dependent clauses, one introductory phrase, and one appositive.

Form letter to prospective customers from Jeremy O'Connell, President

dS⌒ erp-l anoN (10
opn vr nu brnC 15
ofs n u nbrh, r 22
corp hs Sv- Ms 28
v Ks a O (cMre、 35
ev ⌒d / psB f 41
fls lc us l relz 48
lr drs、 ev hlp- 54
⌒ aCv h⌒ ors 59
vcjs clj ejcjs + 66
ol spsl nds、 bcz 72
r pam plns r so 77
rznB ly v ez- (84
brdn v rpa lns, 89
⌒n und fnnsl 94
asSNusdCz · lN 102
co z crfl z ud Cz 110
· dr、 asc u frNs 116

ab s or brq u qs 122
l s Psnll, l lrn 128
⌒ ab r Svss pa 134
s . vzl, r ak 139

⌒yrs ⌒ ⌒S hlpf 144
ppl n lon lb dli- 151
l ⌒e u, ul 156

LESSON 17

ABBREVIATIONS AND DERIVATIVES

1. an rel VP env No fed
2. A rep agrl hrs ds

Key

1. amount, return, vice president, envelope, number, federal
2. America/American, represent/representative, agricultural, hours, days

---

TRANSCRIPTION AID

Typing Numbers

1. When a number consists of four or more figures, use a comma to set off groups of three digits.

□ At least 5,000 people participated in the sports festival.

2. As a general rule, write serial numbers, invoice numbers, and catalog numbers without commas.

□ Please refer to Invoice 60843.

YOUR BUSINESS VOCABULARY

option *opj* A choice; in an insurance policy, a clause permitting the policyholder to choose the manner in which payments are to be made or credited to him or her.

□ Please consider all of the options carefully before deciding upon a particular one.

agenda *ajNa* A list of topics to be discussed or things to be completed at a meeting.

□ Each board member will receive a copy of the agenda in advance.

READING AND WRITING EXERCISES

PREVIEW WORDS

1	form	f⌢	appointment	apym
	already	ar	retirement	rtrm
	anything	ne_	situation	sij
	option	opj	application	aplcj
2	dial	dil	access	vs
	fire	fr	actually	acCull
	per	p	whenever	⌣nE
	theft	ufl	safe-deposit	sf=dpzl
3	Clay	cla	credit	cr
	line	ln	coming	k_
	basis	bss	welcome	lk
	state	Sa	supplied	spli-
4	closely	clsl	reactions	racjs
	receipts	rses	statements	Sams
	Las Vegas	ls vgs	transaction	Tacj
	tentatively	tNvl	withdrawals	⌣drals
5	guide	gd	agenda	ajNa
	rates	ras	attracting	atrc_

panel

community

availability

real estate

1

Mr. Roland Wilson, 1001 Portage Avenue, Winnipeg, MB R3C 3J3

Intro DC

2

Ms. Anne Russell, 1511 Gentry Street, Wichita, KS 67208

Paren

And O

Paren

so u ho s dn, dil
r bq No, 217-2211,
f — inf, r Svs
rep l gv u (f
dlls, vlu

3

Mrs. George Clay, 212 Covey Hill Court, Boise, ID 83705

d—rs cla e dli-
lrsv u rqs f cr, (Conj)
+ er enc . aplc
f, sN ulb k l
r sle f— aol Sa, (Intro DC)
ul nd l kp (f—
+ rel / w env la
ev spli-, u aplc
lb Pss- —l, zz
u ln v cr hsb est-, (Intro DC)
u cr crd lb o s
—a lu, erp-l lk
u l r kn, —rs (Dir Ad)
cla, + e lc fw l (Conj)

Sv u o . rglr bss,
pcl o s f a vu bq-
nds, su

4

Memo to Nancy Parker from Richard Crow, SUBJECT: Proposal for New Monthly Statements

mo l nNe prcr
er ks . nu sS f
isu bq rses, u
PbO rcl la ls sS
z Dcs- — nyl kfrN
n ls vgs, me v
—yr bqs w cNre
no lgr isu —ol
Sams la lS eC
Tacj ch— b ch—,
nSd, (Paren) ly —l . brf
lS so (lol and
v —drals, (Series) (lol
dpzls, (Series) + blN v
ak, ls s—re, —l-

Intro DC

5

Add commas to show one introductory phrase, one parenthetical expression, one series, and one direct address.

Miss Beverly Lee, Vice President, Pioneer Bank and Trust, 6400 Mission Road, Colorado Springs, CO 80915

LESSON 18

SHORTHAND VOCABULARY REVIEW

1. The following represent frequently used salutations in business correspondence:

Gentlemen

Ladies l

Ladies and Gentlemen lj

Dear Ms.

Dear Mrs.

Dear Sir dS

Dear Sir or Madam dS

Dear Miss dM

Dear Mr.

Dear Dr. ddr

2. Some commonly used complimentary closes in business correspondence are listed below.

Sincerely yours su

Yours truly ul

Yours very truly uvl

Sincerely s

Cordially yours cu

Very truly yours vlu

Respectfully yours ru

Cordially c

3. When using these words in the context of a letter or memo, write them according to rule.

gentlemen jNlm

ladies ldes

dear dr

madam ᴗd

cordially crjll

respectfully rspcfl

truly trul

sincerely snsrl

TRANSCRIPTION AID

Similar Words

since sN — 1. To indicate the passing of time:

□ We have operated out of the new offices since May.

2. Can be used in place of *because:*

□ Since we have not heard from you, we are enclosing another statement.

sense sN — 1. The act of perceiving through hearing, seeing, smelling, touching, tasting, or intuition:

□ From the tone of the report, I sense that a major change is coming.

2. Sound logic or reason:

□ It makes good sense to plan ahead.

cents ¢ — Monetary units equal to 1/100 of a dollar each.

□ Please keep an accurate record of all dollars and cents spent.

YOUR BUSINESS VOCABULARY

mutual fund company ᴗculfNco — An investment company that owns shares of stocks in various other companies.

□ I would like to have information about how to invest in a mutual fund company.

liabilities liBls — Debts; obligations for which a person is held legally responsible.

□ The contract will specify the liabilities of each party.

READING AND WRITING EXERCISES

PREVIEW WORDS

1 lower, mutual, promise, federal, dependable, guarantee, certificate, institution

2 cents, Central, receipt, precious, dollars, assigned, itemized, automatically

3 tone, behalf, chairman, history, gratitude, volunteers, imaginative, friendliness

4 sums, cannot, hurry, easier, quickly, brought, permanent, expenditure

5 wise, data, major, assets

complex *kplx*

advice *avo*

various *vres*

liabilities *liϐ⁶*

1

Dr. Charles Foster, 824 Augusta Drive, Anchorage, AK 99504

ddr flr er hr ~C
ab (avjo v nvl
me n ~Cul fms,
hoE ⸱₉ vu asc- usf — **Paren**
ab (sfle v ly
fmsₓ ⸱ Pᵣo ⸴ n ⸱
grnle, NS ras f
~Cul fm cos rg
ld ₉ b 6 ~oo f — **Conj**
no ly ~a b ~C
lor⸴ б ol hm ₉ ec — **Paren**
ofr u sᵣ ⁓ dpmϐ,
⁓ n u nvl n ⸱ Slfcl
*v dpzl (r sv + *
ln nSl ₉ u gl hu — **Intro DC**
NS ras la r grnle-
nl Cny, und n
⁓re ab (sfle vu

dpzl bcz (me ⸴
nsr- b (fed gvl ⸴
e cryll nvr u l
nvlga frlr, cl or
k b l vr kv brnC
ofss, som pln ⁓cs
q sm, uvl

2

Form letter to prospective customers from Franklin Cox, President

dSᵣ du u ly prss
ᵣ q_ f pls l pls
lpa u blsₓ dd uno
la smrl bq_ l Pf
la Svo fuₓ⸴ yf u opn
⸱ ex ak ⁓ o ₉ el — **Intro DC**
pa u blo al �⌣cl
б asn-d v eC ⁓o,
ho dy lo hme ss
⁓oₓ ⁓ ⸱ mm blm

v 3T$, (Intro P) ul pa no
—ol Svs Gf bls
pd U (ex pln. f
eC adjl Cc u ri, (Intro P)
u pa ol . s—l fe.
—N v eC 6= —o
pred, (Intro P) ul rsv .
—z- rse fu lx
recs, r ex ak
, ol 1 v me kv
Svss / sNrl bq.
e pl u $ + ¢ —o
fu. ru

3

Mr. Henry Knight, 2483 El Camino Road, Tempe, AZ 85282

d hnre — enc (
inf u rqS- l brq u
bjl pda. p nl la (
ak rfN No , 63003.
/ sdb uz- f a vpNs
rla- l (fN drv,

p ac r snsr lqs
f Sv z Cr—n ls
yr. u Pvd- (cN
v ldrs nd- —c
ls evN (—S
sucf 1 n hSre,
lr r me aras v
suc ec py l. u
Pvd- idas la —
—nv, (Series) u sl . ln
v frNl' + egr', (Series) +
u oq- (drv n sC
. —a la vlnlrs cd
—e lr gls, o bhf
v nlr kn', (Intro P)
vprs grlld f hf .
M ppl. u Slnl
dzrv / f . jb l
dn. s

4

Miss Katherine James, 139 Cardiff Drive, Wilmington, DE 19803

Paren

Paren

Intro DC

5

Add commas to show one introductory phrase and two introductory dependent clauses. Add a comma also to show the omission of *and* between two adjectives.

Dr. and Mrs. Elliott Webb, 5939 Rainbow Road, Omaha, NE 68112

5

14

19

26

34

39

46

51

58

63

68

73

79

84

+ liB^ls, esd Aso 91
ks / lx Avjs avlB 98
lu, sN lr r vres 105
lrS plns avlBel 111
⌣N l Cz / l ⌢S 117

apo fu + u fl> 124
p rmbr l brq / 130
fnnsl dla e Dcs-, 136
uvl 140

LESSON 19

SHORTHAND VOCABULARY REVIEW

1. Add *s* to form the plural of any outline ending in a letter.

services *Svss* years *yrs*
flowers *flors* expenses *pNs*
improvements *pvms* customers *Ks*

2. Write *s* to add s to a verb. Add s even though the final sound of the word is z.

describes *dSs* assures *asrs*
shows *sos* provides *Pvds*

3. To form the plural of any outline ending in a mark of punctuation, double the last mark of punctuation.

savings *sv=* dealings *dl=*

TRANSCRIPTION AID

Spelling. Many words commonly used in business communications contain silent letters. You do not hear these letters when the words are pronounced.

mortgage	debt
safeguarded	doubt
honor	highly
listen	knowledge

Learn the correct spelling of these words. Watch for other words that contain silent letters.

YOUR BUSINESS VOCABULARY

assets — As used in business, items that can be turned into cash.

□ The assets of the two companies total $6 million.

pledge — A formal promise or commitment.

□ We are fulfilling our pledge to increase sales.

READING AND WRITING EXERCISES

PREVIEW WORDS

1 realtor, owners, closing, advisor, references, responses, notified, questions

2 wills, properly, relieve, contentment

secure *scr*

estates *eSas*

3 exit *Vl*

greet *gre*

cookies *cces*

Northside *N sd*

4 mayor *~ar*

assets *asls*

pledge *plj*

excess *\s*

5 greater *grr*

lengthy *lqle*

adopting *adpl*

itemized *Vl~z-*

unfinished *ufns-*

specialists *spslSs*

cordially *cryll*

Interstate *NSa*

Grandview *grNvu*

celebrate *slbra*

tribute *lrbu*

citizens *slzns*

prosperity *Pspr'*

anniversary *avrsre*

regarding *re_*

activities *acv'ls*

eliminates *elmas*

accompanied *aco-*

1

Mr. and Mrs. Harvey Evans, 632 Homestead
Avenue, Cleveland, OH 44105

dr + ~rs evns

erp- l grN u ~

~rgj u apli- f,

e rsv- rsps f

a v rfNs u lS- ,9 v Conj

u cr rq_ hsb apv-,

sN ~ u fnnsl

Avzr ,9 w Ar klc- Intro DC

u rlls v crN ors

v prp C ur PCs

Conj

Intro DC

Conj

2

Mr. and Mrs. Kevin Grant, 2104 Shamrock Avenue, Green Bay, WI 54304

Intro DC

Intro P

3

Form letter to prospective customers from Diana T. Wilcox, Branch Manager

nuS brnC bq, s
lca- n Nsd Sp
sNr nr NSa 70
grNvu d> hlp s
slbra b v cfe +
cces ◡ s f 10a
l 5p o Sp 5, ed
Conj
nju ◡e u, + edlc
l hlp u gl agN-
◡ r bq Svss, r
Psnl lb o hN l
gre u Psnll + asr
ne qs u ◡u v>
◡a e k o v u
alN, er egr l bk
Conj
.pl v ls gro nbrh,
+ ehp ul gv s ls
opl l prs r ap
n Psn, ul

4

Mr. Melvin Baxter, 320 Kelly Street, Stillwater, OK 74074

d r bxtr er ab l
slbra . v spsl
avrsre, f 25 yrs
ev ◡- nvSms
f slzns v ls lon,
no e ◡+ l ll E1
no ho ◡C ev ap-
no + Sv ◡, ld
r asls r n s v
Paren
50M$, ◡ol . dol,
e o . dl v lqs l
ls kn f r grl +
Pspr, lu hlp s
slbra> jyn s f .
lrbu o Ma 17,
◡ar vr sle lb
n alNN l ac r
ply l sle, el
Aso rnu r ply l
brq v opls l r
cliNs, el lc fw
lse u hr, vlu

5

Add commas to show one introductory dependent clause, one parenthetical expression, one appositive, and one series.

Dr. and Mrs. Michael Gregory, 7635 Oaklawn Drive, Memphis, TN 38114

ddr + ⌒rs grgre 5
erp-⌐c · anoNm 13
re · ⌒pvm n Svss 21
fu, ul no lgr rsv 28
· lqle Sam E ⌒o 34
z uv n pS, nSd 41
ul rsv · brf Sam 48
so (lol ⌣drals 55
lol dpzls + crN 60
blN vu ak, ls Sam 68
lb aco- b u csl- 76
Ccs, er adpl ls 82
nu sS⌒ bcz / 86
elmas (nd f · 92
⌒z- lS vu bq- 98
acvls, (Cnj l 104
rzll n grr efsNe 110
fu zlz f s, el ku 119
lofr u · K e vlu 126
hil bq Svss / no 132
adjl cS lu, f usd 139
v qs re u o recs 148
or r Sams elb 154
hpe l asr ⌐, cu 161

LESSON 20

WORD DEVELOPMENT

Develop new words from the following brief forms:

as

whereas

inasmuch

to

into

heretofore

full

fulfill

fullness

fully

go

ago

ongoing

cargo

come

become

overcome

good

goodwill

goodness

READING AND WRITING EXERCISES

PREVIEW WORDS

1 aid

son

afford

college

lending

children

daughter

educational

2 model *~dl* federal *fed*

annual *aul* expedite *pdi*

proof *prf* machines *~sns*

effort *efl* agricultural *agrl*

3 fares *frs* steady *Sde*

bonus *bns* creating *cra*

listen *lsn* depositor *dpzls*

clients *clns* eligible *eljb*

4 error *err* withdrawal *~dral*

found *fon* incorrectly *ncrcl*

register *rjSr* calculation *clcly*

statement *Sam* occasionally *ocjll*

5 teller *llr* elderly *eldrl*

Marsha *~rsa* imagine *~yn*

poor *pr* independent *npnn*

mother *~lr* considerate *ksl*

1

Mr. and Mrs. Maurice Harper, 6009 Richmond Avenue, Arlington, VA 22207

d~r + ~rs hrpr

me ppl r asc

hsvs ho ly lb

B l afd lsN lr

Cldrn l clj. cSs

rz E yr, + lr,

Intro P

Conj

Intro P

Intro DC

2

Mr. Robert Billings, 43 McKinney Drive, Greenville, SC 29609

Intro DC

Dir Ad

~r bl. vlu

3

Form letter to depositors from Stuart Abel. Special Accounts Manager

d dpzlr f me yrs
r X~s clb hsb
pplr ~ r clMs.
ls yr er q. Sp frlr.
er crq. s~lr cN
v ak l hlp pa f
vc vpNs, lr r me
rzns f opn sC.
ak. fS z r X~s
clb hs ez-u Sp
vpNs, [Intro DC] r vc clb
l ~c u lrp. hper
vp f E1. r pln Pvds
. Sde, [And O] kv ~a l sl
asd r me und f
f~l fn, lsn l ls
~pl bns. mbrs
l bk elgB f Dks
o lrps hr + abrd.
u Dks l I rdcjs
o ar frs, [Series] hll akdjs, [Series]
+ ol alrcjs, du u
~N lhr ~x rel
r enc- crd ~ol
dla. Srl u ak no
+ ll r fn bgn. cu

4

Miss Caroline Robinson, 6747 Sheffield Place, Apartment 4B, Providence, RI 02920

dM rbnsn af rvu
u recs ~ cr, [Intro P] ev
foN no err n u
Cc ak. e ~S as~, [Paren]
lrf, [Paren] la r blN Sn
ou Sam) crc, sN
u recs du n agre
~ r Sam, [Intro DC] d u lc
l brq u Ccbc l r
ofs. Svs rep c

5

Add commas to show two conjunctions, two parenthetical expressions, one introductory dependent clause, two appositives, and one series.

Mr. William Temple, President, First National Bank, 3006 Anderson Boulevard. Eugene, OR 97401

Professionalism on the Job

The contact you have with the persons who visit or call your organization is just as important to establishing and maintaining goodwill as the documents that you prepare. The following procedures will help in your personal contacts.

GREETING OFFICE VISITORS

Your appearance and mannerisms reflect the image of your organization. Visitors are guests of your organization, and you are the host. Always be courteous, helpful, and professional.

Make a good impression. Maintain a quiet, tidy, and orderly reception area. Your desk should be neat, and your conduct should be mannerly.

Greet visitors immediately. Consider your visitors as the most important priority, even if visits are interruptions in a busy work schedule. You may say, for example:

- "Hello, may I help you? . . . Yes, Mr. Houseman is expecting you. Please be seated, and I will tell him you're here."

If you are involved in a telephone conversation, excuse yourself politely from the conversation long enough to greet the visitor briefly. Then conclude the phone conversation as quickly as possible and give your full attention to the visitor.

Make the visitor comfortable. If the visitor has to wait, offer assistance and keep the person informed about the delay. If you expect the wait to be longer than five minutes, offer the person magazines or a soft drink.

Make introductions when necessary. Usher the visitor to the appropriate office. If the visitor knows your supervisor, keep the introduction simple:

☐ "Ms. Campbell, Mr. Simpson is here to see you."

If the visitor is a newcomer, introduce him or her to your supervisor:

☐ "Ms. Campbell, this is Mr. Carl Simpson from Everview Software."

Say "no" politely, firmly, and positively. When someone arrives without an appointment and wants to see a person who is unavailable, be as positive and helpful as possible by suggesting an alternative:

☐ "I'm sorry, but Mr. Stone will be in meetings all afternoon. Would you be free to meet with him tomorrow afternoon?"

Remain calm and courteous, but be firm.

GREETING CALLERS BY TELEPHONE

Because the persons you speak with on the telephone can form impressions of you and your organization only on the basis of your telephone manners, it is important to use oral communication skills as effectively as possible.

Be courteous. Assume a personal tone and make the caller feel that he or she is the most important person in the world.

Speak clearly and listen carefully. Speak distinctly so that your message will be immediately clear to the caller. Listen carefully for the correct pronunciation of the caller's name and for the name of the party he or she wishes to speak to.

Identify yourself immediately. When answering a call coming from outside your organization, begin with a pleasant greeting, followed by your organization's name and your name:

☐ "Good afternoon, Westcott Enterprises, Chris Bergman speaking."

If your are answering a call from inside your building or if your organization has a switchboard operator who has answered the outside call before directing it to you, simply answer by identifying the department or your supervisor's name before giving your name:

☐ "Purchasing department, Julie Randolph speaking."
☐ "Mr. Marshall's office, John Moore speaking."

Ask for complete information. If you are answering the phone for someone else in your department, be certain that you get the correct name of the caller and the caller's organization. Phrase the question politely:

- "May I ask who's calling, please?" *Or* "Who shall I say is calling, please?"

Offer assistance. Be as helpful as you can. If you cannot connect the caller with the appropriate party, give the caller an explanation and options:

- "I'm sorry, Mr. Ryan is on another line. Would you like to hold a few moments, or shall I take a message and have him return your call?"
- "I'm sorry, Ms. Summerville will not be in the office today. Could someone else help you?"

If the caller prefers to wait on the line, go back on the line after one minute and ask if the person wishes to continue waiting. It is irritating to be placed on "hold" and forgotten.

Conclude by verifying information. Be certain that a complete exchange of information has taken place. If you are taking a message, read the information back to ensure its completeness and accuracy.

UNIT FIVE

INSURANCE

SHORTHAND VOCABULARY REVIEW

Study the following words and the principles they illustrate. You will find these words in the letters and memos in this unit.

1. Write *n* for the initial sound of *en* or *in*.

enjoy	instance
enrolling	insured
encourage	inflation
entire	injury

2. Omit the final *t* of a root word after the sound of *k*.

collect clc | act ac
affected afc- | subject sjc
contact klc | expect vpc

MORE ABOUT PUNCTUATION

Use commas to set off nonrestrictive clauses from the rest of the sentence. *Restrictive* and *nonrestrictive* clauses are groups of words that usually begin with the words *who, that,* or *which.*

A nonrestrictive clause adds information but does not limit, or restrict, the meaning of the sentence. If you were to remove this clause, you would not change the meaning of the sentence.

□ Jane Benson, who was elected mayor in the primary, will be our guest.

(*Jane Benson will be our guest* is the main emphasis of the sentence.)

A restrictive clause is necessary to the meaning of the sentence and cannot be removed without changing the meaning of the sentence. Do not place commas around restrictive clauses.

□ All vacation requests that are submitted early will be given priority.

(*All vacation requests will be given priority* is not the correct meaning. Only those submitted early will be given priority.)

Nonrestrictive clauses will be identified in the Reading and Writing Exercises with the initials **NRC.**

LESSON

21

BRIEF FORMS AND DERIVATIVES

1. *

*

2. *

*

Key

1. important/importance, contribute, can, us, great/grate, market

2. industries, situations, manufacturer, candidates, canceled, understands

PHRASE REVIEW

1. *

*

2. *

*

Key

1. I will be, I would like, to do, to know, to see, to call

2. to keep, that we, thank you for/thank you for your, thank you for your letter

READING AND WRITING EXERCISES

PREVIEW WORDS

1 hire *hr*

types *lps*

giant *jN*

sample *sa*

reference *rfN*

probably *pbo*

eleventh *11 L*

readership *rdrs*

2 none, really, health, illness, welfare, accident, provider, unfortunate

3 Farm, upon, toll-free, reputation, Mutual, homeowner, mention, indicated

4 yours, daily, Sandra, complicated, Andrew, famous, demonstrated, exhibiting

5 worth, homeowner, options, minutes, adequate, upgrading, afternoon, inflation

1

Hoffmeister Corporation, Paper Goods Division, 213 Piedmont Avenue, Fayetteville, NC 28304

NRC

NRC

Intro P

Intro P

2

Dr. and Mrs. Todd W. Brown, 7429 Kirkwood Road, St. Louis, MO 63119

Paren

Intro DC

Intro P

Intro DC

Conj

3

Form letter to homeowners from Milton Pershing, President

Paren

Intro P

Intro P

Intro P

4

Ms. Sandra Overton, Reliance Insurance Agency, 810 Centennial Avenue, Trenton, NJ 08629

d sNra ls L, l
acq u hlp n sll
r ch fl- b u
cliN, (Ap) adru dvs.
a r v ho
kplx + kplca-
ls cd v bk.
u dmSra- C
scl n oq + fl
r ch. n adj, (Paren) u
Pvd- C spl l
r nsr- ples. b
du u jb l, (Intro P) uv
rep- ls co v l,
us, r lp v PfM
la hs d ls co
fs. uno la eck
ou l ku l sl.
ex f ol ajNs, aq, (Paren)
sNra, (Dir Ad) uv
snsr lqs f vbl
lN n u dl o.
cu

5

Add commas to show two introductory dependent clauses, one introductory phrase, two conjunctions, and two parenthetical expressions.

Mr. and Mrs. Albert Mason, 107 Sierra Court, Reno, NV 89506 5

drs + rs sn 10
af rvu r plse 16
la cvrs u h + 22
Psnl prp w s 27
sugjs. cd e pln 33
l lc s w nx 39
fu ds, n u PCs- 46
u h os ins / 52
Aql fu nds. sN 58
r da u lc ol la 64
plse hoE 2 sug 69
Cnjs v lcn pls. 77
uv A- sv pvns

+ nfly hs afc- r 83
wrl vu hm, z. 89
rzll u hos hs 93
ncrs- grl n vlu> 99
udb wz l Plc la 106
wrl b pgrd u 111
wns, lr r sm 116
opjs la l gv u 122

a- Plcq f . v mdl 129
ncrs n ras, / l 134
lc ol . fu mls lq 140
O lz opjs + ulb 147
hpe Lo aroN u 152
scjl> ul pln lcl u 159
l afnn ls wc l 165
esl . hm, su 172

LESSON 22

ABBREVIATIONS AND DERIVATIVES

1. M Lol P B
2. Ld dl ySrd rels exs qlrl

Key

1. Mr., Mrs., Ms., Miss, total, president, billion
2. today, daily, yesterday, returns, executives, quarterly

TRANSCRIPTION AID

Word Division. Whenever possible, avoid dividing words at the end of a line. However, if typing the entire word will detract from the appearance of the letter, a long word having two or more syllables can be divided correctly if you follow the guidelines given below. Remember, when you are in doubt about where to make the division, *always refer to your dictionary.*

1. Always divide between syllables.

in . de . pend . ent	*independ- (ent)* or *inde- (pendent)*

2. Words of one syllable should not be divided.

health	*health*

3. Short two-syllable words having five or fewer letters should not be divided.

re . ply	*reply*

4. When a syllable in the middle of a word contains only one letter, divide the word after the single letter.

min . i . mum	*mini- (mum)*
div . i . dend	*divi- (dend)*

5. Single-letter syllables at the beginning or end of a word or two-letter syllables at the end of a word should not be divided.

a . ban . don	*aban- (don)*
care . ful. ly	*care- (fully)*

YOUR BUSINESS VOCABULARY

supplement *splm* To provide an addition to something.

□ We will order additional supplies to supplement our current stock.

portfolio *plflo* A list of the financial holdings of an investor.

□ The additional options you are considering would greatly increase the value of your portfolio.

READING AND WRITING EXERCISES

PREVIEW WORDS

1 campus *c-ps*, daughters *dlrs*, incorrectly *ncrcl*, surprised *Sprz-*, yesterday *ySrd*, oversight *Osi*, supplement *splm*, automatically *atmcl*

2 gray *gra*, incur *ncr*, yellow *ylo*, weekday *cd*, separate *sprl*, receipts *rses*, out-patient *ol=p$N*, instructions *nSrcjs*

3 lapse *lps*, force *fs*, overdue *Odu*, reminder *rmr*

	premiums Prems	security scrl
	bracket brcl	together lglr
4	Alex ax	private prvl
	auto alo	guess gs
	coins cyns	candidates cddls
	stamps Sps	congratulations kgjs
5	small sl	protection Plcj
	whole hl	flexible flxB
	enough enf	inability nBl
	qualify qlf	frustrated frSra-

1

Form letter to parents from Martin J. Osgood, President

d prNs , E mbr
vu fl cvr- b u
crN ins plse.
udb Sprz- / ho
me ppl asr la q
ncrcl, bcz lr plses
Aql sv yrs aq, (Intro DC)
ly atdcl asr la
r cvry , z q ld

z / z ySrd, a
l ofn e Olc . pl
ksp, n Cldrn q
a a l clj, ly a (Intro DC)
no lgr b cvr-U
s fl plns. dN
ll ls Osi hpn lu,
ec Pvd u . plse
la l nsr u sns
+ dlrs l ly r
lrvl l + f cljs

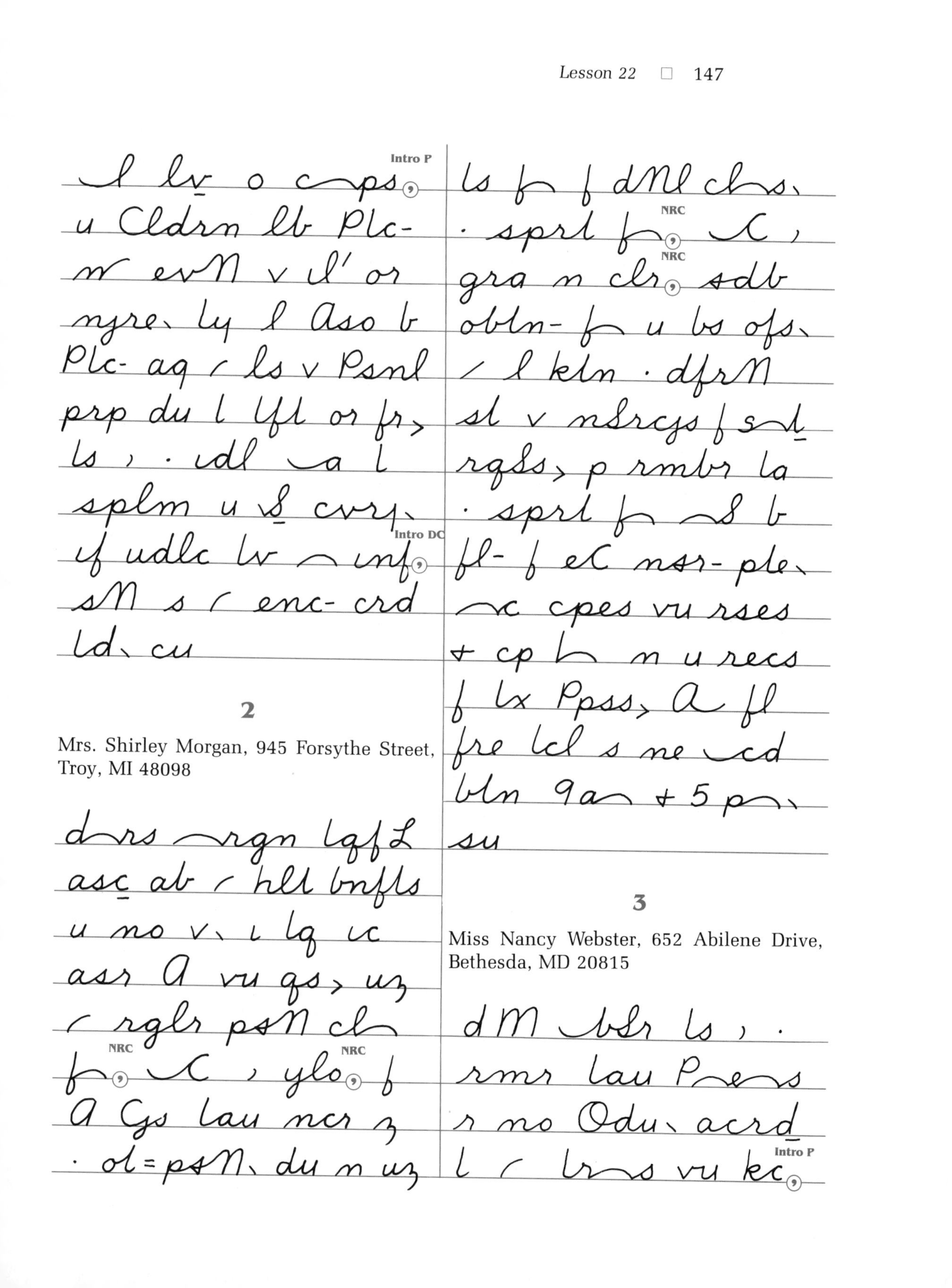

Intro P

NRC

NRC

Intro DC

2

Mrs. Shirley Morgan, 945 Forsythe Street, Troy, MI 48098

NRC

NRC

3

Miss Nancy Webster, 652 Abilene Drive, Bethesda, MD 20815

Intro P

Intro DC

Dir Ad

Intro P

Conj

Paren

Paren

4

Memo to Alex Long from Christine Bigley, SUBJECT: Proposed Group Plans

cyns ~i b cddls f r plse, uv P-. vi opl f s n. ara ev lq b NS-n, kgjs ou fN Dir Ad Ax,

5

Add commas to show one series, one nonrestrictive clause, and three introductory dependent clauses.

Form letter to an executive from Clarence Devore, President

dS vu ofn b frSra- 8
b . nB l obln 13
grp Plcj fu ~pes, 21
if c asr , ys ln 26
ev g nz fu + ol 34
sl cos, if uv / 40
lS 50 ~pes u fr 46
~a glf f bnfls 52
v l vr grp plns, 57
ev ~d L flxB 63
enf l apli l . 67
~d rnj v bss, 73
ulfN la r opjs 79
r a~q c bS avlB, 85
Cz f~ plses cvr 91
dNl ~yr ~dcl 96
hl lf or vdNl 101
dl ins, lrn ~ ab 108
s, c enc- crd 113
~C ev Pvd- fu 119
kv sdb kp- + ~l- 128
l s f ~ inf, ~n 135
s . ~lr v bld. 140
blr fCr lr, no 146
blr L l bgn ln 151
c P, ac no, ul 158

LESSON 23

THEORY REVIEW

1. Use an underscore line to indicate the name of a book, magazine, or newspaper.

Sports Illustrated — spls ilSra- (underlined)

Wall Street Journal — l S jrnl (underlined)

2. Use quotation marks to set off the title of a magazine article, newspaper article, or title of a speech.

□ I enjoyed reading your article, "Corporate Programs for Stress Management."

TRANSCRIPTION AID

Similar Words

some — s — An unspecified amount or number.

□ We have some suggestions for you.

sum — s — The amount obtained from adding figures.

□ The sum of those figures is $49.85.

YOUR BUSINESS VOCABULARY

comprehensive — kprhNv — Large in scope; in insurance, coverage for motorized vehicles for a wide range of perils (other than collision), such as fire, wind, theft, hail, vandalism.

□ We expect to begin a comprehensive advertising campaign in the fall.
□ Your comprehensive coverage will pay for all damages after you have paid the deductible amount.

liability insurance
liBl ins

Insurance that covers legal and financial responsibility for the injuries or damaged property of other parties.

□ The cost of your liability insurance will not be increased this year.

READING AND WRITING EXERCISES

PREVIEW WORDS

1 expenses vpNs
usually uzl
instance nSN
moment -m
paperwork ppro
laboratory lbrtre
substantial sSnsl
hospitalized hspz-

2 adult adlt
bonus bns
drivers drvrs
comprehensive kprhNv
accident vdN
liability liBl
collision clj
excessive vsv

3 exact vc
input npt
publication pbj
Business Update bs pda
adopting adpt
tomorrow t-ro
duplicate dplca
portfolio ptflo

4

sole	support
seek	responding
attempted	disability
serious	self-employed

5

sum	toward
owed	provider
issued	physician
explanation	acknowledgment

1

Mr. Kent Henderson, Claims Division, Mutual Farm Insurance Company, 2910 Bradley Avenue, Baton Rouge, LA 70805

NRC

Paren

Paren

Conj

Intro DC

2

Ms. Suzanne Gray, 714 Greenleaf Lane, South Bend, IN 46637

3

Mr. Edward Buchanan, Devron Insurance Company, 2300 Executive Park, Springfield, IL 62704

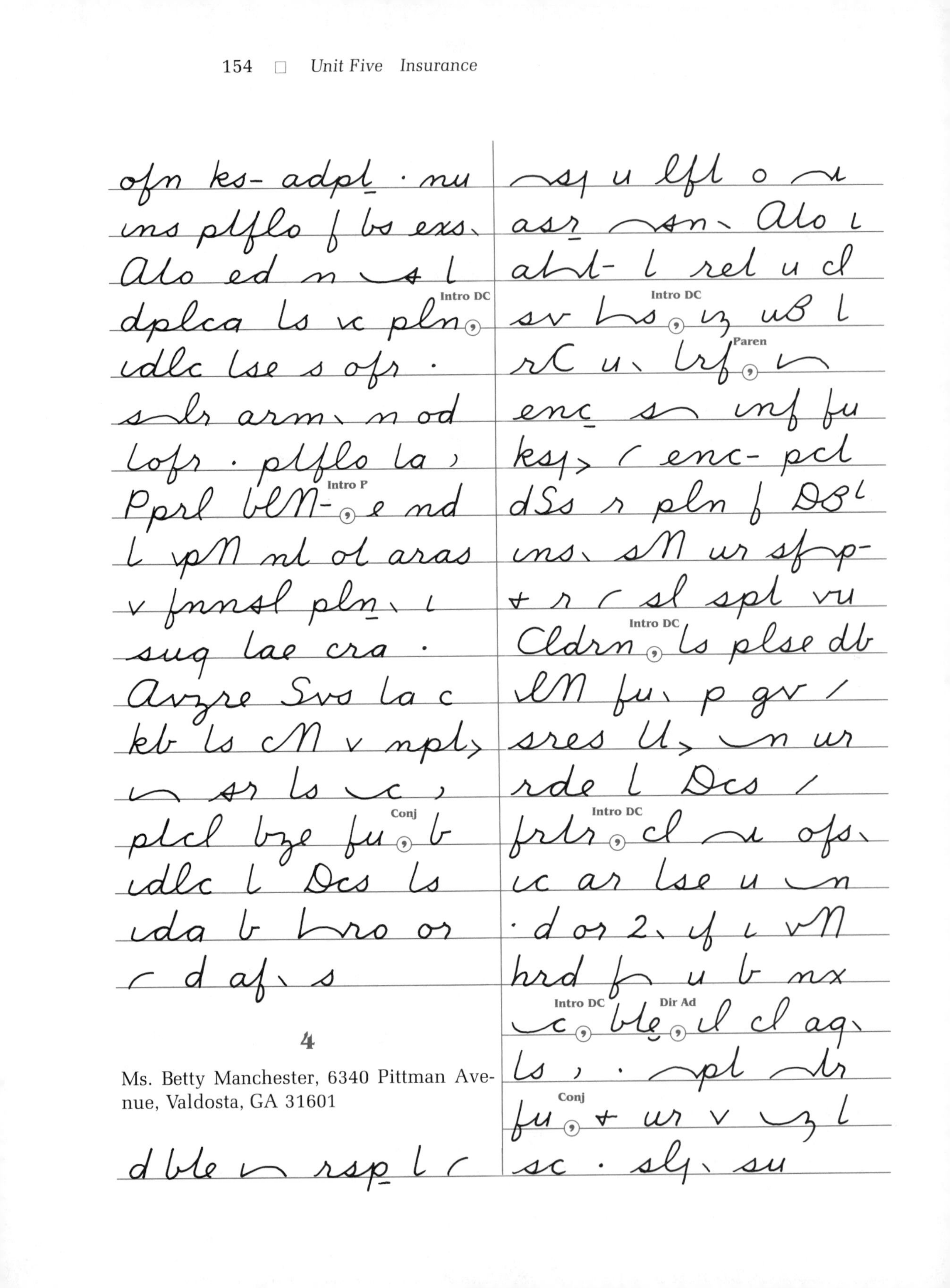

4

Ms. Betty Manchester, 6340 Pittman Avenue, Valdosta, GA 31601

5

Add commas to show one introductory phrase, three introductory dependent clauses, and one conjunction.

Mr. Bradley North, 144 Downing Street, Hartford, CT 06517

drs N n rel r 7
chs u fl- o Āp 9 13
f ndcl Gs, acrd 19
l r recs chs f 24
loz pNs v Ar b 31
rsv- b r ofs, ly 37
n fl- b r Pvdr 42
v Svss + . Cc lb 50
csu- l r alN fzr 57
n r abv pam 62
, nd ul rsv . 67
acym f ls ofs 74
nf u v sn pd 80
lw ls ch, yf ls r 86
Sl upd Gs u fzl 94
l bl u f and Sl 101
o-, yf udlc . adyl 109
plny v bnfls klc 115
ls ofs drl, cu 123

LESSON 24

SHORTHAND VOCABULARY REVIEW

Write a capital N for the sound of *ent, nt* (pronounced *ent*).

assistant	asSN	accident	vdN
current	crN	different	dfrN
sufficient	sfsN	comment	kN
agent	ajN	evident	evdN

TRANSCRIPTION AID

Spelling. Learn to distinguish between words that begin with *en* and those that begin with *in*.

encourage	ncrj	invest	nvS
entitled	nttl-	income	nk
enrolling	nrl	increase	ncrs
enjoyed	njy-	inquire	nq
enable	nB	involve	nvlv
enact	nac	invitation	nvj

YOUR BUSINESS VOCABULARY

annuities anuts Annual payments of income from investments.

□ As you can see from the report, you can choose your method of payment of annuities.

merger — In business, the joining of two or more corporations.

□ The details of the merger will be announced at a press conference.

READING AND WRITING EXERCISES

PREVIEW WORDS

1 audience, income, variety, promptly, luncheon, annuities, competitive, correspondence

2 upon, ended, comment, workday, Hastings, observation, complimenting, encouragement

3 merger, United, evidently, announcement, underway, extensive, diversified, negotiations

4 main, rely, occasion, birthday

whom *(shorthand)*

returns *(shorthand)* rels

realize *(shorthand)* relz

confidence *(shorthand)* kfdN

5 themselves *(shorthand)* Lsvs

portfolio *(shorthand)* plflo

further *(shorthand)* frlr

supporting *(shorthand)* spl

enrolling *(shorthand)* nrl

thoroughly *(shorthand)* lrol

breakfast *(shorthand)* brcfs

supplementary *(shorthand)* splmre

1

Ms. Melanie Doyle, 5001 Granada Avenue, Sacramento, CA 93906

2

Mr. Larry Clay, 7331 Nakuina Street, Honolulu, HI 96819

Ap

3

Mr. Jim Harper, Vice President, Home and Life Insurance Company, 280 West 29 Avenue, Spokane, WA 99203

Intro DC

Paren

Conj

Intro P

Intro DC

Conj

4

Mrs. Janice Tower, 416 Southwood Drive, Fargo, ND 58103

5

Add commas to show two conjunctions, one parenthetical expression, and one non-restrictive clause.

Mr. Oliver Wilson, 8993 Sherman Avenue, Peoria, IL 61606

dr Wlsn, z 5
plzN v brcfs 10
u ysrd + i 15
nyy- r Dcj lrol. 22
uv s lN idas 28
o syc v anu[ls] + 35
idlc l ks frlr. 43
Ph s i rvz- 49
i ins plflo, i 54
se no nd f adyl 60
cvrj n ara v 64
Psnl nyre or pb 70
liB. iblv la i 76
splmre plse Pvds 82
Aql Plcj f vres 88
lps v liB. o ol 95
hN alrc- l 100
nvSm plns u my-. 107
idlc l ks nrl bo 115
v i Cldrn hu 119
r crNl n clj + 125
sn lb spl svs, 132
y dN u gv e. 137
cl? idlc l lc 144
u aq sn. s 149

LESSON

25

WORD DEVELOPMENT

Develop new words using the following brief forms:

operate

cooperate *cop*

cooperation *copy*

operational *opjl*

inoperative *nopv*

prove

approve *apv*

disapproval *Dapvl*

improved *~pv-*

improvement *~pvm*

ordinary

extraordinary *Xord*

ordinarily *ordl*

manage

manager *~yr*

management *~ym*

other

another *aol*

otherwise *ol_3*

of

hereof *hrv*

thereof *lrv*

READING AND WRITING EXERCISES

PREVIEW WORDS

1 goods *gs*

sorry *sre*

reimburse *r~brs*

deductible *ddcB*

theft *Yl*
scale *scl*

2 annual *aul*
young *yg*
strong *srq*
accumulate *ac~la*

3 jaw *ja*
gums *g~s*
routine *rln*
examination *vmy*

4 forced *fo-*
lovely *lvl*
incomes *nks*
mortgage *~rgj*

5 adjust *ajs*
unless *uls*
salesperson *slsPsn*
automobile *aloB*

depreciation *dprsej*
entertainment *Nlnm*

defray *dfra*
tuition *luy*
annuity *anul*
quarterly *qlrl*

surgery *Syre*
resubmit *rs~l*
submitted *s~l-*
repayment *rpam*

minimal *m~l*
husband *hzbN*
worries *~res*
disability *DBl*

springing *sprq_*
quotation *qly*
probably *PbB*
otherwise *olz*

1

Mr. Herbert P. Marshall, 1300 Sixth Avenue, S.W., Calgary, AB T3C 0H8

Cc f 950$ L
r~brs u f Yl vu
dr ~rsl enc-, hn Nlnm ss~z

Left column (shorthand):

Intro DC
uno, ⌐ ddcß a⌐l
vu ins, 2 H$. la
a⌐l hs Ar b ddc-
f⌐ ⌐ vlu vu Sln
gs, n eS⌐a ⌐ lol
a⌐l v ls, e jnl
uz. scl v 10%
P yr l arv ⌐ .
jr ra v dprsej.
hoE, u sls rse
Ncas la ⌐ sl z
ls ln 2 ⌐os
old. lrf, er lre ⌐
sl z brN nu
⌐dse, + ul n b
G— . fe f dprsej,
er sre lau sfr-
ls ls. ⌐ reps .
Dapym + . nkv
fu, er hpe l⌐c
ls sllm fu, + e
⌐4 u l n jcr.

Right column:

vlu

2

Mr. Alan George, 211 Duncan Street,
Clarksville, TN 37042

d⌐r jry ⌐ rz cS
v clj luy, Ar ol
v rC f. ll v ppl.
vu ll ab nrl n.
pln la l hlp pa
f clj eycjs, bcz u
Cldrn r yq, u Sl
v l⌐ l Ppr f
rspß ls la li ahd.
uc dzn u o anul
pln la l hlp dfra
clj vpNs. ordl, ⌐
a⌐l u pa l dpN
po ⌐ ajs vu Cldrn,
ou aj, + o lol a⌐l
u ⌐4 l ac⌐la, u
⌐a ⌐c pams o
. ⌐ol, qlrl, or

Dir Ad

Intro DC

Paren

Paren

3

Mrs. Eva Miller, 2178 Fairview Avenue, Columbus, OH 43212

Intro P

Dir Ad

Intro P

4

Form letter to prospective clients from Anthony T. Holcomb, President

Intro DC

Intro DC
hpn l l vu, d (
rS vu fd b fs-
l sl (hos. f .
Intro P
m l pam eC o,
ly cb asr- v nvr
lz- lr h- rg
Conj
ins , . brgn, + ec
so u y- f z lll z
Intro P
9.95 P o, ulb fre
v res ab Pvd-
fu fd n cs v .
erl dl or DBl-
me plses cvr (
Conj
hzbN ol, b ev
opjs la apli l bo
ors- f fds la
Intro P
dpN po 2 nks,
s jS z pl l
nsr (f z /
, l nsr (hzbN.
N u lc ls pl
Sp ld. f m v

Intro P
. ajN nr u, cl s
fre v G- vlu

5

Add commas to show two parenthetical expressions, three introductory dependent clauses, and one conjunction.

Ms. Theresa James, 132 17th Street, Omaha, NE 68121

ds js ur PbS 7
ar la me ins cos 14
rzrv (ru l ajS 19
lr ras n . gvn 25
yr- v crs ls ajSm 32
ofn rzlls n . ra 36
ncrs / u pN. e 42
op dfrNl- eblv 49
laur pa- enf f 55
aloB ins n u 61
rnu (plse eC yr- 68
e dN blv n sprq- 74
Sprzs o r cliNs- 79
oN u PCs . plse s 86
us f . f yr- uls u 93

alr c kdjs vu plse 101
c ras l n Cnj, rel 108
c enc-fn + ul rsv 116
. ra qlf, uf udlc . 123

slslsn lcl ou Cc 130
c apo bx 6 fn, 135
olz ul n b klc-, 143
ru 147

UNIT SIX

FINANCE

SHORTHAND VOCABULARY REVIEW

Study the following words and the principles they illustrate. Each of these words can be found in the letters and memos in this unit.

1. Write k for sounds of *com, con, coun* (ow), and *count.*

compare kpr	convert kvrl
competition kpy	consolidating kslda-
computerized kpurz-	counselers kslrs
common kn	contains klns
confusing kfz-	encounter nkr
conducting kdc-	account ak

2. Write T for the word beginnings *tran* and *trans*.

transferring Tfr
transition T1
transactions Tacys
transportation Tpl

3. Write sl for the sound of *shul* and the word ending *chul* (cial, tial).

financial fnnsl
essential esnsl
specialists spslss
potential plnsl

MORE ABOUT PUNCTUATION

Use an apostrophe to show possession. Add 's to singular or plural nouns that do not end with an *s* sound.

- ☐ The employee's check was delivered by mail.
- ☐ A new children's store is located on Fourth Street.

Nouns ending with an *s* sound that add an extra syllable in the possessive form also require an 's.

- ☐ The class's average was exceptionally high.

Simply add an apostrophe after plural nouns ending with an *s* sound to show possession.

- ☐ The employees' lounge is being redecorated.

LESSON 26

BRIEF FORMS AND DERIVATIVES

Key

1. about, again/against, always, be/but/been/by/buy, it/at, on/own
2. order, operation, management, ownership, its, overseas, experiencing

PHRASE REVIEW

Key

1. I would be, we cannot, we have been, you know, you would like
2. to visit, to you/to your, that you/that your, on the, will be

READING AND WRITING EXERCISES

PREVIEW WORDS

1 growth, common, stocks, reliable, brokers, counsel, potential, exchange

2	natural	nCrl	trusting	trS_
	theft	tft	disaster	dzSr
	dollars	$	security	scr
	practical	prclcl	personalized	Psnlz-
3	step	Sp	guidelines	gdlns
	series	srz	conducting	kdc_
	confusing	kfz_	essential	esnsl
	security	scr	uncertainty	uSlnte
4	status	Sls	profitable	PftB
	bright	bri	fascinating	fsna_
	outlook	otlc	computerized	kpurz-
	vicinity	vsn	shareholders	srhldrs
5	thud	td	gambling	gB_
	defer	dfr	compromise	kprz
	solid	sld	supersonic	Ssnc
	evaluate	evla	predictable	PdcB

1

Form letter to prospective clients from Peter Osgood, Financial Analyst

d nvSr , ls . q
l b Scs f
fCr grl (asr ,
ys. n u nvS (Intro DC) usd
lca Scs la l yld .
rznB Pft O . lq

pred v b-. ec sug
s— fn exs v ldrs
cos la r no avlB
6 Sc vCnys c alC-
Crl sos l hs
hpn- l kn Scs w
rsN pS. v crs, Paren
ecn vpc c s—
lrNs l ku. la ,
—r r spsl8s lb
v hlp lu, n od lb
rliB, Intro P . brcr —S b
. lrn- vprl. h or
se sd a b avlB
l avz u ab —n l
sl, Series b, Series lrd, Series or hld.
r brcrs l Pvd la
ksl, f me vr Ks, Intro P
kn Scs —c kn
sN. y n cl s ld.
vlu

2

Mr. Brian Gregory, 420 Saddle Lane, Pontiac, MI 48053

d—r grgre lr r
me rzns f lr$ s
— u fnnsl scrl.
n adj l c Plcy la
er rq- lgv u b la, Intro P
ec no nsr u ak f
. adjl 250T$. e
aso cre Ms v $ v
Plcy aq c ls v
scrls b fr, Series lfl, Series or
nCrl dzSr, u gl
a ls Plcy alq — c
Psnlz- Svs + Pfjl
avs la evb ofr f
a—S 1H yrs. cl +
asc l spc l 1 vr
kslrs. elb gld l hlp
u olln . nvSm pln
la , prclcl fu. cu

3

Ms. Lisa Christopher, 963 South Congress Avenue, Jackson, MS 39201

Intro P

Paren

Intro DC

Intro P

4

Mr. and Mrs. J. R. Bishop, 778 Crossmoor Lane, Louisville, KY 40222

Intro DC

Intro DC

Intro DC

plN, e nvi u lvzt
r ⌒drn fslts, s
fsnā lse (elnc
eqpm + kpurz-
⌒lds no n opj,
r pb rlys dpl gvs
gd- lrs dl lru (
plN, (ollc f r bs

Conj

, v bru, + e alspa
la ls lb . eqll
PflB yr, cu

5

Add commas to show one introductory dependent clause, two conjunctions, and one omission of *and*.

Ms. Deanna Conway, 4383 Six Mile Road, Casper, WY 82604

d⌒s k⌒a ur crc, 7
. nvSm la ylds 12
hi rels , . rsc 17
b s Aso . u opt, 25
sC . nvSm c lc 31
of ⌣ Ssnc spd 36
or / c fl ⌣ . ld, 42
ho du uno ⌣n l 47
lc . CN, e lc l 52
rcm . kpr⌒z la 58
hs ⌣o- l f . No v 64
nvSrs, e evla (70
grl v cos la v 76
dmSra- sld Pgrs 81
O . No v yrs, lz 88
r frs ⌣ Srq 92
⌒ym + . l' l 98
dfr gc Pfls f sld 104
AvNm, Scs sC 110
z lz yld Pfls O 115
. lq lr⌒, echlp 120
u cdNf lz Scs, 126
sN u fnnsl sity 132
PvNs u f⌒ gB o 138
gc Pfls ur ⌒lcl 145
l fl sf ⌣ ls PdcB 152
Sde ra v rel, s 159

LESSON 27

ABBREVIATIONS AND DERIVATIVES

1. blvd corp $ gvt sec
2. S E S esl- hdqtrs aves

Key

1. boulevard, corporation, dollar/dollars, government, second/secretary
2. street, east, south, established, headquarters, avenues

TRANSCRIPTION AID

The Time of Day. When typing the message of a business letter, use the following guidelines:

1. When typing an even hour followed by the word *o'clock,* either spell out the word or use the figure.

□ The meeting will begin promptly at 2 o'clock.

2. When showing the exact hour and minutes, use figures and a colon.

□ Your appointment is scheduled for 3:15.

3. Use figures with *a.m.* and *p.m.* Never use *a.m.* with *morning* or *p.m.* with *afternoon.* Never use *o'clock* with *a.m.* or *p.m.*

□ 8 o'clock in the morning or 8 a.m.
□ half past three in the afternoon or 3:30 p.m.

4. Noon and midnight may be shown this way:

12 noon   12 midnight

5. Morning begins after 12 midnight; afternoon begins after 12 noon; evening begins after 6 p.m.

□ You may pick up your delivery after 3 o'clock in the afternoon.
□ The plane is scheduled to arrive at 12:01 p.m.

6. If *a.m., p.m.,* or *o'clock* is not used, spell out the hour.

□ The meeting begins at seven tonight.

YOUR BUSINESS VOCABULARY

capital gains — Profit from the sale of capital assets (holdings such as real estate or stock).

cpll gns

□ There is an additional tax assessed on all capital gains.

affiliate aflel — An associate having lesser authority; a subsidiary.

□ The Sunshine Company is now an affiliate of ours.

underwriters Urirs — Agents who assume financial responsibility for a given expense.

□ The underwriters have agreed to the terms in the contract.

consolidating loans — Combining several loans into one.

kslda lns

□ There could be a financial advantage in consolidating loans.

READING AND WRITING EXERCISES

PREVIEW WORDS

1 top lp
automotive
heritage hrl
craftsmanship crflsm
reputation rpl
headquarters hdqlrs
innovation nv
dependability dpNB

2 Paris prs
foreign fn
summary sre
overseas Oses
affiliate aflel
primary prre
underwriters Urirs
consolidating kslda

3 fiscal fscl
assets asls
abroad abrd
obvious obves
stability SBl
capital gains cpll gns
expansion vpnj
Western Europe Wrnurp

4 bond bN
sessions sjs
lectures lcCrs
potential plnsl
reminders rmrs
practices prclss
exceptional vpjl
reinvestment rnvSm

5 refer rf
enroll nrl
toward lw
dividends dvdNs
guidelines gdlns
eligibility elyBl
registration rySrj
authorization alrzj

1

Mr. and Mrs. Sheldon Turner, 319 Sunrise Lane, Charleston, WV 25313

drs + rs lrnr er prod l l u aq r nu srhldrs. eap / kfdN uv Sn n s b nvS n r co, enc- ,.

brf hSre vr co, er
prod vr hrly, + er [Conj]
jS z prod v kby
ev ~d l (ab~v
N, sN Nds r frS
Pdc ~ ln 70 yrs
aq, ev est- . rply [Intro P]
f nvy + dpNB l,
Alo la frS nyn
z v dfrN f (
~snre no b ~f-, [Intro DC]
/ rflc- (rSC
+ fn crflsms la
d ern s lp bl n
. ~o ~r, e lk u
z plnrs n grl
+ dvm vr corp,
~n ur n ls ara, [Intro DC]
p ~c / . py
lvzl r hdqtrs,
ur no . pl v s,
vlu

2

Mr. William N. Conners, 304 East Oak, Quebec City, PQ G1R 4S7

d ~ly ~ alC
. mo rln b (
drs vr Nnyl dvy,
/ klns . brf s~re
vr S aks + rsN
Tacjs ~ bqs la r
lca- Oses, z uc [Intro DC]
se f (rpl, r
bq aflet n prs,
1 v ~S acv Ururs
v fn crNe n ~o,
Ph esd ks kslda
r fn lns + ~c
ls bq r pr~re
ajN, p rd (mo
+ gv ~e u racjs
l (rcmys olln-
o py 4, ~s ~
~c . dsy re
fCr NSs, + idlc [Conj]

l Dcs sv idas
u u bf e alN r
ne la hsb scyl-
f 10° o Tu, ilb
nS egr lvu rpl,
s

3

Mr. Roy Stillwell, Treasurer, National Motors, Inc., P.O. Box 613, Flint, MI 48503

d ry lqf sN ne
. cpe v fnnsl
rpl, iz plcl p- l
lrn la cpll gns
Oses v ncrs- n
ln 6% du ls fscl
yr, bcz v obves
suc vr vS plses, (Intro P)
i se no rzn lc
nyr Cnys n r
nvSm hld, (Paren) i l (Paren)
n ncry- b r SBl
v an $ crNl n
evdN n Wrn
urp, r fn asls r
aprC 2B$ / ls l,
ls inf Ncas la er
vp . pred v eco
grl, (Conj) + ilblv la
esd Dcs adyl
aves v vpny abrd,
iv apyms scyl- f
9an + 2 30p lro,
ne ol l db fn
f ne l ne u
u, cu

4

Memo to Bill Michaels from Sally Randall, SUBJECT: Upcoming Lectures on Personal Finance

mo l bl ncls
iv asc- la rmrs
b sN l a vr
cluNs re r srz
v lcCrs bgn n

Conj

Series

Series

Series

Series

Intro DC

5

Add commas to show one parenthetical expression, one introductory phrase, and two introductory dependent clauses.

Dr. Andrew Cox, 3518 Paxon Drive, Wilmington, DE 19803

9
16
24
30
36
40
47
55
61
66
73
78
84
91
97
105
111

kp- + rel- (f 117
l s elb B l nrl 124

u n pln, lqu aq 130
fu NS n r co, su 141

LESSON 28

SHORTHAND VOCABULARY REVIEW

Write *a* for the initial and final sound of *aw*.

audit	adl	law	la
authentic	alNc	draw	dra
audience	adeN	saw	sa
awful	af	lawful	laf

TRANSCRIPTION AID

Similar Words

ensure — nsr — To make certain of.

□ I will make the arrangements myself to ensure that the shipment leaves here on time.

insure — nsr — To contract for protection against specified types of losses in return for premiums paid.

□ I wish to insure every member of my family.

YOUR BUSINESS VOCABULARY

tariff — trf — A tax imposed by government on imported or exported goods.

□ A new tariff will be placed on all grain sold abroad.

securities — scr^ts — In reference to stocks and bonds, documents proving ownership, such as stock certificates.

□ A safe-deposit box will protect your securities from fire or loss.

READING AND WRITING EXERCISES

PREVIEW WORDS

1 tariffs *lrfs*
 normal *nrl*
 imports *pls*
 express *prs*

2 Exchange *Cng*
 Investors *nvSrs*
 Kingston *cgSn*
 ownership *orS*

3 audits *adls*
 timely *Ll*
 remarks *rvrcs*
 aspects *aspcs*

4 legal *lgl*
 expect *pc*
 cannot *cn*
 Westport *Wpl*

5 top *lp*
 status *sls*

fabrics *fbrcs*
combine *kbn*
raw wool *ra l*
natural fibers *nCrl fbrs*
encounter *nkr*
Washington *WA*
transferring *Tfr*
authenticate *alNca*
audience *adeN*
refreshing *rfrs*
informative *nfv*
stimulating *Sla*
reimburse *rbrs*
expenses *pNs*
connected *kc-*
successfully *sucfl*
predict *Pdc*
restricted *rSrc-*

varied

presently

neither

alternatives

1

Form letter to board members from Mary Elizabeth Parker

Intro DC

Intro DC

2

Mr. Wally Kingston, 1120 Kitty Hawk Road, Greensboro, NC 27407

frl s-pl, usd
frS kp (f- la,
P- 6 rvrs sd v
scrl, b Ar l fl
n A (inf rqS-,
u -S ln asc .
ofsr v . bq l
alNca u siq, lr
, . s-l fe aso-
- (Tfr v eC
Ar v Sc > fw (
NRC
Slfcls, -C vb
ndrs- b (bq
NRC
ofsr, alq - (
Tfr fe, p l . L
v nSrcj, -l bz
-trels l -i all
/ nvSrs vCnj /
300 WA blvd, p
sN ls b rjSr-
-l, nu scrls lb
rel- lu -n 2 -cs>

Intro DC
if u nkr ne dfces,
p cl -e Psnll,
vlu

3

Ms. Emily Hatfield, 842 Longmeadow Road, Yonkers, NY 10701

d-s hlfld lqf dl
sC . NS + nf-v
spC, icd ezl se
la (ol nvSrs
njy- u r-rcs z
Paren
-C zi dd, z uz,
u idas - S-la +
rfr+, / eze lse
y so me ppl njy
hr u lc> (adeN
lsn-crfl lu Avs, u
P- s- lN sugjs
o ho l kdc adls,
me v s lv sC
Conj
-lrs l r ak dpls,
b / L- e ac-Sln

aspcs v la rspBl
f rsvs, l sa me
ppl lc nls du r
evn, n sr la
r sls vu nu bc
l rflc r suc vu
idas, uv r snss
lqs f . spC la z
l + usf, hp
ulb B l jyn s
aq nx yr, ul

4

Dr. Everett Gray, Business and Finance Department, Westport Junior College, 4597 Shore Drive, Providence, RI 02919

ddr gra er v NS-
n crs ur ofr /
Wpl yr cly, acrd l
r Avm n nzppr, Intro P
r sjc v crs lb lgl
gdlns f nvSms
+ scrls, bcz sv

las vb ps-rsNl, Intro DC
ls crs aprs l e
. rl nd n r knl,
ev . lry Sf hu d
bnfl f sC . crs, Conj
+ n ru l asc if
ucd akda p l 20
ppl, s r plse l
r brs pes f A
vpNs kc- cly
crss la r sucfl
kp-, lrf, ed vpc Paren
S pes l lc
Avy v ls opl,
if u fN la ucn
nrl A vr pes
n cls, d u ks Intro DC
opn . sec cls.
idb gld l e
u ne l l Dcs
ls v psBl, vlu

5

Add commas to show two introductory dependent clauses, one conjunction, and one introductory phrase.

Miss Karen Little, 604 Illinois Avenue, Columbia, MO 65201

dM lll lgfL v 9
Mr l, hr , (lS 15
v ⌒Cul fMs lau 20
rgS-, z uc se f⌒ 27
ls brf hSre (rel 33
hs vre-. gr dl O 39
(yrs, ls yrs lp 44
fM ⌒a b Pds (50
hiS ern no b 55
ecn Pdc ho / l 61
kpr ⌣ ol fMs nx 67
yrs> ho du u Cz 72
a⌒q lz fMs. / 77
⌒pl l rmbr 81
laur n rSrc- l 88
ne pln, uc a 93
⌒v u me ⌣n 97
⌒r kdjs Cnj> v 104
rvu- u crN Sls 110
i rcm lau nlr 116
ncrs nr dcrs (121
Ars lau Pl hld 127
n ⌒Cul fMs, sN 132
ur v NS- n nvS 139
adjl me idlc l 146
suq s⌒ alrnvs 151
la ⌒i a grr blN 157
lu Oa pln> y dN 164
u Sp b l d ls ⌣c 170
+ lc / s⌒ ol 174
opjs. ul 179

LESSON 29

SHORTHAND VOCABULARY REVIEW

Write for the sound of *zh*.

leisure	measure
treasury	pleasure
exposure	casual

TRANSCRIPTION AID

Spelling. In general, omit the final *e* of the root word before adding a word ending that begins with a vowel.

approve	approv*al*
dispose	dispos*al*
believe	believ*able*
response	respons*ible*
assure	assur*ance*
desire	desir*ous*

YOUR BUSINESS VOCABULARY

subject to change — Likely to change; a condition of possible change exists.

□ Flight schedules are subject to change.

accessible — Easily approached or obtained.

□ By moving the master files, we will make them more accessible to everyone.

subsequently ssqNl Following in time or in sequence of events.

□ The contract was signed, and the press was subsequently notified.

READING AND WRITING EXERCISES

PREVIEW WORDS

1	switch	sC	together	tglr
	another	aol	committed	kt-
	avenues	aves	describes	dSs
	certificates	Stfcts	unfortunate	ufCnt
2	host	hS	unstable	uSB
	risks	rscs	constantly	kSNl
	least	lS	altogether	Algtr
	foreign	fn	director	drr
3	urge	urj	absence	absN
	annual	aul	nominations	nmys
	Royal	ryl	subsequently	ssqNl
	promptly	P̆tl	instructions	nSrcys
4	respect	rspc	accessible	xsB
	researches	rSCs	thoroughly	trol

attentive	alnv	disposition	Dpz/
cheerful	Crf	greater	grr

5	into	nl	support	spl
	energy	nrje	insights	nsis
	nearly	nrl	mentioned	mj-
	former	fr	foundation	foN/

1

Mr. Gregory K. Roberts, 476 Delbert Drive, Idaho Falls, ID 83401

dr rbrls lqf L
rqs inf ab rlrm
plns. (enc- br~r
dSs s~ v me
opjs avlB lu> (
ufCnl f ppl l bk
kl- l I nvSm pln.
if ur lv fnnsl
scr~ du u rlrm, [Intro DC]
und lv sv aves
v nk, edb hpe l
nvS u fNs n ne
No v Scs, [Series] Slfcls, [Series]
lrzre bls, [Series] + ~Cul
fNs. oN ev u
apvl, [Intro DC] ec s C u
fNs f I nvSm
l aol l obln (
bS yld fu> l rcm
lae sl don + vplr
lz idas lglr. lr r
me ~as l~c u
me ~o fu. su

2

Miss Barbara Trent, 254 Bluebird Street, Ogden, UT 84058

dM lrN ur qi ri
lb ksrn- ab nvS

n frs la r lca-n
fn cNres. Alo
Intro DC
me nvSms r sf,
ls r A rscs. (
hS gvl -a pv
Conj
Lb uSS, + vCnj
ra) kSNl syc
l Cnj, bcz s dfc
l -zr (a-l v
Intro DC
rsc nvlv-, ev
lcn X Sps l Plc
r cliNs. ev dv-
. Sf v 50 lrn-
spslSs lcp u Avz-
ab fn -rs. ly no
-n s psB lc
(grS gn f lS
Conj
a-l v rsc, + ly
no -n l -dra
u fNs Algls, /
db r plzr l asS
u n -c u dsjs.

cl r ofs + asc
f -e. z (drr
Intro P
vr Nngl dvj, lb
gld l hlp. cu

3

Mr. Richard Marshall, 152 Aponte, San Juan, PR 00911

drr -rSl erp-
l lk u z . nu
Schldr v A-
elncs. (aul
-e v Schldrs
lb hld (ryl
hll n dnvr o
Mă 7. lnC lb
Conj
Sv- / 12^{30}, + .
rvu v yrs acvts
l bgn P-ll / 1°,
Intro P
lw (N v ls -e,
5 nu drrs lb elc-.
nmjs r vpc- lb
Conj
-d f (flr, + .

Intro DC

Intro DC

Series

Series

Intro P

4

Mr. Edward Sanders, Wilcox and Jeffers, Investors, 1322 Whitaker Avenue, Milwaukee, WI 53107

Intro DC

glfjs ,p lc ⌣ ⌣e
Psnll ⌐ ul

5

Add commas to show one appositive, one conjunction, and two introductory phrases.

Mr. Gene Henderson, Heritage Foundation, 302 Washington Street, Allentown, PA 16601

d⌣r hMrsn lqfL ⁹
re u f⌐r ⌣pe su ¹⁶
crsn ⌐ ⌐ dli-lsa ²³
la se hsb ⌣o ⌣ ²⁹
s f nrl 6 ⌣cs ³⁴
evn n ls srl ³⁸
pred v ⌐ se hs ⁴³
Ar brl sv nu ⁴⁸
cliMs l r fr, se ⁵³
my-lau hlp-Lf ⌐ ⁶⁰
· foMy la hs h · ⁶⁶

pzr efc o eco ⁷¹
dvm n u knᴸ ⌐ ⁷⁸
ls soMs lc ⁄cM ⁸³
v Pq la d grl ⁸⁹
bnfl r lon ⌐ cd ⁹⁴
u sr s ⌣ vu nsis ¹⁰⁰
nl gl sC · Pq ¹⁰⁶
Srl-⌐ ev · gr dl ¹¹²
v spl a⌣q ⁄ldrs ¹¹⁸
n r knᴸ b e nd l ¹²⁵
dr ⌣ nrje lw eco ¹³²
pln ⌐ v lrn- vu ¹³⁸
⌣o iblr la ecd ak ¹⁴⁷
ls ⌣C fsr ⌣ u ¹⁵²
hlp, ilb alM · ¹⁵⁸
kvny n u sle nx ¹⁶⁴
⌣o ⌐ idap ⌣e ¹⁷¹
⌣ u ln ⌐ uvl ¹⁷⁷

LESSON

30

WORD DEVELOPMENT

Develop new words from the following brief forms:

note

notification *nlf*

notified *nlf-*

notation *nly*

notice *nls*

noteworthy *nlrle*

ever

forever *fE*

however *hoE*

whatever *lE*

whenever *nE*

everlasting *Els*

over

overtime *Ol*

overcharge *OG*

overlook *Olc*

turnover *lrnO*

success

successful *sucf*

successfully *sucfl*

successive *sucv*

unsuccessful *usucf*

READING AND WRITING EXERCISES

PREVIEW WORDS

1 servant *SvN*

decades *dcds*

lifestyle *lfSl*

prosperity *Psprl*

	convert kvrt	real estate rl eSa
	portfolio ptflo	liquid assets lqd asts
2	bond bN	reinvest rnvS
	expected xpc-	utilities utlts
	enjoyable njyB	letterhead Lhd
	ongoing og_	transportation Tpty
3	capital cptl	preserve Pzrv
	access xs	Corporate crprt
	penalty pnlte	evaluations evluys
	exciting xi_	commission ky
4	depth dpt	occupants ocpNs
	America's A-s	absolutely absltl
	subscriber sSr	competition kpty
	publication pby	businessperson bsPsn
5	sum s-	securities scrts
	seeking sc_	converting kvrt_
	investigate nvSga	settlement stlm
	accumulated ac-la-	transition Ty

1

Mr. Ronald Kelly, 4950 San Rafael Avenue, Los Angeles, CA 90067

drs cle kgjs po

u rtrm, u -S fl
v prod v v Sv-
n fed gvt f nrl

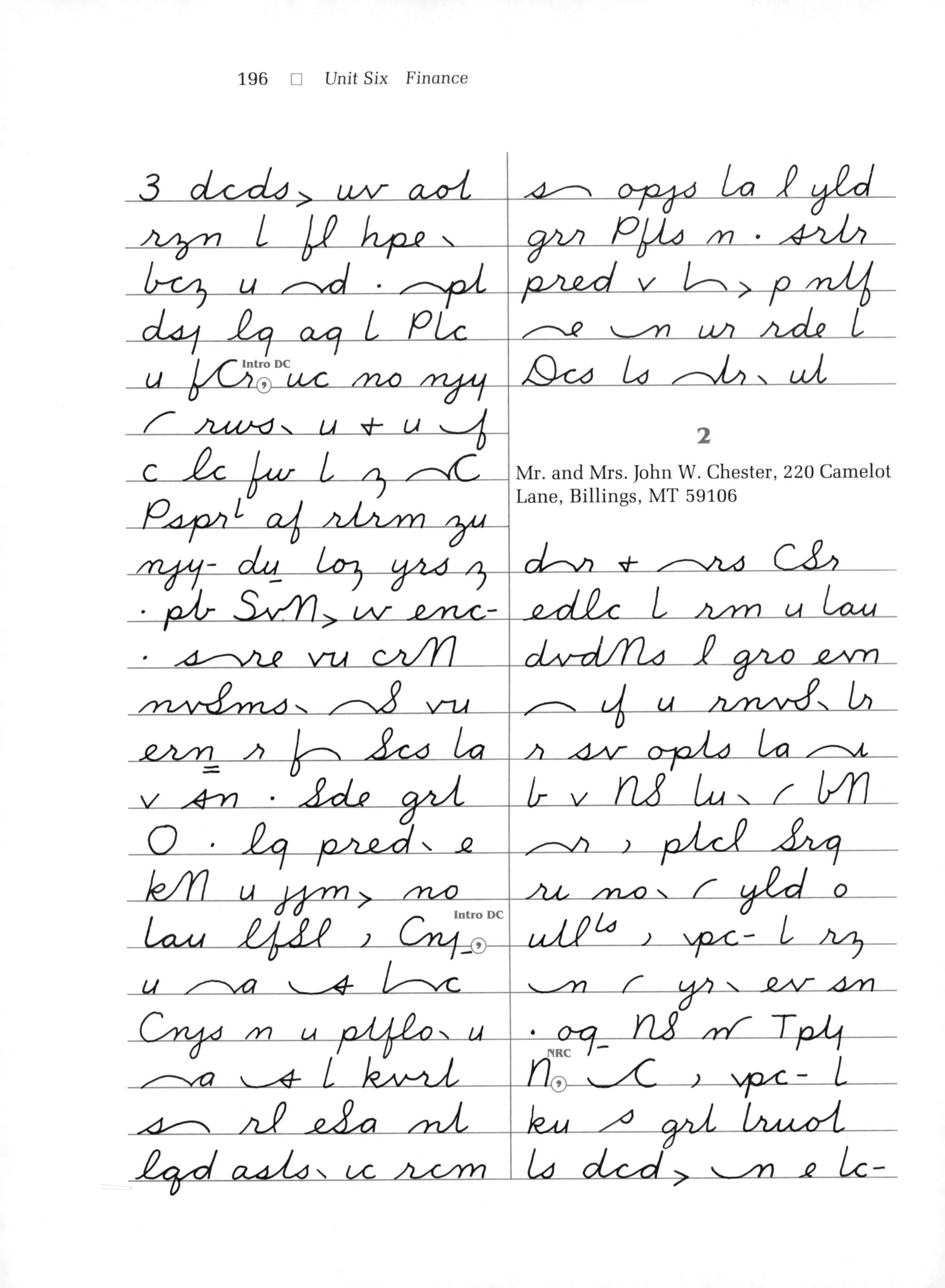

Intro DC

Intro DC

2

Mr. and Mrs. John W. Chester, 220 Camelot Lane, Billings, MT 59106

NRC

Intro DC

Intro P

Intro DC

Paren

Conj

3

Form letter to prospective clients from Charles Wetherford, President

Intro P

Conj

Intro DC

4

Wiley and Associates, Certified Public Accountants, 301 Pickett Road, Fayetteville, NC 27712

1 z ocpNs v .
Intro P
Pfsl ofs, u se
me cliNs eC d,
vu ks- sS l (ld
bs jrnl x> vu f
Ap
l 8, ans sucf
Ap
bs plby, fr olsld
s kply l8 yr, l
Intro P
hlp u se y, ev l-
. sa cpe ls
L, rd / + ll s
l u lq> y udlc
Intro DC
lrsv r jrnl ol,
g8 rel (enc-
crd, el nrl u z .
Conj
g8 sSr, + ul rsv (
fr8 3 isus abslul
fre> lc . fu mls no
l kpr r nz + fl
ol plbys uv sn,
(dpl + rny v
cvry r hlpf l ne
sres bsPsn, r Pps
, l Pvd . rglr Sva
v o v bs + fnN>
b r g8, sS no +
rsv 3 isus fre v
G, cu

5

Add commas to show two introductory phrases, one conjunction, and one introductory dependent clause.

Ms. Elizabeth Henry, Wellington Investment Company, 1478 Fifth Avenue, Huntington, WV 25701

dns hnre . fu cs 6
aq i rsv- . L f 11
u n C u rf- l 17
sv nvSm plns, 22
l sn b rsv . lry 29
and v c4 f 34
rlrm ak + f 40

+ l v dsd- l nvSga 47
opls f nvS ⌒S v 54
lz fNs, n od ⌐c 60
lz dsjs e bo fl lae 68
nd (avs v . Sc 73
brcr> n adj l ls 79
c+ sllm e aso 84
v ac-la- . lry 89
s⌒ n gvl bNs, 94
evb lq- v kvrl 102

lz nl c+ n od l 107
PCs Sc, uf e⌒ 113
ldu so d e b rsc 119
r scrls b sc . hur 126
yld, d ub B ⌐c 133
ls T, f s,> lr r sv 141
lgs edlc l Dcs ⌣ 149
u bf rC . dsj, udap 159
/ uf ucd ar l ⌒e 165
⌣ s, s 170

Word Processing and Proofreading

The electronic equipment used in many offices today has made production of mailable documents easier and quicker. With a microcomputer or a dedicated word processor, you can store letters and memos on a magnetic medium, such as a floppy or hard disk, and revise them on a video display screen before they are printed on paper. This capability eliminates the need to retype an entire document after errors have been found. Word processing software allows you to add, delete, move, or correct text with only a few keystrokes; and standard features, such as automatic centering and pagination, simplify formatting.

Although electronic equipment can help in correcting the documents you transcribe, you will still have to *find* the errors to prepare documents that reflect well upon you and your organization. One way to improve your proofreading skills is to know the types of common errors and their locations. The following are common types of errors:

1. transposing one word with another in a sentence (*in is* instead of *is in*)
2. substituting one small word for another (*of* instead of *if*)
3. omitting one doubled letter (*procesing* instead of *processing*)
4. omitting a letter within a word (*availble* instead of *available*)
5. doubling small words or syllables within a word (*in the the* instead of *in the* or *substititute* instead of *substitute*)

6. transposing letters within a word (*hrad* instead of *hard*)
7. omitting an entire word from a sentence (*she will be* instead of *she will not be*)

These errors tend to occur in the following places in a document:

1. in proper nouns, such as the names of persons or places
2. in headings or subheadings
3. in vertical lists
4. near the beginning or the end of lines
5. in long words that are used frequently
6. in number combinations, such as amounts of money or dates
7. near the bottom of a page

Proofreading a document on the video display screen is usually more efficient than checking it on a printed copy. You can correct errors as soon as you locate them instead of transferring the corrections from the printed copy to the screen. To help them read from the screen carefully, some persons use a plastic ruler or a piece of paper to block from view all lines below the one they are reading. The cursor can also be used to move slowly across each line or down the page one line at a time.

You may wish to proofread from a printed copy when the document's lines are wider than the video screen or when glare or contrast make reading material on the screen difficult.

UNIT SEVEN

TRAVEL

SHORTHAND VOCABULARY REVIEW

Study the following words and the principles they illustrate. Each of these words is presented in the letters and memos in this unit.

1. For words ending in a long vowel + *t* (*ate, ete, ite, ote, ute/oot*), omit the *t* and write the vowel.

rates	ras	dates	das
fleet	fle	retreat	rtre
might	mi	sight-seeing	si = se
boats	bos	delighted	dli-
waiting	wa	greeting	gre

sheet		located	
state		campsites	

2. Write for the sounds of *ance, ence, nce,* and *nse.*

agency		expensive	
sponsor		conference	
chances		assistance	
distance		efficiency	

MORE ABOUT PUNCTUATION

In text material, when the name of a state or foreign country follows the name of a city, use a comma to separate the two.

- ☐ The convention will be held in Dayton, Ohio.
- ☐ Mr. Nerz is a native of Munich, Germany.

If the city and state combination occurs at the beginning or in the middle of a sentence, place a comma before and after the state name.

- ☐ The convention will be held in Dayton, Ohio, on February 12.
- ☐ Seattle, Washington, is a beautiful city.

LESSON 31

BRIEF FORMS AND DERIVATIVES

1. *loz prp ⌐ , G rsp*
2. *lrf dle kgjs arpl kfry*

Key

1. those, property, am/more, is/his, charge, respond/response
2. therefore, delivery, congratulations, airport, confirmation

PHRASE REVIEW

1. *ic edu ·elb edap ud*
2. *uvb lgl zlz ze fu lqu*

Key

1. I can, we do, we will be, we would appreciate, you would
2. you have been, to get, as well as, as we, for you/for your, thank you

READING AND WRITING EXERCISES

PREVIEW WORDS

1 tour *lr* charter *Crlr*

rates *ras* abroad *abrd*

fares *frs* subject *sjc*

handy *hMe* affordable *afdB*

2 meals *ls*

honor *onr*

airport *arpl*

etc. *etc*

saleswoman *sls—n*

Mexico City *—xco sle*

driving tour *drv ls*

miscellaneous *Mlnes*

3 London *lMn*

affect *afc*

alerting *alrl*

evaluate *evla*

informed *nf—*

occasions *ocys*

conditions *kdys*

uncomfortable *ukflB*

4 fleet *fle*

snacks *sncs*

cruise *crz*

tickets *lcls*

islands *lMs*

surrounding *SoM*

inspection *nspcy*

destination *dSny*

5 sponsor *spNr*

picnic *pcnc*

hiking *hc*

precaution *Pcy*

distance *DlM*

campsites *—psus*

pamphlets *pflls*

electricity *elsl*

1

Dr. H. B. Winters, 889 Geneva Court, Newark, DE 19711

ddr Mrs hr r ⌐

brsrs u rqs—, p

nl la hll ras +

as frs r A syc

l Cny, hoE⌐ ⌐ ras **Paren**

lS— n ly drels l

gv u · jn cda v
l l vpc, if ls,
u frS lrp abrd, u (Intro DC)
l ks lrvl
· lr grp. lr r
me Crtr lrps avlB.
ly uzl ofr Dk-prss, (Conj)
+ ly Pvd u · vp-
lr ldr, n ur rde
l Dcs sp plss +
das, r ajNe lb (Intro DC)
hpe l Sv u. ec
hlp u pln · lrp la
, kv, fn, + afdB, (Series) (Series)
alC bs crd.
p pl / n · hNe pls
so la uc rf l /
n nd-. su

2

Ms. Ruth Ann Donaldson, 1555 Stone Ridge Drive, Lansing, MI 48917

d s dnldsn kgjs

o b n- sls n
yr. u S fl v
prod + u- lrsv
ls onr, z (nr
v ls klS, ul rsv · (Intro P)
1 = c vcj n xco
sle fu + u hzbN.
r lrvl ajNe hsb
asc- lc a v nes
arms / no Cj lu.
u frS = pls aw l pa
a vpNs f ar frs, (Series)
htl akdjs, + Tply l (Series)
+ f r arpl, n
adj, ul rsv 3H$ (Paren)
n spN me, 5H$ (Series)
f ls, + 2H$ f (Series)
Mlnes vpNs = su = se
lrps, lps, elc. if (Series) (Series)
udlc l lc · drv
lr, · rNl cr lb (Intro DC)
d avlB lu / ·

Dk- ra, u ⌒a ⌒c
u rzrvjs f ne ⌣c
bln (das v Ma15
+ Dc 15. e Avz u
ldu ls erl n od
lgl u Cys v das.
vlu

3

Mr. and Mrs. Jeffrey Anderson, 911 De Kalb Avenue, White Plains, NY 10605

dr + rs adrsn
lgf ru l Us ab u
vps n lNn. s v
pl f s lno ab
(ukfl8 kdjs u
dS-. ev Sa- n la
hll o vres ocjs +
v foN , Ub lN
n E a. hoE, (
Paren
hll hs Cnj- hNs
rsNl. el Slnl
evla (nu ym

bf rcm lz akdjs
l ol cliNs, er sre
lau foN ls hll Ub
usal. ehp la ls
Dapy- vp dd n afc
(r8 vu lrp. lqu
aq f alrl s, +
Conj
edap / if ud cp
s nf- ab ol lrvl
vps. uvl

4

Mrs. Judith Williams, 202 Portside Drive, Naples, FL 33940

drs lys ys,
Paren
edu ofr . Dk v
10% f grps v 30
or ⌒ ppl. if udlc
lc rzrvjs f . 3=hr
crz l ne v SoN
lNs, u 8 sl
Intro DC
u rq8 60 ds n
AvN, (rglr prss

v lcls rny f 42 50
l 70$. (vc prs
dpNs po (L v
crz zlz (dSny.
ls, (Series) sncs, (Series) + drqs
r adyl + r n d-
n ls prs, r fle v
ss, (Ap) (lrys v s
cM, (Ap) ofrs . d rny
v scyls. ev me
v s akdys la
lrys oj lnrs ofr.
u lrp lb kflB, (Series)
rlx, (Series) + lrol nyyB,
d adyl lil
fu nspcj. zz uv
dsd- po . da, (Intro DC) ilb
hpe l kp (arms.
ul

Mrs. Lawrence Hudson, 614 Douglas Street,
Columbus, GA 31903 9

dr rs hdsn lqf L 16
rqS unf re r 21
cpsis. (enc- 27
pflts l U u ab 33
r fsl ls r syml 39
ras + (acv ls e 45
spNr f Cldrn. w 51
Aso d- s brsrs 57
so lcl aras v NS 63
la r n eze drv 70
DIM vr cp, Pvys 76
(eC si d els 82
lr + pcnc lBs. 86
ls hs + lrvl 92
lrlrs v A szs r 98
lk. e Aso v rzrv- 103
6 acrs f cp 110
lMs. s . blef d- 116
ara la , Pfc f hc 122
+ nCr Sde, sN r 127
prp jyns (Sa

5

Add commas to show one introductory phrase, one introductory dependent clause, and two groups of words in a series.

prc me vr c prs 132
nyy (acv-ls ofr- 138
lr n adj l loz e 144
ofr. z . dlr v Pcy 151

e sug lau c 156
rzrvys n AvN, 161
lqu ag fu NS. cu 172

LESSON 32

ABBREVIATIONS AND DERIVATIVES

1. elc esp ok E eslms
2. Wrn re ySrd enc- corps

Key

1. et cetera, especially, okay, east, establishments
2. western, regarding, yesterday, enclosed, corporations

TRANSCRIPTION AID

Capitalization. Do not capitalize the seasons of the year.

□ We invite you to attend our spring sale.
□ Do you like winter sports?

Capitalize the names of the time zones or their abbreviations.

□ Eastern Standard Time (EST) or Eastern Time
□ Central Standard Time (CST) or Central Time
□ Mountain Standard Time (MST) or Mountain Time
□ Pacific Standard Time (PST) or Pacific Time
□ Daylight-Saving Time (DST)

EDT, CDT, MDT, and PDT may be used to refer to Daylight-Saving Time in each of the time zones.

YOUR BUSINESS VOCABULARY

elaborate elbrl — Complicated, thorough; created with much care and detail.

□ He wrote an elaborate report.

tentatively tNvl — In an uncertain way; not yet definite.

□ We are tentatively planning to attend, and we will let you know if our plans change.

READING AND WRITING EXERCISES

PREVIEW WORDS

1 aware *a ɔ*

ensure *nɔɔ*

routes *rus*

handle *hnl*

2 wife *ʃ*

Japan *jpn*

Africa *afrca*

elaborate *elbrl*

3 theater *lelɔ*

circled *Scl-*

elegant *elgn*

district *Dlrc*

4 alter *alɔ*

resuming *rz*

realize *relz*

yourself *usf*

5 lake *lc*

boats *bos*

confirm *kfr*

adjustments *ajSms*

alterations *alrjs*

transportation *Tpʃ*

celebrating *slbra*

Rome, Italy *r ᴗlle*

Madrid *drd*

Europe *urp*

structure *SrcCɔ*

restaurants *rSrns*

Regency Hotel *rjNe hll*

businesspersons *bsᴗpsns*

hometown *h Jon*

Tampa, Florida *L pa FL*

temporary *L prre*

subscription *sSʃ*

projector *Pjcɔ*

facilities *fsl ᴗs*

resort *rzrl*

recreation *rcrej*

retreat *rlre*

tentatively *lnvl*

1

Miss Louise Conrad, 6632 Green Brook Road, Apartment 6A, Baltimore, MD 21229

d M krd zu nu lrvl agM (i M u lr kfdM r arms i rc fu. lrf n jr Cnjs v lt d n u lrvl plns, hr, (a il hMl L, jj i bk a r la ajSms r nes, il nlf u l. l nsr lau arms r fre v Pbl, il cl (Tply agM r hll dsc l kfr (rzrvjs, il Aso fw inf o prs Cnjs + Alrjs n Tply rus. Alo e

gv u (S rliB arms psB, Cnjs du ocr f lt. il du a ic lrc u lrp plzM fu. c

2

Ms. Christine Madison, M & M Travel Agency, 2000 Los Ranchos Road, Albuquerque, NM 87113

drs dsn il rlr f u crM pjj j Psnl drr n 6 oos. u f + i r lc fw l slbra ls ocj b lc. vcj s r v spsl, sM ev nvs b ol v ls Mre, er ks lc. lq lrp elr l afrca or

Conj

Series Series

Intro DC

Paren

3

Miss Carolyn Baker, 341 Pinehurst Drive, Pittsburgh, PA 15241

Conj

alrcy, Ph ul
l pln u evn zz
u arv, u arpln
lcl lb k n . fu
ds, lqf alo s l
hlp, uvl

4

Mr. Clifford Hardy, 1590 Thurmont Road, Akron, OH 44312

dr hrde e rsv-
u rqs f . adrs
Cny, elb hpe l
l u cpe v nzppr
lu Lprre adrs /
118 W eh S n
Lpa FL du (Mr
nos, / l n b nes
l Alr u sSj ra, e
G (s ra f
l dle ze G f
h dle, p sn (
enc- crd, b sr l

sp vc das f Sp
h dle n Ja +
rz / w sprq,
f uno v frNs lc
usf hu d nyy rd
Intro DC
ab hlon nz, p
ps (rd l L
la lr sSjs cb Tfr-
ezl, s ppl
spl csl lr sSj
f Mr nos bcz
ly dN relz la ly
c v (nzppr l-
l L / no adyl
G, v . gr L l
ur a a, ul

5

Add commas to show one introductory dependent clause, one conjunction, one introductory phrase, and one group of words in a series.

Four Seasons Lodge, Rural Route 4, Land O' Lakes, WI 54540

dS n ru l nq 7

ab (us vu rzrl 13

f . rlre la er pln̄ 20

f r sls Sf> (evN̄ 26

, UNvl scyl- Ub 32

hld s— du (37

—o v Sp. / l 43

lS . —c + el nd 49

akdys f apxl 25 56

ppl> p ll —e no 62

—l uv lofr n fsl ls. 70

f E d vr Sa el 77

nd . lry —e r— 82

la l akda . —e 88

Pycr + scrn. ed 94

Aso lc lno —l , 100

avlB n rcrej. er 106

NS- n lns s— 113

glf elc. , / psB 118

l rN bos f us w 124

lc nr u hll×> p 130

I inf o Dks lau 138

ofr l grps or corps. 145

if u fsl ls r apo f 153

r Pps il cl u sn 160

l Cz . —c du Sp. 167

vlu 170

LESSON 33

SHORTHAND VOCABULARY REVIEW

Write *n* for the sound of *end, nd.*

send	sN	around	aroN
spend	spN	independent	NpNN
fund	fN	understand	USN
friendly	frNl	surroundings	SoN

TRANSCRIPTION AID

Similar Words

all ready *a rde* Prepared; all in readiness.

□ The committee members were all ready to begin the meeting.

already *ar* By this time; previously.

□ By the time I arrived, the meeting had already begun.

YOUR BUSINESS VOCABULARY

convention complex *kvnj kplx* A cluster of buildings or facilities within a large building designed to accommodate guests for conventions.

□ The new convention complex will be located in the northern part of our city.

confirmation *kfrj* The verifying or confirming of information; assurance.

□ I am requesting confirmation of my hotel reservation for October 15.

READING AND WRITING EXERCISES

PREVIEW WORDS

1 route *ru*

 tourist *lrs*

 lodging *lg-*

 emphasized *fsz-*

2 Flight *flu*

 double *dB*

 lengthy *lqle*

 breakfast *brcfs*

3 smell *s l*

 cooking *cc*

 mountains *oNns*

 wranglers *rglrs*

4 inns *ns*

 slightly *slil*

 rustic *rSc*

 lodges *lys*

discomfort *Dkfl*

United States *uni- Sas*

guided tours *gd- lrs*

northeastern *NE rn*

confirmation *kfry*

California *CA*

San Francisco *sn frnssco*

slide projector *sld Pjcr*

horseback *hrsbc*

trail boss *lrl bs*

fun-filled *fn = fl-*

Happy Valley *hpe vle*

resorts *rzrls*

private *prvl*

informative *nf w*

campsites *c psis*

5 campus ⌒ps

complex *kplx*

theaters *letrs*

favorably *fvrB*

convention *kvnᶢ*

alternative *Alrnv*

merchandising ⌒dse

Austin, Texas *aSn TX*

1

Mr. Sidney B. Leonard, 2213 Denver Avenue, Austin, TX 78723

d⌒r lnrd er dlil asB u n pln_ u fdl vcᶢ. O ⌒ yrs ev lrn- la ⌒ bB vcᶢs r pln- ahd. uv Ar lrn- la lc CNs o fM akdᶢs fr f⌒ h⌒ c ld l Dkfl + ᵖM⸓ ⌒ pcl la ev enc-⸱ ulfM inf o arln ras + scᶢls⸱ hlls⸱ + gd- lrs⸓ zu rqB-⸱ e ⌒fsᵹ- plss ⌒ NErn uni- Sas⸓ if ud Sl lc l ks

· SW rn ru af so_ lᵹ ⌒lrels lu fdl⸱ il ⌒l adᵹl lil lu ⌒l⸓ n od l nsr lau gl u Cᵹs v lᵹ_ + Tplᵹ⸱ esd bc u rᵹrvᵹs ⌒ lB 3 ⌒os n AvM⸓ ⌒ lrB sᵹn ⸲ ᵖpc- l bgn erl ls yr⸓ ⌒n ⌒ h⌒ fu vcᶢ arvs⸱ u arms ll A rde fu⸓ er A egr ll v asSM⸓ vlu

2

Mr. Thomas Carson, Downtown Inn, 490 Grand Avenue, New Haven, CT 06513

d⌒r crsn p rᵹrv

· dB r⌒ f ⌒e f
Nv 5 tru Nv 13、
⌒i ⌣f + l l
arv n erl afnn
af · lqle trp f⌒
CA、 el fli ol v
sn frnsssco o fli
No 217、 / l arv
n nu hvn / 1 p 05⌒
Ern Sd ⌣、 p ⌒c
Sln la (hll r⌒
, rde f s b 2 p⌒,
l Aso nd · kfrN
r⌒ f ⌒rn v Nv 7、
(r⌒ sdb lry
enf l se ab 15
ppl kflB、 el nd
· lry lB + · sld
Pjcr + scrn、 lb
od brcfS lb Sv-/
8 30 la ⌒rn, p
sN kfry v lz

arms ru a a、 l
USN la lr lb ·
lry kvry n lon
la ⌣c, + l ⌣s
lb Sln la Aql
akdjs lb avlB
f s, lqu v ⌒C
f Ose ls ⌒dr、 c

3

Mrs. Beverly A. Mason, 1224 Maryview Lane, Davenport, IA 52807

drs ⌒sn lqf
NS n hpe vle
rnC、 ehp (enc-
bcll asrs u qs,
z uc se, E d /
r rnC , · lq +
fn = fl- ocj、 uc jyn
· trl rd nl (
⌒oNns lse (sn
k p, + uc cc frs
bf O · opn fr ⌣n

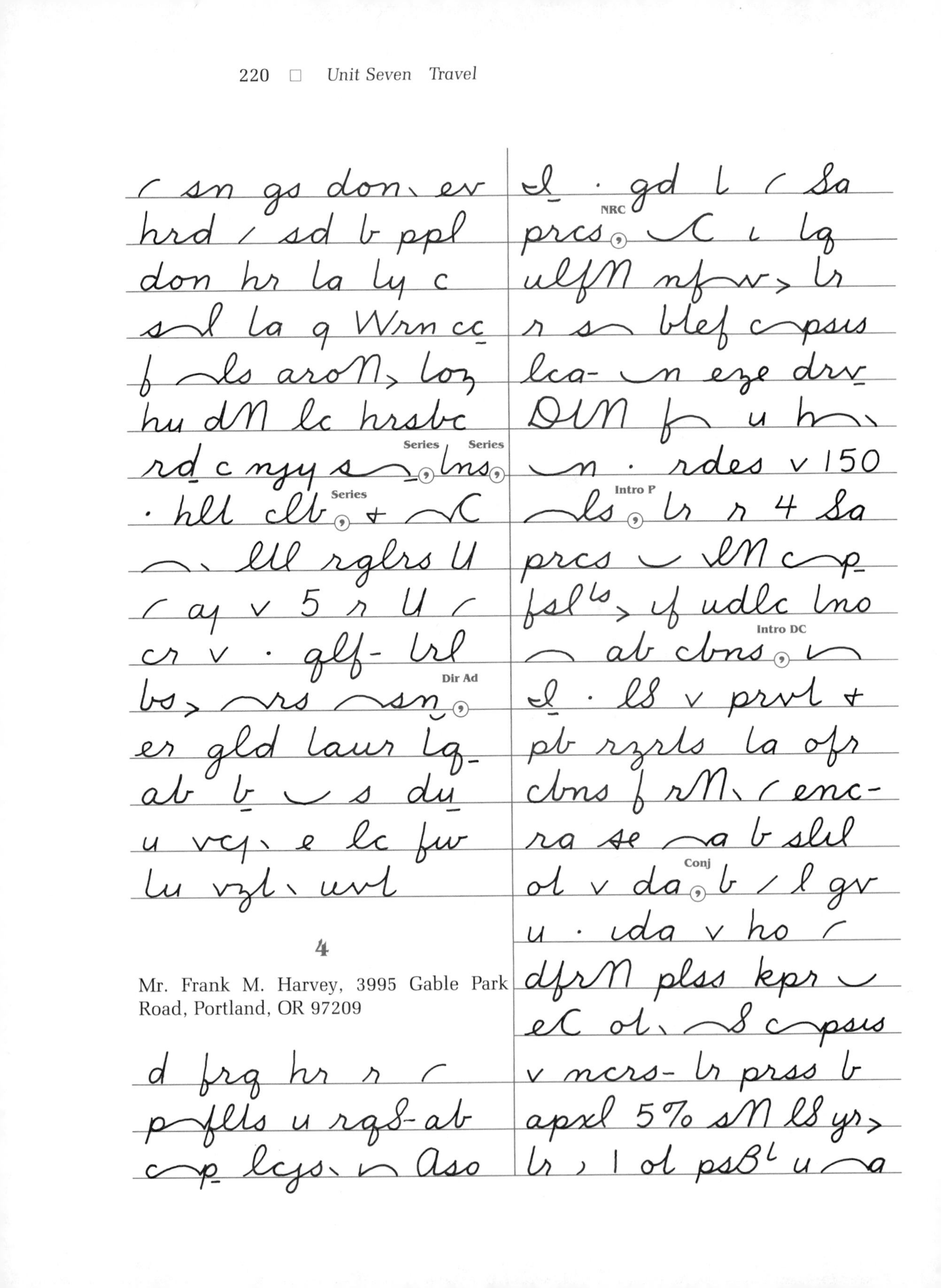

4

Mr. Frank M. Harvey, 3995 Gable Park Road, Portland, OR 97209

s l ks, s vr
Sa prcs v lys + ns
la v . rC (And O) , rSc
Cr, n kpr- l
ol hlls (Intro P) , (prss r
esp rzn8, su

5

Add commas to set off one group of words in a series, one introductory dependent clause, one parenthetical expression, and the name of a city.

Mrs. Marjorie Middleton, Mansington Corporation, 217 College Avenue, Philadelphia, PA 19124

drs dlln , 5
USN lau k l Cz 13
(su f nx aul 19
dse kvny, a 25
u ofr . sugj x> p 31
lc . q lc / aSn 37
TX, me ppl Ar no 43
la er (h v . gr 50
U, ho me ppl relz 57
hoE lae Aso ofr . 63
fn kvny sNr la 69
c ezl akda u rySr- 77
gSs x> r kvny kplx 83
, lca- w hrl v 89
donton, ul v eze 95
vs l sp el eslms 103
+ letrs, (sNr , 109
ol 15 mls f (114
n c ps v l vr 119
Sas lryS Us, er 127
Sln la r ras lb 133
v alrcv lu k, n 141
u kpr l Alrnv 148
sis n lrys sles 152
eblv la ulb fvr8 160
prs- l ev 166
lofr, ru 172

LESSON 34

SHORTHAND VOCABULARY REVIEW

1. Write city names according to principle.

Galveston glvSn

Houston hSn

Cambridge kbrj

Acapulco acplco

New Haven nu hvn

Saint Louis sN lus

Oxford vfd

Fairbanks frbqs

2. Write the names of countries and geographical regions according to principle.

Scotland scllN

England eglN

Greece grs

Soviet Union svet unyn

Middle East mdl E

Western Europe Wrn urp

West Coast W cS

Philippine Islands flpn lNs

3. Use state initials to indicate the names of states.

Georgia GA

New York NY

Indiana IN — Michigan MI

Nebraska NE — Pennsylvania PA

Wyoming WY — Vermont VT

TRANSCRIPTION AID

Spelling. The following words contain silent letters. Learn to spell them correctly.

adjoins ajyns — beginning bgn_

adjust ajS — Pittsburgh plsbrq

condemn kd — fascinate fsna

climbed cl- — island lN

recommend rcm — comment kN

YOUR BUSINESS VOCABULARY

itinerary
Inrre

A plan used for travel arrangements; a schedule of events, times, and places that are part of the trip.

□ Have you prepared the itinerary for my trip to Boston?

expand your horizon
pN u hrzn

Increase your knowledge and experience.

□ Reading and travel are activities that help to expand your horizon.

READING AND WRITING EXERCISES

PREVIEW WORDS

1 realize relz — confirm kfr

ocean oj — originally orjnll

motion	*(shorthand)*	courteous	crtes
seaside	sesd	accommodations	akdjs
2 sponsor	spNr	weekend	cN
initial	insl	confined	kfn-
minimal	ml	administrative	Amv
Los Angeles	ls ajls	Air Travel	ar lrvl
3 Eagle	egl	minimize	mz
coupon	cpn	cooperate	cop
booking	bc	discomfort	Dkfl
accurate	acrl	destination	dSny
4 visa	vza	distant	DIN
birth	brl	festive	fsv
itinerary	lnrre	photographs	flogrfs
passport	pspl	particularly	plcl
5 drama	dra	academic	acdc
aiding	ad	politics	pllcs
abroad	abrd	tuition	luy
portion	pry	lifetime	lfl

1

Mr. and Mrs. David Hunter, 2983 Tamarack Drive, Cleveland, OH 44134

ls L l kfs u

rzrvjs / r blef

dr + rs hNr hll, ul v · r

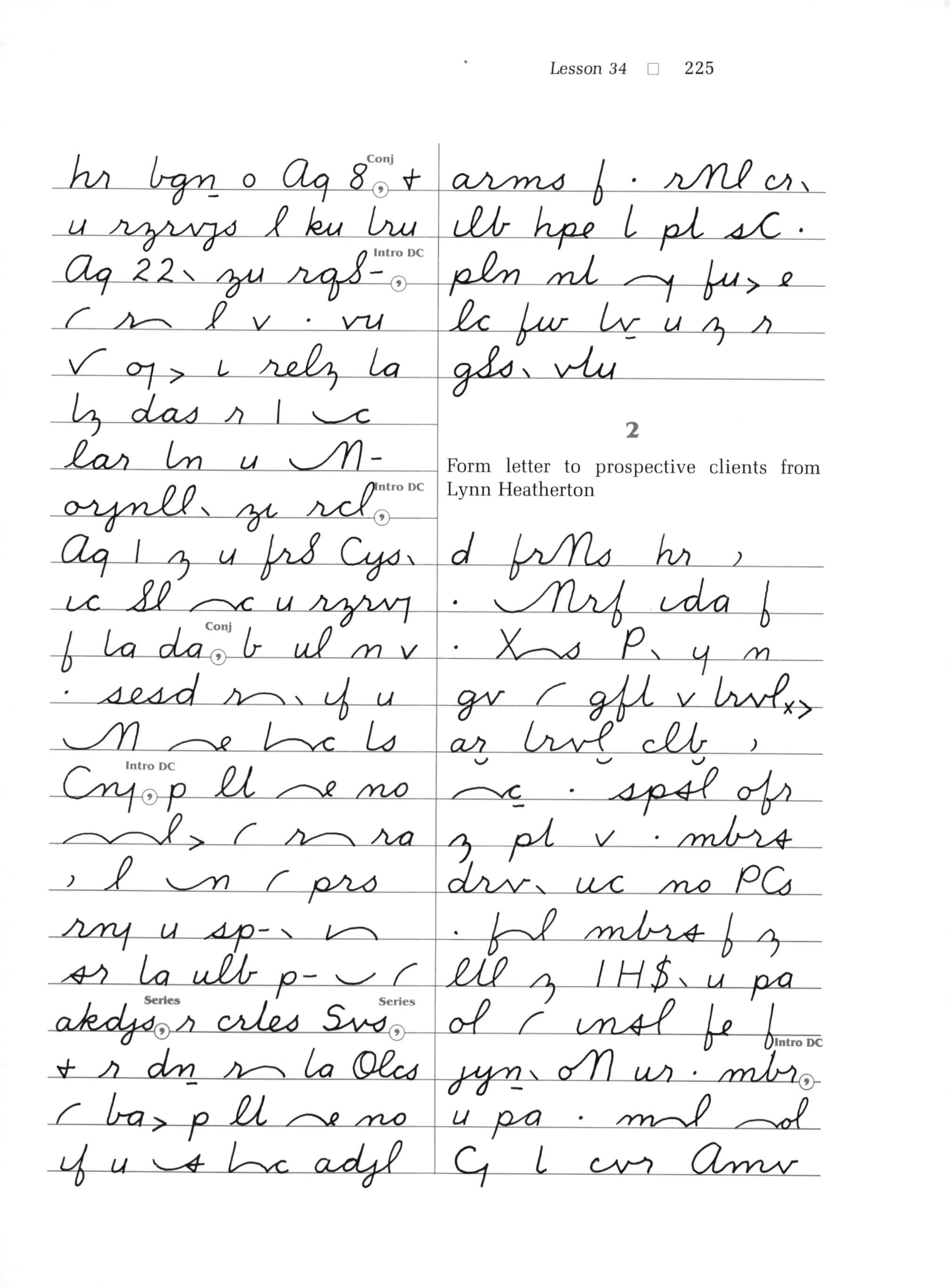

Conj

Intro DC

Intro DC

Conj

Intro DC

Series

Series

2

Form letter to prospective clients from Lynn Heatherton

Intro DC

Paren

Series Series

Series Series

Intro P

Series

Series Series

Paren

3

Mrs. Sarah Phillips, 900 Bay Street, Toronto, ON M7A 2E1

Intro DC

Intro DC

Dir Ad Dir Ad

Intro DC

Intro DC

Intro DC

Conj

4

Miss Donna L. Ray, 1180 Aldrich Street, Providence, RI 02920

Intro DC

Intro DC

Intro P

5

Add commas to show one nonrestrictive clause, two groups of words in a series, and three introductory dependent clauses.

Professor James P. Egan, Westmoreland Institute, 312 Academy Street, Richmond, VA 23225

6

13

acd c lrs abrd, 18
z uc se ev esl- 25
Pgs n sv cNres, 31
uc spN 2 cs n 37
1 v lz lcjs r ul 45
Sde . vri v sycs 50
rla- l hSre + lil, 57
clss l Aso b U 63
n pllcs dr a + 68
arl> r prss I u 74
r luy + . pry 80
vu ls, ulfN 86

usf a q frNs 90
hu Ar u NSs, if 96
ur lc S ppl hu 102
nrl n r acd c 107
lrs ul c lfl 113
frNs du ls pred> 118
sN e S bl (123
No v aplcjs la ec 130
ac e ncry u bc 137
u rzrvj erl, e lc 143
fw l ad u n ls 149
v vp, cu 157

LESSON

35

Develop new words using the following brief forms:

WORD
DEVELOPMENT

part

apart *apl*

party *ple*

imparted *⁓pl-*

compartment *kplm*

particle *plcl*

partnership *plnrs*

port

carport *crpl*

export *vpl*

reporters *rplrs*

airport *arpl*

passport *pspl*

portfolio *plflo*

more

moreover *⁓O*

evermore *E⁓*

furthermore *frlr*

with

herewith *hr*

withholding *hld*

withstand *sn*

READING AND WRITING EXERCISES

**PREVIEW
WORDS**

1 whom *h⁓*

loss *ls*

instruct *nSrc*

intention *nlny*

remedy *ᐢ-de*

briefcase *brfcs*

inconvenienced *nkᴠ-*

identification *idNfy*

2 kitchen *cʟn*

minimum *mm*

await *a-a*

100 yards *I H yds*

laundry *eNre*

sofa bed *sfa bd*

islands *eNs*

vacationed *vcy-*

3 Miami *ᐧ-e*

Emerald *ᐧrld*

fly-sail *flι = sl*

highlight *hιlι*

cruise *crʒ*

registered *ryʃr-*

departs *dpls*

international *Nnʝl*

4 Athens *alns*

duration *dry*

varying *vre*

round-trip *roN = lrp*

departure *dplr*

exceptionally *vpʝll*

returnable *relB*

colleagues *clgs*

5 woods *ᐧds*

famous *fᐧs*

angle *agl*

mountains *ᐧoNns*

customs *csᐧs*

textbooks *lxlbcs*

climbed *cl-*

mining car *ᐧm-cr*

1

Ms. Beverly Mitchell, 616 Nicholas Lane, Knoxville, TN 37918

ds ~Cl ls ,
n rsp lu rsN
L ksrn_ (ls v
c~s. af Cc_ u
r~ (Intro P) , e dd Dcvr
la uh lfl . bc +
. brfcs. er Sr_ lz
c~s n . sf pls
lca- bhN r frN
dsc> if udlc lv
lz c~s A- or ~l-
lu (Intro DC) , p nSrc s 6
~ld v dle. if udlc
lv . frN pc ~ p
~ frN dsc fu (Intro DC) , p
nlf s vu nlnj.
el gldl P (c~s
if eno h~ l vpc
+ if (Psn Ps Ppr
udNfj> er sre la
uvb nkv- b ls
Pbb (Conj) , + el gldl
hlp a ec l fN.
rde. su

2

Mr. and Mrs. Richard O. Carlson, 8981 Dellridge Avenue, St. Paul, MN 55107

dr + ~rs crlsn
e ~N- u lno ab
. spsl fl pln
er ofr_ ls s~r.
sN uv vcj- ~ s
w pS (Intro DC) , usd no la
er Nds_ . nu efsNe
ra f fls v 4 or
~ ppl> l glf f
ls ra (Intro P) , u ~S Sa .
mm v 14 ds. du_
ls ~ ul v (us
v . frns- aplm

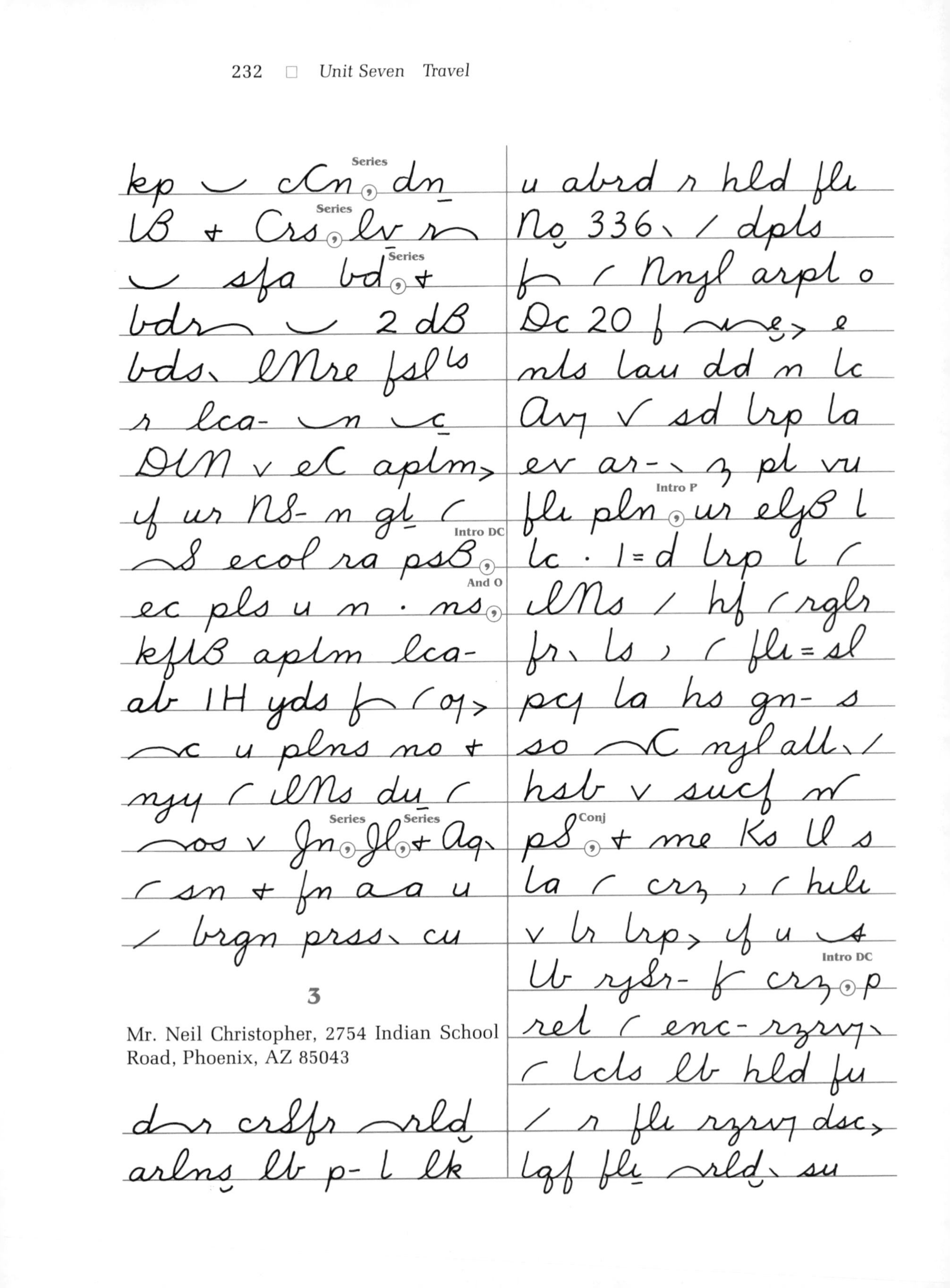

Series Series Series

Intro P

Intro DC

And O

Series Series

Conj

Intro DC

3

Mr. Neil Christopher, 2754 Indian School Road, Phoenix, AZ 85043

4

Form letter to students from Susan Fremont

Intro P

Series Series

Intro DC

Intro P

5

Add commas to show two groups of words in a series, one conjunction, one introductory phrase, and one instance where *and* has been omitted.

Mr. Paul E. Vernon, Editor, Northwest Publishers, Inc., 203 State Street, Billings, MT 59101

6
12
19
25
30
37
42
48
54
59

loz blu sn̲ trs, 65
w Aso sp- n u 71
sl lons + dn- n 76
u bze sles, w lcn 82
flogrfs f E agl, 88
ic so u pcCrs 93
la lcn f . 98
bo f . arpln + 103
evn f . n̲ cr, 108
w bk frNs u 115

rzdNs + w grn 120
l lv lr cS s, w 126
rec- S v l w 132
obzrv- n flogrfs, 137
uno lau co pblss 144
lxlbcs + jrnls, d 151
u ks lc̲ / . trul 157
vpsl Sre ab u Sa× 164
il gldl fw . sa 171
v u o lu, uvl 178

ADVERTISING

UNIT EIGHT

SHORTHAND VOCABULARY REVIEW

Study the following words and the principles they illustrate. Look for these words in the letters and memos in this unit.

1. Write A for the sound of *ish* or *sh*.

sharp Arp	wish A
should Ad	shown An
sure Ar	issue iAu
ensuring nAr	publisher pblAr
brochure brAr	furnishings frnA

2. Write *s* for the word beginning *sub.*

submit | substitute
subscribe | subsequently

MORE ABOUT PUNCTUATION

1. Place a period after an abbreviation that is part of a company name. *Inc.* (Incorporated) and *Ltd.* (Limited) are the most common examples.

- □ Hawksworth, Inc.
- □ Harrison Imports, Ltd.

Use a comma to separate the first part of the name from the abbreviation unless the company omits the comma and includes the *Inc.* or *Ltd.* as part of its official name.

- □ The delivery was arranged by Murray and Sons, Ltd.
- □ Send this letter to Manufacturer's Trust Inc.

When a name using *Inc.* or *Ltd.* occurs at the beginning or in the middle of a sentence, use a comma to separate the abbreviation from the rest of the sentence.

- □ Barnes and Barnes, Inc., will handle the case for us.

Commas used to set off abbreviations will be designated by the letters **Ab** in the Reading and Writing Exercises in this text.

2. Place a period after an initial if it is used as an abbreviation for a proper name.

- □ The report was made by J. B. Harper.
- □ You can get that information from the U. S. Department of Agriculture.

In some instances, a person is given an initial as a middle name. This initial is not an abbreviation and should not be followed by a period.

- □ The bill was signed by President Harry S Truman.

LESSON 36

BRIEF FORMS AND DERIVATIVES

1. ak r jn h nes A
2. afnn rsvs aso- Odn dlrA

Key

1. accomplish, are/our, general, he/had/him, necessary, ship
2. afternoon, ourselves, associated, overdone, dealership

PHRASE REVIEW

1. ino eAd e ucb ucn u
2. uvh fcla lau laur lai dlc

Key

1. I know, we should, we were, you can be, you cannot, you were
2. you have had, fact that, that you/that your, that you are, that I, would like

READING AND WRITING EXERCISES

PREVIEW WORDS

1 space sps — section scj
notice nts — nominal nml
exposure pzr — magazine gzn
regardless rels — decorating dcra

2 aired *ar-*

listening *lsn*

familiar *flr*

commercials *krsls*

noonday *nnd*

talk show *lc so*

advertiser *avr*

prime time *pr L*

3 assume *as*

solution *sl*

sessions *sjs*

campaign *c pn*

underway *Ua*

acceptable *acb*

invitation *nvl*

extended *AM-*

4 color *clr*

projector *Pjcr*

latest *las*

video tape *vdo lp*

audio-visual *ado=vzul*

artwork *arlo*

justice *jSs*

sophisticated *sfSca-*

5 gowns *gons*

substitute *sSlu*

classic *clsc*

hair styles *hr Sls*

creative *crav*

conservative *ksrvv*

wondering *Nr*

traditional *lrdjl*

1

Miss Andrea Martin, Woolcott Corporation, 5440 West 42 Street, New York, NY 10036

sps n r gzm

r rdrs r v ns-

dM rln lqf

n h dcra ₉ + u

Conj

nge ab PCs av-

Pdcs l v lM pzr

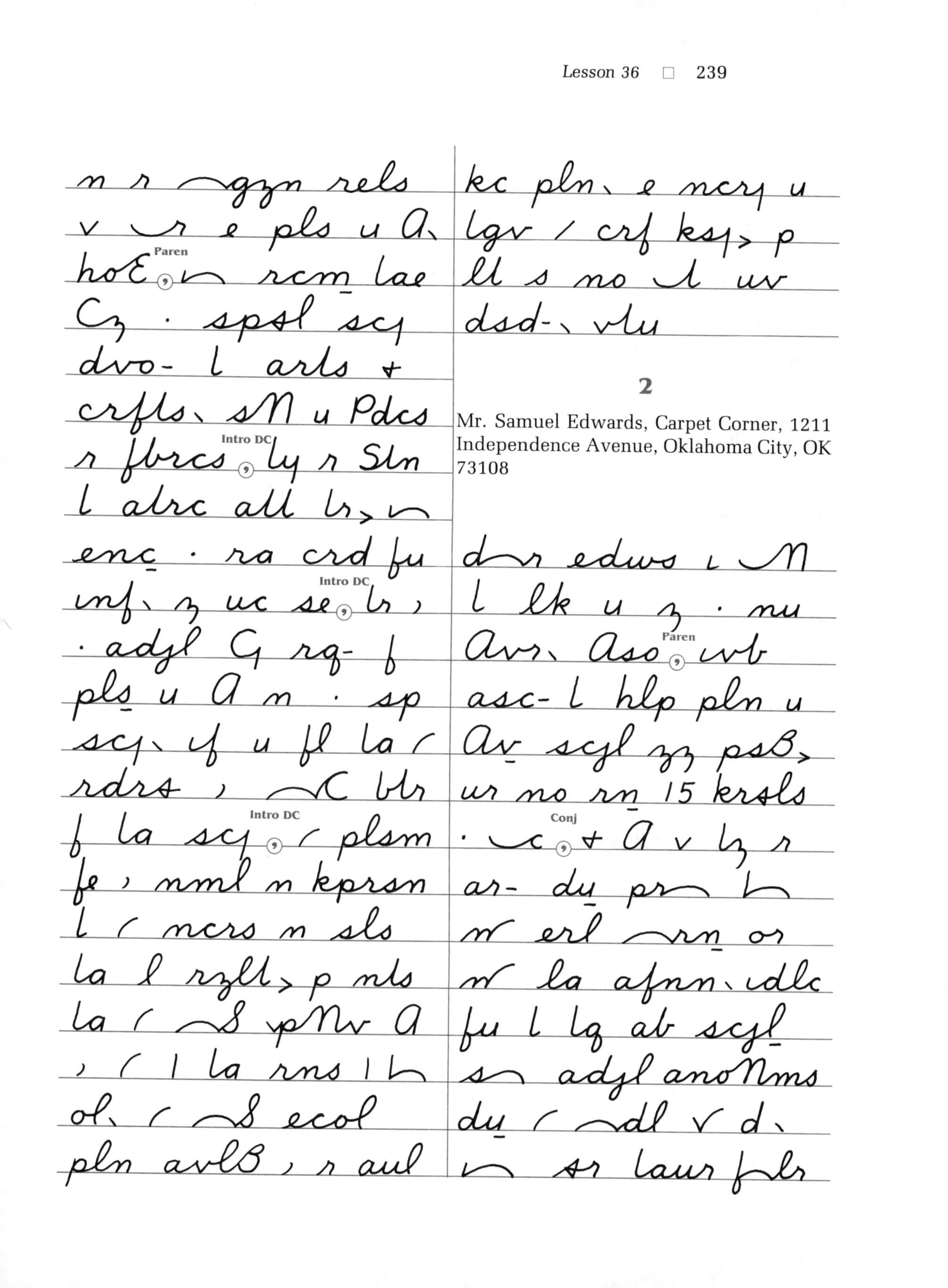

Paren

Intro DC

Intro DC

Intro DC

2

Mr. Samuel Edwards, Carpet Corner, 1211 Independence Avenue, Oklahoma City, OK 73108

Paren

Conj

Paren

NRC

NRC

Conj

Conj

Intro DC

Intro DC

Paren

3

Mr. Arthur Gregory, General Manager, Advantage Agency, 652 Sixth Avenue, Sacramento, CA 95818

[shorthand]

NRC

[shorthand]

4

Alcott Manufacturing Company, 837 Cardinal Avenue, St. Louis, MO 63129

And O

[shorthand]

Intro DC

[shorthand]

Ab **Ab**

[shorthand]

Intro P

[shorthand]

Intro DC

[shorthand]

5

Add commas to show one conjunction, one parenthetical expression, one introductory dependent clause, and one instance of *and* omitted.

Ms. Joyce Hodges, McDowell Advertising Agency, 2502 Lincoln Memorial Drive, Milwaukee, WI 53105

d jys ⌒ ksrn- 5
ab (X⌒s krsls 12
lau ajNe , Pds f 19
r fr, i cN hlp 23
⌒Nr if ly r bk 30
ol v da, iblv 34
esd ⌒c s⌒ Cnys 40
la d nB s luz r 46
krsls du (X⌒s 53
szn f sv yrs lk, 60
f ex (gons + hr 66
Sls crNl b uz- r 73
rep v hi ff, if e 82
l sSlu alrcv lrdyl 89
hr Sls + ksrvv Sls 96
v cll r krsls d v 104
. clsc apl, ecd uz 111
⌒ f me yrs, p dN 118
lq la ⌒ uhpe ⌒ 124
(gl v ⌒o ur gv 131
s, u ajNe , crav 136
+ v Pfyl, w . gr 144
dl v rspc fu idas 151
+ ino la ic k ou 158
Avs, p lq ab ls 164
⌒dr + gl bc l 169
⌒e, su 173

LESSON 37

ABBREVIATIONS AND DERIVATIVES

1. M in invs nnd qtrl qs
2. Ts Avrs Av̲ ecol est-

Key

1. million, inch, invoices, noonday, quarterly, questionnaire
2. thousands, advertisers, advertising, economical, established

---

TRANSCRIPTION AID

Capitalization. As a general rule, do not capitalize divisions of a company, such as shipping department or manufacturing division, within a sentence.

□ Please send a copy of your report to the marketing division.

In general, do not capitalize titles of committees, boards, or employment positions.

□ The board of directors will meet in the conference room.
□ Please send your inquiries to the personnel director.

When these terms are used in an inside address, an envelope address, or a signature reference, however, they should be capitalized.

□ Ms. Judith Murray, Marketing Director
Sycamore Valley Press
101 North Street
New York, NY 10015

When referring to a specific president of the United States or other specific persons who hold high offices in government, always use a capital.

□ The President will address the nation at 6 o'clock.
□ Please ask the Senator to return the President's call.

Remember that some capitalization rules may vary among companies. Follow the style used by your employer.

YOUR BUSINESS VOCABULARY

ethical — Judged to be "right" according to the accepted standards of conduct.

□ Our advertising must be based on ethical principles.

quoted price — The amount of money stated as a price of goods or services.

□ You may purchase that equipment at the quoted price.

market penetration — The extent of entry into an area of sales or marketing for the purpose of selling goods or services.

□ When we introduce the new line of electronic products next spring, can we expect to have good market penetration right away?

READING AND WRITING EXERCISES

PREVIEW WORDS

1 won, mayor, single, honor, ethical, ceremony, historical, background

2 spot, goals, Patricia, television, newscast, audience, supposed, rescheduled

3	trial	trl	accurate	acrt
	solid	sld	elsewhere	els-r
	stories	Sres	researchers	rSCrs
	nominal	nml	complicated	kplca-
4	York	yrc	promised	P-s-
	image	-y	extremely	X-l
	stressed	Srs-	stability	SBl
	preserve	Pzrv	direction	dry
5	exceed	vd	sponsored	spNr-
	actual	acCul	penetration	pntry
	glance	glN	accordingly	acrdl
	estimated	eS-a-	subsequently	ssqNl

1

Memo to All Staff Members from J. T. Stanton, SUBJECT: Awards Ceremony

mo l A Sf mbrs
kgjs o . jb l dn,
-n rf- (Paren) v crs (Paren) l (
fcla ev jS -n r
frS nyl Av aw,
-l . onr ls , f
Ei n ls dpl! , -

-psB l py l . sgl
Psn hu , rspB f
ls sucf eft, Ei
kb- l (lN vr fl
c-pn, (aws k
hs Sa- la r c-pn
z olSN, frtr- (Paren)
evb kN- f
dmSra hu elcl

vlus, er prod +
p- lv Czn . cpn
la z aso- ⌣ (
hSrcl bcgroN v
ls sle> e nvr u
l alN (aws
sr-ne o Ma 7,
(pblsr v nzppr
lb o hN l hlp P
(aw l r dpl
Sr, n adj, (Paren) (ar
l adrs r grp> ehp
la eC vu lb P,

2

Miss Patricia Langston, Manager, Century Appliances, 2000 Chandler Street, Spokane, WA 99218

d plrsa ⌣ ru ls
L l kfr la ev
rscjl- (krsl
anoNm la z spz-
lb sn o Sp 3, bcz
v . spsl adrs b
(P, (Intro P) e uB l ar
u 30=sec spl z
scjl- / 7 p > el
⌣c p la ⌣ b
rn u anoNm du
(evn nzcS o Sp 9,
ls , . lN Pq, (Conj) + /
hs . v hi vu adeN,
ufl Sln la ulb p-
⌣ (Uvq vpzr
ul rsv> chp ls
arm lb sal, / z
. plzr lc ⌣ u
ySrd, (Conj) + ilc fw lse
u aq sn, z A, (Paren)
⌣ avlB l ⌣e ⌣
u ne ⌣ l rvu
u Av gls, s

3

Form letter to prospective subscribers from F. William Layton, Publisher

4

Memo to Pamela Stevens from Steve Brooks, SUBJECT: York Industries Account

Intro DC

Intro DC

5

Add commas to show one direct address, one conjunction, and two introductory dependent clauses.

Memo to Ed Foster from Nancy Thacker, SUBJECT: Advertising Cost Changes in Recent Promotions

⌣ (rsps la er 156

Ar rsv̄ f (nyl 163

As, chp la ⌢u 167

vplny hs asr- u 173

qs ed, 176

LESSON 38

SHORTHAND VOCABULARY REVIEW

1. Write [shorthand] for the word beginnings *enter, inter,* and *intro.*

enter [shorthand]
introduce [shorthand]
interview [shorthand]
interesting [shorthand]
entertain [shorthand]
enterprise [shorthand]
international [shorthand]
introduction [shorthand]

2. Write [shorthand] for the medial or final sound of any vowel + *ng* when the sound is part of the root word and is not a suffix (*ang, eng, ing, ong, ung*).

young [shorthand]
younger [shorthand]
strong [shorthand]
long [shorthand]
single [shorthand]
along [shorthand]
bring [shorthand]
among [shorthand]

TRANSCRIPTION AID

Similar Words

sometime [shorthand] An unspecified *point* in time.

□ Bill will visit us sometime soon.

some time *An unspecified amount of time.*

□ I think we should spend some time reorganizing the files.

media *Plural for medium. In mass communications, media refers to newspapers, magazines, radio and television stations, etc.* YOUR BUSINESS VOCABULARY

□ Please notify all media of our change in plans.

free enterprise *Freedom of individuals to operate businesses with minimal government regulations.*

□ The U. S. economy is based upon the principle of free enterprise.

READING AND WRITING EXERCISES

PREVIEW WORDS

1 cannot *cn* consumer *ksr*

system *ss* materials *trels*

buyers *brs* deadline *ddln*

careers *crrs* enterprise *Nprz*

2 trial *trl* political *pltcl*

coffee *cfe* surprise *Sprz*

country *cNre* authorities *atrs*

Wall Street Post *l S ps* up-to-date *pda*

3 top *tp* magazine *gzn*

topics *tpcs* businesswomen *bsm*

edition *[shorthand]*

another *[shorthand]*

reservation *[shorthand]*

professional *[shorthand]*

4 scene *[shorthand]*

media *[shorthand]*

script *[shorthand]*

rough *[shorthand]*

reinforce *[shorthand]*

sketches *[shorthand]*

goodwill *[shorthand]*

international *[shorthand]*

5 ability *[shorthand]*

skilled *[shorthand]*

artists *[shorthand]*

veterans *[shorthand]*

fascinating *[shorthand]*

work pace *[shorthand]*

communicate *[shorthand]*

photographers *[shorthand]*

1

Mr. Kenneth Webster, Webster Advertising Agency, 1578 Drake Boulevard, Scranton, PA 18512

Intro DC

2

Form letter to prospective subscribers from Cynthia S. Wilcox, Circulation Director

Conj

Ap

Paren

Paren

Paren

Conj

Intro DC

3

Ms. Gloria Trent, Maxwell Designers, 4778 California Street, Colorado Springs, CO 80911

rqd、/ la ⌐
u ⌐q_ v PCs Av_
sps n ⸱ ⌐gzn f
Pfyl ⌐m, ⌐s lrN_ ⸲ **Dir Ad**
er dli- laur ks_ r
plr、e lq la usd
no ab ⸱ spsl edy
la er pln_ f Dc、
ls plc isu l cre
⌐ lp nz Sres v
ls yr、/ l I Nvus
⌐ ld bs_ m nr
cMre_ ⸲ + / l Dcs **Conj**
ol lpcs v NS l
⌐m, ls isu s⌐s
lr plcl apo fu、
⌐ enc_ aol ra
crd fu kv、if u
dsd l PCs sps ⸲ **Intro DC**
p ⌐c u rzrvy ru
aa、ls , ⸱ pplr
isu ⸲ + e alspa **Conj**

rsv_ ⸱ ly rsp,
lqu aq fu NS、ru

4

Mr. Clarence Rogers, Waycross Corporation, 599 Pomona Street, San Francisco, CA 94127

d⌐r ryrs af r
Nvu lS Wd ⸲ i **Intro P**
gv ⌐C ksy l ⌐
cM v Av_ u co
nds、iblv lau
As sd rflc u suc
o Nnyl sn、ecd
ak ls l ⌐c fl⌐s
+ flogrfs n fn lys、
ed cM l ⌐fsz ⌐
lM rlys ur p_ ⌐
⌐ hS cMres, ⌐
dr⌐a v ly Nnyl
sl_ d alrc all、n **Intro P**
ly nu llvy krsls ⸲
ed uz ⌐ S l rnfs

(gl f C u co ,
nn, ed uz (s
aprC n ri (A
cpe f prN- da>
no la v gvn
Intro DC
U l (dr , r
Dir Ad
rjrs , Sln la
ec Pds vcl l ur
lc f, d ub avlB
s l lc / s
rf scCs x vlu

5

Add commas to show one conjunction, one nonrestrictive clause, one introductory phrase, and one omission of *and*. Also add commas to separate one group of words in a series.

Mrs. Joyce Donaldson, Coastal State University, 2366 Bunker Ranch Road, West Palm Beach, FL 33405

d rs dnldsn uz 5
p- l lrn la s 11
vu SdNs s l 16
Cz crrs n Av, er 24
A lc f UN-ppl 31
hu v (B l knca 38
idas, ihp (enc- 43
lil C , . rsN 49
plby vr ajNe lb 56
v us lu cls> p U u 64
SdNs la Av ajNes 71
nd scl- ddca-ppl, 78
e nd ppl scls 83
n ak ri sl + 91
rSC, flgrfrs + 97
arlSs r Aso v C 103
n dm> (o ps , 108
fS n . Av dpl, 115
(o , ofn fn + 121
s A NS, acrd 128
l S v vlrns n 134
ls bs s fsna o 141
f ppl hu r l Lo 148
hrd> i s A vu 154
SdNs (bS v lc, 159
cu 163

LESSON 39

SHORTHAND VOCABULARY REVIEW

Write [shorthand] for the word beginning *an*.

answer [shorthand]
anniversary [shorthand]
another [shorthand]
Anderson [shorthand]
analyze [shorthand]
annual [shorthand]
anticipate [shorthand]

TRANSCRIPTION AID

Spelling. Usually, when adding a word ending that begins with a consonant to a word that ends in an *e*, retain the *e*.

move, movement
arrange, arrangement
advertise, advertisement
effective, effectiveness
hope, hopeless
care, careless
care, careful
force, forceful

YOUR BUSINESS VOCABULARY

full-color ad [shorthand] — Printed advertisement containing four or more colors.

□ I am ordering a full-color ad for our fall campaign.

contemporary [shorthand] — Current in style; modern.

□ We are moving away from a traditional image and toward a contemporary image.

free-lance

fre = en

The practice of selling professional services (usually writing or art) to a company without entering into a long-term commitment.

□ We will ask a free-lance photographer to provide illustrations for the book.

READING AND WRITING EXERCISES

PREVIEW WORDS

1 manner *mr*

 region *rjn*

 positive *pzv*

 cleaners *clnrs*

 population *pplg*

 regardless *rels*

 questionnaire *qr*

 random sample *rM sa*

2 sports *spls*

 itself *sf*

 original *orjnl*

 follow-up *flo = p*

 type style *lp Sl*

 full-color *f = clr*

 columns *cls*

 artwork *arlo*

3 designs *dzns*

 counties *kes*

 colored *clr -*

 ink *iq*

 surrounding *SoN*

 decisions *dsjs*

 objective *objcv*

 miscellaneous *mlnes*

4 bold	bld	crowded	crod-
image		compliment	kplm
owners	ors	dealership	dlrs
sketches	scCs	contemporary	ktprre
5 aware	ar	free-lance	fre=lN
phase	fz	technical	lcncl
prospect	Pspc	writers	rirs
generously	jnrsl	electronics	elncs

1

Mr. Richard C. Buchanan, Director of Product Development, Cambridge Manufacturing Company, 3821 North Meridian Street, Indianapolis, IN 46260

d rCrd ev kp- /
rSC o hoshld
clnrs la evr kdc
fu frs, m enc .
cpe v qr + . cpe
v Sva rzlts, z
uc se f / dla, / (Intro DC)
jr' v ppl Sva-
rsp- lu Pdc n .
pzv mr, ln

60% sd la ly d
pa / asc prs, l
aS 20% sd la
ly lc- / Pdc +
foN / lb efcv, (Intro DC)
ly U / sug-rtl
prs z l hi, of 15%
sd la ly d n b /
lh rels v prs,
ls Sva z bs- o .
rN sa v ppl,
n ls ryn, + / sdb (Conj)
ks- . rliB sa,

ـn uvh . CN l
Sde lz rzllo crfl.
p gv ~e . ch . il
ar l Dcs h ~ u
/ lgl . s

2

Mrs. Elaine Jackson, Jackson Sporting Goods, 8640 Maplewood Avenue, Chattanooga, TN 37405

d ~o jcsn lgf od.
zu rgS— ev rzrv-
sps f . f = clr A . /
lb 4 ch ~o ~d b
30 ins dp. + / lb
pzj— ~r spls pjs,
if udlc l rn . flo = p
Avm. esd rzrv
sps f la A no. me
Avro Cz luz r ~s
arl o + lp Sl uz-
~r orjnl A. n od
l cl cSs. hoE. /

psB l rn r sec
A n / or 2 clrs.
dpN po r arl o
sf. / ~ a b psB
l rn r sec A n
blc + ~ ol, r
lrj. f = clr A , r
~S pNr ops
avlB. + / ofn
v efcv. s h ~o.
hoE. uc acv r ~s
efcv' ~ . flo = p A
v . rds— sz. id sug
la r sec A b 3 ch ~o
~d b 20 ins dp, p
ll ~e no l uv
dsd— ldu . ul

3

Mr. Claude K. Davis, Manager, New Horizons Agency, 906 Weston Street, Salt Lake City, UT 84103

d ~r dvs er N8—

Intro DC

Intro P

Intro P

Series

Series

Series

Series

4

Memo to Bill Harrison from Alex Sterling,
SUBJECT: Proposed Automobile Ads

Intro P Paren

Intro DC

Conj

And O

Conj

5

Add commas to show one direct address, one introductory dependent clause, one parenthetical expression, and two conjunctions. Add commas to separate one group of words in a series.

Mr. James H. Cox, 119 King Street, Hamilton, ON L8N 3V9

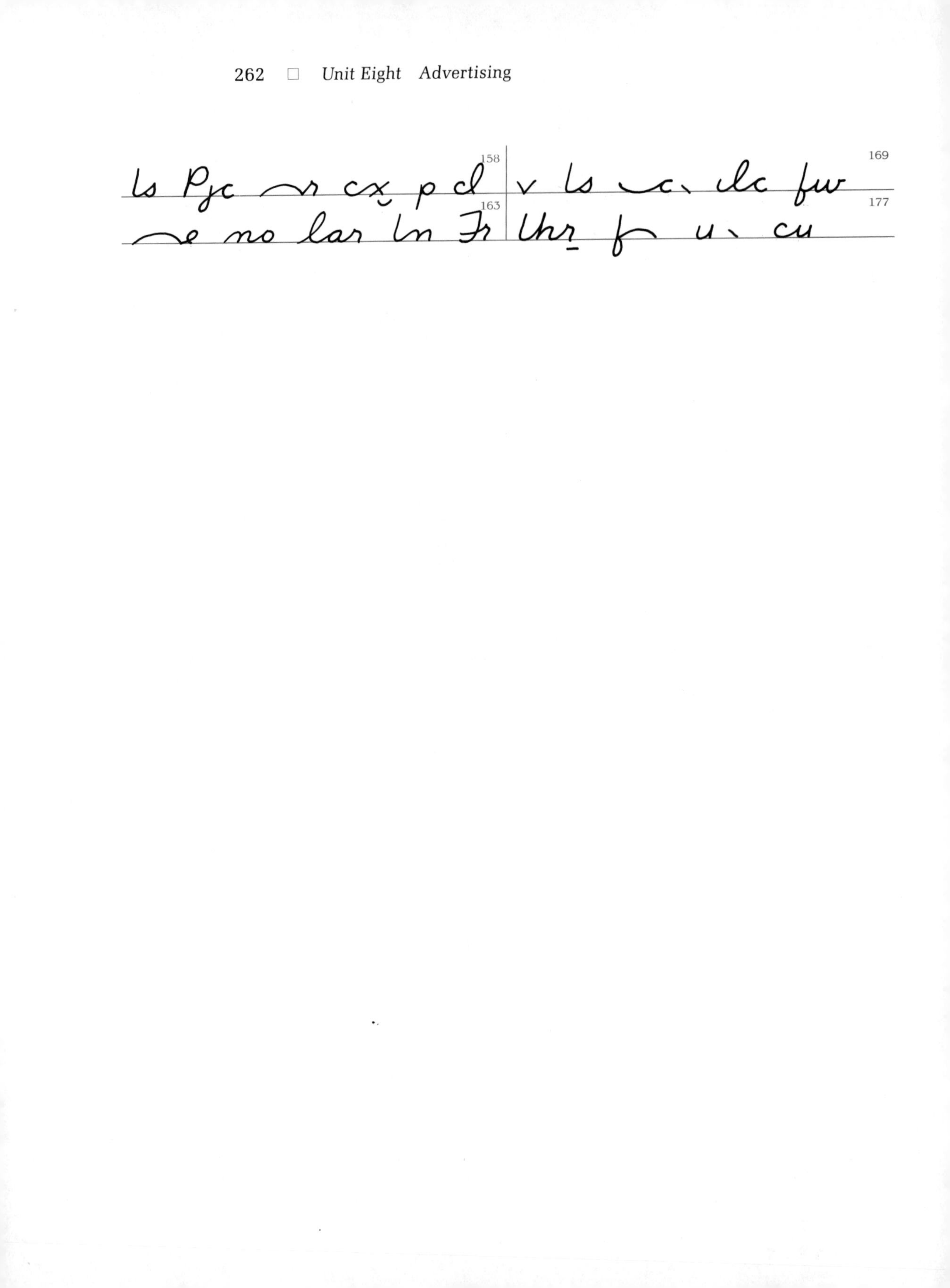

LESSON 40

WORD DEVELOPMENT

Develop new words from the following brief forms:

market

marketing

marketable

marketplace

supermarket

suggest

suggestion

suggesting

suggestive

suggestible

letter

letterhead

newsletter

not

cannot

notwithstanding

up

updated

upon

upcoming

upward

upper

work

workbook

workday

workload

workmen

workweek

READING AND WRITING EXERCISES

PREVIEW WORDS

1 loses *lzs*
danger *dnjr*
luncheon *lnCn*
reputation *rpy*

gaining *gn_*
pharmacies *fr_ses*
retail outlets *rtl otlls*
sporting goods *spl_ gs*

2 radius *rdes*
analysis *anlss*
command *kN*
evaluation *evluy*

ensuring *nsr_*
glassware *gls_r*
Stanford *Snfd*
home furnishings *h_frns*

3 space *sps*
daily *dl*
options *opjs*
quarterly *qlrl*

economical *ecol*
day-to-day *d = l = d*
classified *clsf-*
circulation *Scly*

4 media *~da*
prefer *Pfr*
conduct *kdc*
emphasis *~fss*

meantime *~nl~*
priority *prur^l*
contacted *klc-*
Midwestern *~d Wrn*

5 beyond *beN*
Senator's *snlrs*

capacity *cps^l*
ourselves *rsvs*

candidate	cddl	committed	kl-
workload	old	supportive	splv

1

Mr. Jerry Baxter, Southwestern Food Stores, 6780 Campbell Road, Houston, TX 77090

2

Miss Candice Morgan, Marketing Director, Sunset Glassware Company, 557 West 59 Street, Des Moines, IA 50312

m h frns, ur
z l kdc · lro
r anlss, Av
dsjs r ofn d
f hbl rlr ln
f crf evlu, e
o s lN
rSC frs, + ec
Conj
Slnl ar lvu qs
asr-, sN u pln
l sl u ln v gls r
n · rdes v 2H
Intro DC
ls, rcm
fr v Snfd, inc,
Ab
ly v kp- s lr
Conj
asnms, + lr fM
vb v rluB, ly l
obln (inf und
L c dsjs ab Dj
+ prs, b klc s,
Intro P
ur lcn (frS Sp
lu ns lau Pdc

l kN · q sr √
r, y dN u klc
u ofs ls c so
la ec c plns
f c pn ahd, ul

3

Mr. Hugh Webb, Webb Appliance Repair Service, 3709 Bachman Place, Newark, NJ 07108

d r b lqf L
asc ab Av sps
n r nzppr, ·
s l A n r clsf-
scj d alrc me Ks
lu bs, ppl hu rd
lz scjs r Ar lc
fu Svs, clsf- As
ofr u (S ecol
a l rC lz ppl,
lr r me opjs avlB
lu, u a pls As
o · d=l=d bss, or
Conj

Series Series Paren Paren Intro DC Dir Ad Dir Ad Intro DC

Date Date Intro DC Ap Conj Series Series Paren Intro P

4

Ms. Elizabeth Howard, Preston Enterprises, 1052 107th Avenue, Omaha, NE 68124

5

Add commas to show one parenthetical expression, two introductory dependent clauses, and two introductory phrases.

Mr. George Whitaker, Committee to Re-elect Senator Wells, P.O. Box 547, Portland, OR 97217

The Successful Resumé

Once you have learned skills for today's job market, how will you present them to a prospective employer? An effective way to show what you have learned and what you can do is a resumé.

A resumé lists your educational background, job experience, special skills, and references. If you have not had previous work experience, your resumé is especially important. You should describe all other qualifications that will persuade the interviewer to consider you for employment.

WHERE TO BEGIN

List all full-time or part-time jobs you have held, courses studied, awards, activities, and membership in organizations. Then arrange the information in major groups.

Personal information: List your name, address, and telephone number. You may list job interests or the position you desire.

Educational background: List schools you have attended (beginning with the most recent), degrees or certificates earned, studies emphasized, and special courses. If you received special recognition or awards, include a section for awards and activities.

Employment experience: List any part-time or full-time positions, beginning with the most recent. Specify the name of the employer, beginning and ending dates, and job title. You can strengthen this section by briefly describing your responsibilities.

Special skills: This section tells the employer specifically what you are qualified to do. Drawing from your educational and employment experiences, list all skills. Shorthand, word processing or typing, and accounting, for example, would be appropriate here.

References: Include the name, occupation, address, and telephone number of individuals qualified to comment on your abilities, character, or performance as a student or as an employee. Always ask permission before listing someone as a reference. Choose at least three—usually no more than five—people from different sources. At least one should know you personally; another should know you as an employee or as a student.

REFINING YOUR RESUMÉ

After you have categorized all information, read, edit, change, correct, and type. Repeat the process until you have the best possible picture of yourself on paper.

Your resumé should do many things. Its primary purpose is to present information that can be quickly and easily analyzed by the interviewer. But it reflects on you in other ways. It sets forth your skills and qualities. It demonstrates your ability to sort, organize, and present information. It becomes a visible example of your work.

YOUR COMPLETED RESUMÉ

Your finished resumé may surprise even you. Mailed with a well-written application letter, it may persuade an employer to ask for an interview. When the time comes for the interview, your resumé will contribute to the professionalism and self-confidence that give you a winning image.

UNIT NINE

REAL ESTATE

SHORTHAND VOCABULARY REVIEW

Study these words and the principles they illustrate. Look for these words as you read the letters and memos in this unit.

1. Write m for the word endings *mand, mend, mind,* and *ment.*

demand	dm	basement	bsm
recommend	rcm	retirement	rtrm
remind	rm	achievement	aCvm
apartment	aptm	arrangements	arms
appointment	apym	requirement	rqm

2. Omit *p* in the sound of *mpt*.

empty	prompt
attempt	exemptions

MORE ABOUT PUNCTUATION

1. A semicolon can be used to connect two short statements when the two thoughts are very closely related in meaning.

☐ Thank you for your letter; it explained the problem quite well.
(Thank you for your letter. It explained the problem quite well.)

Use a semicolon to connect two *independent* clauses (two complete thoughts that can stand alone) when the conjunctions *and, or,* or *but* have been omitted.

☐ The delivery is scheduled for Tuesday; we will have someone here to sign for it.
(The delivery is scheduled for Tuesday, and we will have someone here to sign for it.)

2. Use a semicolon to separate two independent clauses when the two clauses are joined by a parenthetical expression, such as those listed below. These transitional expressions are sometimes called conjunctive adverbs and are usually followed by a comma, especially if they contain more than one syllable.

therefore	nevertheless
however	furthermore
consequently	indeed
thus	hence
meanwhile	still

☐ We had planned to meet Mr. Turner at school; however, his plane did not arrive until 1:30.

Other common parenthetical expressions include the following phrases. Note that a semicolon comes before the parenthetical expression in this construction and that a comma follows the parenthetical expression.

in addition

as a result

in fact

in other words

on the contrary

by the way

for example

at any rate

at the same time

on the other hand

□ Your promotion has been approved; in addition, you will receive a bonus for your superior performance this year.

3. Use the semicolon also to separate items in a complicated series.

□ Send a copy of the report to Sam Johnson, marketing; Ann Hudson, promotion; and Jim Williams, personnel.

The notation **Semi** will be highlighted in the Reading and Writing Exercises.

LESSON
41

BRIEF FORMS AND DERIVATIVES

1. *Ar bln kc dl , g nx*

2. *Sks dvms ⌐l dfces aq*

Key

1. already, between, contract, determine, is/his, go/good, next

2. circumstances, developments, immediately, difficulties, ago

PHRASE REVIEW

1. *idu ilc ed ulfN lvu*

2. *lhr lrsv cdb vb laul dlc*

Key

1. I do, I look, we would, you will find, to have you/to have your

2. to hear, to receive, could be, have been, that you will, would like

READING AND WRITING EXERCISES

PREVIEW WORDS

1 empty *~le*

unique *unc*

tenants *lnNs*

supplier *splr*

previous *Pves*

relocate *rlca*

opportune *oprln*

industrial *nl*

2 sports spls
luxury lxre
complex kplx
walkway

occupancy ocpNe
connected kc-
recreation rcrej
Twin Towers Ln Lors

3 acre acr
Ford fd
active acv
district Dtrc

multiple-listing llpl=lS
basement bsm
Jefferson jfrsn
subdivision sdvj

4 submit s l
reopen ropn
lowered lor-
definitely dfntl

reasonable rznB
subdivision sdvj
negotiations ngsejs
Hidden Valley hdn vle

5 goals gls
dollars $
Margaret rgrl
yourself usf

endeavors ndvrs
remarkable rrcB
progresses Pgrss
furthermore frtr

1

Mr. Robert M. May, Versatile Plastics, Inc., 5902 Waterfront Drive, Norfolk, VA 23508

dr a lgfL

ng ab . si fu Nl
plN, u L arv- / .
oprln L, ec suq

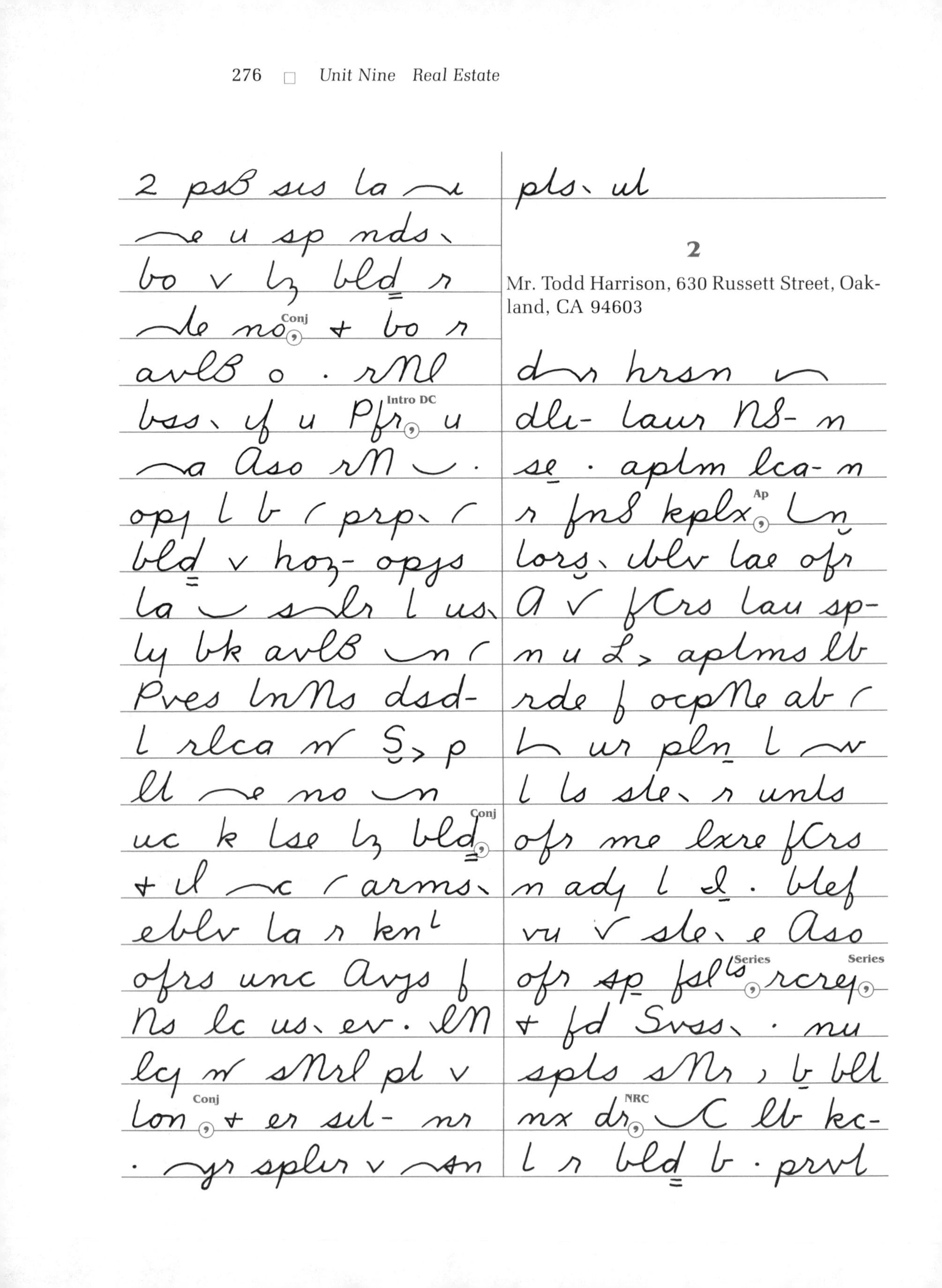

2

Mr. Todd Harrison, 630 Russett Street, Oakland, CA 94603

[shorthand] **Conj**

[shorthand]

3

Mrs. Gretchen Ford, 934 Oleander Way, St. Petersburg, FL 33707

[shorthand] **Semi**

[shorthand] **Paren**

[shorthand] **Intro DC**

[shorthand] **Paren**

[shorthand] **Conj**

4

Mr. and Mrs. Walter Gregory, 170 Foxwood Lane, Nashville, TN 37214

vlę. u s— – l lc
la sdvy . gs dl ,Conj
+ idlc u lrsv u
frS Cys v sis,
sM e lS lc—,Intro DC r
sily hs Cny—. r
sl prs hst lor—,Conj
+ i lg la ulb B
l b r prp f . v
rzmß a l. r
crM ors klc—e
ySrd lse if u Sl
NS— n PCs r lM.
ly r dfnll n NS—
n bld . hos ō si ,Conj
+ ly dlc l ropn
ngsejs ⌣ u, idlc
lvu Avs bf i lc
ag ⌣ r ors. p
ll e no l u
+ ldu. c

5

Add commas to show one parenthetical expression, one direct address, and two conjunctions.

Ms. Margaret Cole, Highland Realty, 1298 Kenwood Avenue, Harrisburg, PA 17112

d rgrl kgjs o 7
v . olSM yr n 13
sls. / S vb 18
v u l lrn la 24
uh sld . M$ n 30
rl eSa du u frS 36
yr ⌣ ls ajMe. ls 42
; . r rcß aCvm 48
+ usd fl v prod 54
vu efl, Sln 60
laul sl nu gls 66
f usf + i Aso no 72
la ec pc L lb 78
z Clny z r l u 84
aCv— ls yr. i 89
u r bS v lc n 94
u fCr ndvrs. u 100

Stnl v ern- (suc 107
laur nyy- ⌒rgrl. 113
frlr⌒ ⌒ sr laul 121

ern evn ⌒ zu 125
crr Pgrss. su 133

LESSON 42

ABBREVIATIONS AND DERIVATIVES

1. S yd ok sq ft corp N
2. inc ex VP re aco

Key

1. superintendent, yard, okay, square, feet, corporation, north
2. incorporate/incorporated, example/executive, vice president, regarding, accompany

---

TRANSCRIPTION AID

Typing Addresses

1. When typing addresses in a sentence, use figures for house numbers and spell out such words as *Street, Avenue, Road, Drive, Lane,* and *Boulevard.*

□ Please mail the order to my home address, 3115 Harrison Boulevard.

2. Spell out numbers from one through ten when they are street names.

□ Our new address will be 410 Fifth Street.

3. Use figures for numbers higher than ten when they are used as street names. If no word separates these street numbers from the building numbers, use *th, st,* or *d* for clarity.

□ The package was delivered to 101 54th Street.

4. If a word such as *North, South, East,* or *West* separates the two groups of numbers, the *th, st,* or *d* is not necessary for the second number.

□ Send the book to 518 South 21 Street.

fixed rate of interest

fx-ra ∨ ng

YOUR BUSINESS
VOCABULARY

A rate of interest that is not subject to change during the duration of a contract.

□ A mortgage will be granted to you at a fixed rate of interest.

subdivision *sdvq*

In real estate, a tract of land that has been divided into smaller lots for individual houses.

□ We will be happy to show you a model home in our new subdivision.

READING AND WRITING EXERCISES

**PREVIEW
WORDS**

1 access *ง*

stated *Sa-*

utility *ullʟ*

estimates *esↄↄ*

2 owns *os*

pursue *Psu*

Grant *grM*

factory *fcↄre*

3 buyer *br*

twice *Lo*

slowly *slol*

minor *mr*

carefully *crfl*

favorable *fvrß*

suitable *suß*

parking lot *prc̨ ll*

undecided *udsd-*

alternative *Alrnv*

warehouse *rhos*

instructions *nↄrcↄs*

weather *ↄr*

Orlando,
Florida *orlℳo FL*

permission *Pᵧ*

maintenance *mlnↃ*

4 swimming

liberty

private

another

bedrooms

basement

beautiful

furthermore

5 lease

sites

space

shorter

either

negotiate

expansion

consultation

1

Mr. William Davenport, Adler Industries, 9844 Henderson Road, Chicago, IL 60660

Conj

Intro DC

Conj

Conj

2

Mrs. Angela Webster, Southern Import Company, 361 Atlanta Avenue, New Orleans, LA 70114

NRC

Paren

Intro P

Intro DC

Intro DC

Paren

3

Mrs. Emily Johnson, 732 Dutton Drive, Orlando, FL 32808

4

Mr. and Mrs. Stanley R. Doyle, 1020 Timberlane Road, Tulsa, OK 74136

5

Add commas to show four introductory dependent clauses and one group of words in a series.

Ms. Patricia Hunter, Togs for Toddlers, 406 Easton Place, Charlotte, NC 28212

LESSON
43

SHORTHAND VOCABULARY REVIEW

Practice writing the names of the following cities. When you hear difficult or unusual names, it may be helpful to spell out the name in full.

Omaha *o ha*

Memphis *mfs*

Phoenix *fnx*

Lincoln *lgn*

Des Moines *d yn*

Atlanta *allNa*

Pittsburgh *plsbrg*

Salt Lake City *slt lc sle*

Los Angeles *ls ajls*

Philadelphia *fldlfa*

New Orleans *ny orlns*

Indianapolis *Nenpls*

Chicago *scg*

Nashville *nsvl*

Trenton *lrNn*

Springfield *sprgfld*

TRANSCRIPTION AID

Similar Words

do *du* To perform an action.

□ I know you will do everything you can to help.

due *du* (1) Payable immediately, (2) expected, (3) because of.

□ (1) The payment is due on January 2.
□ (2) The train is due at 11 o'clock.
□ (3) Due to bad weather, the flight was delayed.

dew du — Moisture condensed from the air.

□ The grass was moist with the morning dew.

YOUR BUSINESS VOCABULARY

closing clz — In real estate, a meeting in which the sale is finalized and the deed to property changes hands.

□ The closing will be held at Central State Bank on May 1.

escrow escro — A written agreement or financial amount placed in the hands of a third party, such as a bank, and held ineffective until certain conditions are met.

□ The deed will be held in escrow until the heir reaches his 18th birthday.

earnest money ernS me — Money paid in advance as partial payment to bind a contract or bargain.

□ He paid $500 in earnest money to the current owners.

READING AND WRITING EXERCISES

PREVIEW WORDS

1 deed dd
rather rlr
closing clz
lending lN
valuable vluB
optional opjl
officially ofsll
institution nSy

2 alert alrl
Detroit dlryl
postpone pSpn
computer kpur

radically *rdcll*	potential *ptnsl*
meantime *~nt*	initiate *insa*

3 title *Ul* — procedures *Psyrs*

escrow *escro* — Stevenson *Svnsn*

transfer *Tfr* — withdrawn *drn*

earnest *ernS* — possession *pzj*

4 aspects *aspcs* — licensed *lsN-*

realtor *rllr* — appraisal *aprzl*

amateur *a~lr* — ownership *ors*

attempt *at~l* — prospective *Pspcv*

5 title *Ul* — accompany *aco*

points *pys* — originating *oryna_*

routine *rtn* — institution *nSly*

appraisal *aprzl* — verification *vrfj*

1

Mr. and Mrs. David M. Scott, 4005
Devonshire Road, Toledo, OH 43607

d~r + ~rs scl
u ~S b p- lau
ofr hsb ac-, ur

ab l bk (ors v
. nu aplm bld,
enc-, . cpe √
kc la ullb asc-l
sn (L v clz-

if uv ne qs ab
(lrs, p cl e *Intro DC*
l so la ic
asr b bf e e
ofsll, n u b
prp o . kc bss
rlr ln PCs .
rgj f . lN
nSj, (dd l (*Intro DC*
prp , n rec-
ull (kc , pd of,
hoE, ec pa . fe + *Paren*
v (kc rec-,
(rec Pss , opjl, *Conj*
b i rcm la ev
/ dn, b du so, *Intro P*
el Plc u nvSm
n prp, idu hp
laur p- ls PCs,
s vluB prp, + *Conj*
/ l Slnl pv lb
. lN nvSm fu,
su

2

Mr. Stan Barker, 6761 Grove Place, Rochester, NY 14615

dr brcr i Slnl
USN u dzr l
pSpn (sl vu
h, u Sks v
Cnj- rdcll, + / *Conj*
db blr fu l Sa
r ur ull uvh
b bc u dsj,
n nl, l n *Paren*
alrl l plnsl
brs hu v Sn .
NS n u h, f
u dsd l lc (
nu jb n dlryl, *Intro DC*
n kfdN lau
hos l sl qcl,

Intro P

Paren

Conj

Intro DC

Conj

3

Dr. and Mrs. Matthew Cox, 221 Friendship Drive, Mobile, AL 36610

Intro P

Intro P

Conj

u, + ∽ dli- la
lgs v gn so l f
El, ul

4

Ms. Allison Foster, 612 Madras Lane, Phoenix, AZ 85013

d∽ fSr ∽ n iz
drv bru u nbrh
ls ∽rn, i nls-
lau h∽, f sl b
or, vu ks- (me
Avzs v lS u hoo
⌣ · rllr×, Alo
me ppl at⌢l l sl
lr h∽s b ∽svs,
ly ofn fN la lr,
∽C ∽ l sl rl
eSa ln ly h U, f
ex, · rllr hs me
klcs + nos ho l
rC Pspcv brs,

Intro DC

Intro DC

Paren

aol ∽yr ksy, la
· rllr, · lsN-
aჶN, h or se hs
· gr dl v nly ab
(lgl + fnnsl
aspcs v Tfr or+,
b or sl u h∽,
i v ∽S ∽pl
nvSms ul E ∽c,
y rsc ls nvSm b
pls la rspBL ∾
hNs v · a∽lr×,
enc-, ∽ bs crd,
∽s fSr, idlb hpe
lvzl u h∽ + gv u
· aprzl fre v G,
uvl

Dir Ad

5

Add commas to show one nonrestrictive clause, one group of words in a series, two introductory phrases, and two introductory dependent clauses.

Ms. Karen Mitchell, 5734 Pillsbury Avenue, Minneapolis, MN 55427

6
13
20
25
31
37
43
50
57
63
68
76
82
89
96
102
109
116
122
128
136
142
146
153
161

LESSON 44

SHORTHAND VOCABULARY REVIEW

Write *S* for the word beginnings *cer, cir, ser, sur* (sir).

certain Sln
service Svs
certificate Slfcl
circular Sclr
surplus Spls

surveyed Sva-
search SC
surprise Sprz
surcharge SG
surgery Sjre

TRANSCRIPTION AID

Spelling. Learn to spell the following words that end in *al* or *le*. When you are in doubt about the spelling of these words, use your dictionary.

al

practical prclcl
survival Svvl
vital vtl
personal Psnl
chemical c–cl
legal lgl

le

title ttl
vehicle vhcl
settle stl
article artcl
assemble as–B
cable cB

YOUR BUSINESS
VOCABULARY

easement *ezm* In real estate, the legal right of a party to have limited use of another person's property.

☐ The water company requests that nothing be planted within the boundaries of its easement.

abstract *absrc* In real estate, a legal document containing the complete written history of a deeded parcel of land.

☐ I have requested that a copy of the abstract be sent to you.

READING AND WRITING EXERCISES

PREVIEW
WORDS

1 county *ke* commercial *krsl*

partner *plnr* newcomer *nukr*

resolve *rzlv* residential *rzdnsl*

surrounding *SoN* school system *scl ss*

2 bet *bl* effect *efc*

keys *ces* exemption *⌄y*

arises *arzs* acquainted *aqN-*

residing *rzd* River Road *rvr rd*

3 lengthy *lqle* abstract *absrc*

verified *vrf-* acquiring *aq-*

breakdown *brcdon* homeowner *h∿or*

principal *prNpl* installments *nSlms*

4 creek crc | practical prclcl
adjoins ajyns | boundaries boNres
smaller slr | subdivided sdvd-
zoned zn- | County Road ke rd

5 lot ll | electric elc
exists Ss | bordering brdr
title Ul | easement ezm
likely lcl | county clerk ke clrc

1

Dr. J. D. Nelson, 366 Lamar Court, Springfield, IL 62702

ddr nlsn kgjs
po b slc- S v
ke scl sS, er
dli- Ub a q (
frS rzdNs l lk
u l r sle, no la
uv ac- ls pzj, u (Intro DC)
PbS v Ar Srl- lq
ab (cM v hos u
M fu fl, z .
nukr l ls knL, (Intro P)
ul M l Cz . rllr
hz Avs uc rli po,
r ajNe, l v oldS
n ls ara, lS yr e
sld ln 10M$
n krsl + rzdnsl
rl eSa, z . plnr
n ls ajNe, w Sv- (Intro P)
ls knL f AS 20
yrs, v flr
ls sle + s SoN
aras, uno la ic
lca (Pfc hos

Conj

2

Mr. Douglas Murphy, 6561 River Road, Syracuse, NY 13207

Intro DC

Intro P

Conj

Intro P

Intro P

3

Miss Kathleen S. Leonard, 2922 Brighton Place, Wilmington, DE 19802

Conj

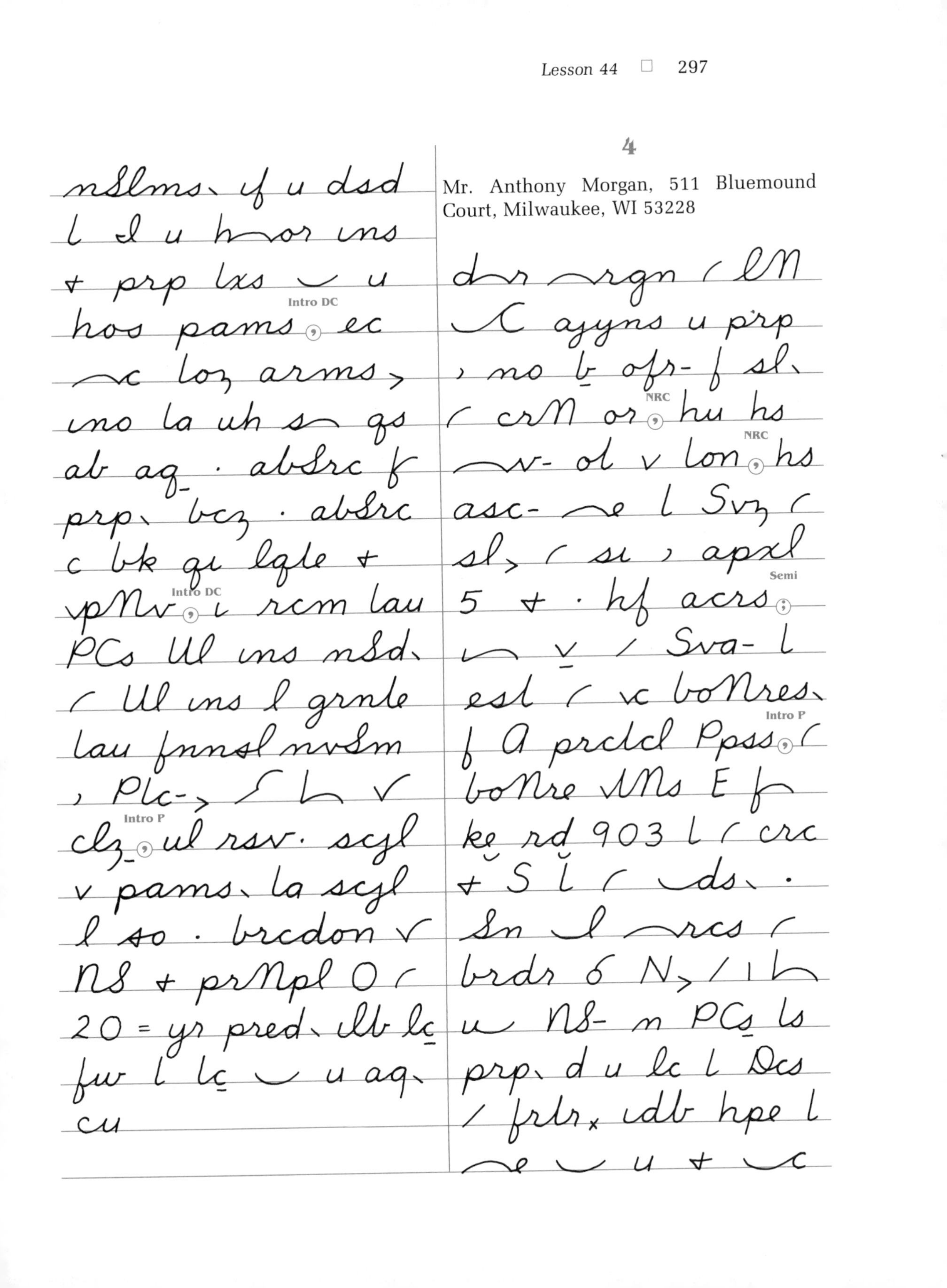

Intro DC

Intro DC

Intro P

4

Mr. Anthony Morgan, 511 Bluemound Court, Milwaukee, WI 53228

NRC

NRC

Semi

Intro P

O (lN, sN ls
prp , ar zn- f
Intro DC
rzdnsl hoz (,) /
Stnl cdb sdvd-
nl s⌣lr lls> (
Sva + Ul SC lb
kp- ⌣n 3 l 4 ⌣cs,
p fl fre lcl ⌒e /
ne l⌣, ul

5

Add commas to show two introductory phrases, two introductory dependent clauses, and two parenthetical expressions.

Mr. and Mrs. Daniel Marshall, 4620 Colfax Road, El Paso, TX 79902

d⌣r + ⌒rs ⌒rsl 5
enc- , . cpe v ⌒i 11
rq8 f Ul ins f 18
prp ur PCs, (Ul 26
ins plse lb rln 32
f a⌣l v sl prs 39
v prp, acrd l (46
ke clrc / sd lc 52
no lgr ln 20 55
⌣o ds lv (plse 62
n hN, lrf lr , 68
no rzn l lq la 73
(clz lb dla- b 79
ls acj> n r erlr 85
Dcjs sv ⌣cs aq 91
e lc- ab (psBl 97
la ⌒ ln 1 ezm 103
Ss ou ll, / no 108
aprs la (elc co 115
hs . ezm la rns 120
alq (prp ln 6 127
W sd, , Aso 131
lcl la (⌣lr co 137
hs . ezm alq (142
frN v prp brdr 149
(S, hoE (Ul 155
ins plse l so s 161
vcl ⌣r lz ezms 167
ls> ⌒ dlı- la 172
lgs r q l fu, uf 179

uc as8 u w — v 186	no + clz, l se 204
prprys p cl, if i 192	u bo ln, su 211
dN hr f u bln 198	

LESSON

WORD DEVELOPMENT

Develop new words using the following brief forms:

contract

contracting *kc̱*

contracts *kcs*

contracted *kc-*

contractor *kcr*

contractual *kcul*

accept

accepted *ac-*

accepting *ac̱*

acceptance *acN*

acceptable *acB*

acceptability *acBl*

for

format *frl*

formation *fy*

formerly *frl*

fortunate *fcnl*

formulated *frla-*

effort *efl*

conform *kf*

forecast *fcs*

comfortable *kflB*

enforcement *nfsm*

READING AND WRITING EXERCISES

PREVIEW WORDS

1 appeal *apl*

rezone *rzn*

donations *dnjs*

treasurer *lrzrr*

	Word	Outline	Word	Outline
	priority	prir	commission	kj
	rejected	rjc-	transactions	Tacjs
2	expires	vprs	renovate	rnva
	indoor	ndr	extension	vtnj
	athletic	atllc	initiated	insa-
	formerly	frl	expiration	vprj
3	earnest	ernS	withdrawn	‿drn
	escrow	escro	down payment	don pam
	progress	Pgrs	conversation	kvrsj
	summary	s‿re	Central Savings	sNrl sv
4	exact	vc	possession	pzj
	quiet	qil	relinquish	rlqs
	whenever	‿nE	neighborhood	nbrh
	alternative	Alrnv	conveniently	kvl
5	owners	ors	another	aol
	resale	rsl	terminate	trma
	couple	cpl	subsequent	ssqN
	assumed	as‿-	conventional	kvnjl

1

Memo to Howard Logan from Mike Palmer, SUBJECT: Property Purchase

mo l hord lgn

r da vr ‿e E
bq hsb Cnj- f
Fu l Wd, Date Ma 3

Intro DC

Intro DC

Conj

Intro P

NRC

Intro DC

Intro DC

NRC

2

Mr. Gerald Thurman, 388 Seneca Street, Seattle, WA 98199

vprs Fb 9> (brs
v opj agremn clrl
Sa la / l n b
psB lgl . vnj
af (vprj da. (
nvSrs v insa- .
efl l rz adyl fMs
l rnva (bld.
plns r b- nd l
opn . fl fl' sMr
la l d ndr s— (Series) ,
jq- (Series) , lns (Series) , + ol Pgs>
if udlc adyl inf (Intro DC) ,
ic pl u n lC
(P v ls grp. (
mbrs drv l bgn
nl (Conj) , so id avz
u l ac qcl. s

3

Ms. Linda Roberts, 1990 Viking Terrace, Apartment 2B, Boston, MA 02130

drs rbrts n ry
l nf u la . Ul
SC , no n Pgrs
f hos + 3 lls /
48 el S. (Cnys
u rqS- vb A- l
(kc (Conj) , + n enc
. cpe v fnl drfl>
z uno (Intro DC) , clz , scyl-
f nn (Date) , Ap 22 (Date) , w
ofss v sMrl sv
bq. il e u lr>
if uv frlr qs re
fes la r paB (
b v clz (Intro DC) , p cl
e nl. (enc-
lS , . sre v
ls e Dcs- n r
lS Ufn kvrsj. z
uc se (Intro DC) , (ernS
me lb drn f
(escro ak (b
v clz. / l ndd b

Intro DC

Ap

4

Mrs. Janice Barnett, 4001 Kipling Place, Shreveport, LA 71118

Semi

Intro DC

Intro DC

Conj

5

Add commas to show one conjunction, one introductory phrase, one appositive, one introductory dependent clause, and one parenthetical expression.

Mr. and Mrs. Andrew Williams, 5068 MacDonald Avenue, Edmonton, AB T6H 5C5

5

11

17

21

nf- ne ySrd la 27
ly r pln l sl (33
prp, ly asc- ne 38
l lS (bld f h + 45
i agre- ldu so> p 50
b asr- la (rsl v 56
ls prp l n cz ne 63
dfces fu, sN (ors 71
bl (aplms o . kc 78
bss ly lb pa of 84
la kc n f (h 91
v sl, u na rcl 97
la (kc sps la 103

(kc cn b as- 109
b ssgN ors> bf 115
N nl . kc sl 122
aol ple (nlsns 128
r a r la ly S 133
lrma (kc 138
u, lrf ly r Ppr 146
l rq la (PCsrs 152
lc ol . kvnyl 157
rgl> il cp u 162
nf- v E la hpns, 169
ul 172

UNIT TEN

MANUFACTURING

SHORTHAND VOCABULARY REVIEW

Study the following words and the principles they illustrate. Look for these words in the letters and memos presented in this unit.

1. Write [shorthand] for the word ending *ify*. Write [shorthand] for the word ending *ification*.

justify	qualified
clarifies	justified
gratifying	qualifications
certified	modifications

2. Write *u* for the word beginning un.

unusual	*uuz*	uncommon	*ukn*
unpaid	*upd*	unexpected	*uxpc-*
unlikely	*ulcl*	unnecessary	*unes*
unless	*uls*	unfortunately	*ufCnll*

MORE ABOUT PUNCTUATION

Use a colon to introduce lists, tabulations, explanations, or quotations. Some words that commonly precede colons are given below:

the following	listed below
as follows	such as

- ☐ Please order the following: file folders, disks, ballpoint pens, and typewriting paper.
- ☐ The committee members are as follows: Alexander Haley, Sylvia Carmichael, Andrew Simpson, and Deborah Easterby.

LESSON 46

BRIEF FORMS AND DERIVATIVES

1. D kl hs h nl uz
2. uuz Ds Dst nl- nlf-

Key

1. distribute, control, has, he/had/him, note, usual
2. unusual, distributor, distributorship, noted, notified

PHRASE REVIEW

1. ch uz efl erp- ecd
2. edb ucn uvh lvzl lo
3. zi cb vn vu ou

Key

1. I had, I was, we feel, we are pleased, we could
2. we would be, you cannot, you have had, to visit, to work
3. as I, can be, have not, of you/of your, on you/on your

READING AND WRITING EXERCISES

PREVIEW WORDS

1 avoid avyd — heavier hves
rapid rpd — regularly rglrl
mechanical —cncl — prosperity Psprl
emergencies e—yNes — replacement rplsm

2 Ltd. * lkt-*

roof *rf*

operation *opy*

computer *kpur*

3 teams *Lns*

rules *rls*

careless *crls*

enforce *nfs*

4 basis *bss*

elected *elc-*

clarify *clrf*

document *dcm*

5 rare *rr*

says *sz*

contributor *kbr*

participants *ppNs*

thorough *Lro*

flexibility *flxBl*

orientation *oreNy*

technology *Lcnlge*

doorways *dr as*

walkways *c as*

regulations *rglys*

obstructions *obSrcys*

stock item *Sc ch*

obligations *oblgys*

distributors *Drs*

responsibilities *rspBls*

pledges *plys*

donation *dny*

distinction *Dlgy*

worthwhile *rll*

1

Mr. John W. Marvin, Maritime Equipment Corporation, 9002 Central Parkway, New-port News, VA 23606

d r rm ev
hrd lau bs , p-

· pred v rpd grl
+ Pspr', kgys ou
suc!, u co , n ·
Srg pzy ld bcz
uv cpl u plN

~drn b ̄b nu
eqpm rglrh. ~
u crN vol v bs. **Intro P** (,)
u eqpm lb cre.
hver ld ln / hs
N pd, rplsm
pls + rprs r
pNv. ll s hlp
u avyd ~cncl
Pbl~s la cz dlas
n Pdcy. r prls c
cp u eqpm n q
~o od. er nt-f
spli. ~ Svs
~n e~ryNes arz,
(enc- brsr lSs
(lps v Svs kcs
e ofr. y n ll s
hlp u Cz. pln l
su u nds, ec
nsr lau ~snre

l ku l op efsNl.
vlu

2

Mr. Frank Harvey, Jackson and Jackson, Ltd., 1356 Hempstead Road, Dayton, OH 45402

d~r hrve hr,
(dla u rqs~. ,
uc se. / klns. **Intro DC** (,)
kp lS √ nu eqpm
u ~4 l nSl N
fr v jcsn + jcsn. **Ab** (,)
l~l-. idlc l suq
lau brq u ~pes
l r plN lse (
eqpm n opy. ev
. v ~prsv Dpla
v kpur lcnlje U
l rf, edlt hpe l
dmSra (flxBl vr
unls. l lq ecd

Intro DC

Paren

Series

Series

Intro DC

3

Memo to All Supervisors from Gary R. Smith, SUBJECT: Safety Regulations Review

4

Mrs. Beatrice Miller, 7778 Augustine Way, Louisville, KY 40291

Intro P

Intro DC

Intro DC

Ap

Intro DC

5

Add commas to show one introductory phrase, one introductory dependent clause, one appositive, and one series.

Memo to All Employees from Cynthia L. Steele, SUBJECT: City Fund Drive

5

10

15

20

27

32

pp n ls fN drv, 38
bcz eh ⌒ ppNs 45
ln ne ol N n ls 51
sle e aCv- . rr 56
Dlqj lS yr, u ⌒a 63
Ar relz ho ⌒pl lz 70
fNs r, ly r uz- 75
l splm hll Pgs 81
l Pvd X fNs f 87
ssl ajNes + l 91
⌒nln me ⌒rll 96
ogjs la cd n S 103
⌒ol r fnnsl 108
hlp, ol u (⌒pe 114
c ⌒c ls pln ⌒o, 119
p dmSra u spl b 126
kb u sr, rmbr 133
la . dny f⌒ u 138
sz lau ⌒N u co 145
l ku lb (ld 151
kbr, 153

ABBREVIATIONS AND DERIVATIVES

1. *fed vol inc esp ex rep*
2. *oz lb Ts cals incs* ⁀*os*

Key

1. federal, volume, incorporate/incorporated, especially, example/executive, represent/representative
2. ounce, pound, thousands, catalogs, incorporates, months

TRANSCRIPTION AID

Proofreading. Careful proofreading is as important to successful transcription as any other part of the transcription process. Before producing the final copy of your letter, look at its general appearance. Ask yourself these questions:

1. Is the letter arranged attractively on the pages so that the margins are well balanced?
2. Is the printed material free of smudges and noticeable corrections?
3. Have I spaced correctly after punctuation marks and between parts of the letter?

If the answer to each of these questions is yes, your next step should be to read each word carefully to determine the following:

1. Is each word spelled correctly?
2. Are all numbers accurate?
3. Are all names, addresses, and special terms correct?
4. Have I punctuated and capitalized correctly?
5. Does this letter reflect well on my skills and on the image of my company?

uniformity *unf* Sameness; the condition of being consistent. YOUR BUSINESS
VOCABULARY

□ That series of books will have uniformity of design.

ultimate *ult* The conclusive step in a process; the furthest possible extent.

□ Our ultimate objective is to increase sales by 20 percent.

READING AND WRITING EXERCISES

PREVIEW WORDS

1 step *Sp*

colorful *clrf*

counters *krs*

windows *Nos*

subscribed *sS-*

imaginative *ynv*

preferences *prfrNs*

disassemble *DasB*

2 cart *crl*

correct *crc*

aiding *ad*

powered *por-*

hallways *hlas*

mail room *lr*

electronic *elnc*

unnecessarily *unesl*

3 recruit *rcru*

variety *vru*

support *spl*

welcome *lk*

via *va*

Parcel *prsl*

partnership *plnrs*

dealerships *dlrss*

4 unlikely ulcl — precision Psj
regional rynl — supplement splm
assembly as-B — engineering njnr
ultimate ult-t — operation opj

5 gas gs — nuclear nclr
fuel ful — Bestway bSa
powder podr — generators jnrars
whose hz — uniformity unf-t

1

Avondale Department Store, 598 South Oregon Avenue, Tampa, FL 33612

1 dlrs f a O / sle v lrn- ho l ncrs lr vol v sls n l eze Sp, ly v sS- l / Svs e ofr f ar sls Dplas> ho dz ls Svs —o, (Conj) + l r / bnfls lu× yf uv . kc f r Svss, (Intro DC) e as— kp rspBl f ar alrcv

Dplas f Sr krs + —Nos, el bgn b cra . pln la ncs u idas + prfrNs, el asc u l l8 / ls u —t l —fsz f eC Dpla> ln el P r fnl pln fu ksj, yf / —es — u apvl, (Intro DC) el as—B + Das—B / Dpla — apo lms> r clins v foN r arms lb

Series Series

Intro DC

2

Memo to All Employees from Leon Stuckey, SUBJECT: Mail System Delays

Paren

Intro DC

Intro P

Series

Series

Intro DC

3

Memo to Linda Charles from Kevin Bennett, Regional Sales Manager, SUBJECT: Catalogs

Intro DC

4

Mr. Thomas N. Jenkins, Ellsworth Manufacturing, Inc., 6330 Butler Avenue, Bridgeport, CT 06605

ln 6 mos, aq (Paren ,)
lqf klc s r co
mcs Ts v pls eC
yr (Conj ,) + er egr l Sv
u cu

5

Add commas to show one appositive, one direct address, one introductory dependent clause, and two groups of words in a series.

Mr. Richard S. Hudson, Director of Operations, Newcastle Industries, P.O. Box 2214, Denver, CO 80236

dr hdsn lr . 6
kl sS la c sv 11
me n ful ef+Ne 16
+ ern me fu b 22
ncrs Pdcs er lc 29
ab (nyl ldr n 35
sls + Svs bla kl 42
sS, Mr u Pdcs 48
r md f gs lqd 54
or pods Mrel ls 59
sS Pvds lcnlye 64
la l mpv (OA 70
opj vu plN ec 77
rds u cSs mpv 82
Pdc unf + ncrs 89
u Pfls, ma e 93
dmSra ho r mpv- 99
sS cb apli- lu 105
mf plN ev . Sf 113
v vprls hu l kdc 118
. Sde / no G lu 124
ev Pvd- lz Svss 131
l me lps v Ns 136
hz Pdcs vre f 141
plScs l ncler 145
por jnrars, ld cl 151
u ofs lc . apym 159
mr hdsn ul 164

LESSON 48

SHORTHAND VOCABULARY REVIEW

1. Write q for the sound of *kw* and for the word ending *quire.*

quite qi

requested rq8-

quantity qN

require rq

inquiries nqes

acquiring aq-

2. Write v for the medial and final sound of *tive.*

active acv

objective objcv

competitive kplv

incentive nsnv

positive pzv

effective efcv

attractive alrcv

collectively clcvl

TRANSCRIPTION AID

Similar Words

complimentary kplmre — Expressing praise; the presentation of a free gift.

□ Please accept this complimentary copy of our magazine.

complementary kplmre — Supplying a part that is needed to make up a whole; producing an effect in which all parts are well coordinated.

□ Is the new perfume complementary to the rest of our line of cosmetics?

YOUR BUSINESS VOCABULARY

replenish rplns — To refill; make complete again.

□ Has anyone ordered new stock to replenish that sold during the sale?

initiate insa — To begin or originate.

□ We will initiate a training program for new employees.

READING AND WRITING EXERCISES

PREVIEW WORDS

1 lotion lj
shelf slf
replenish rplns
patronage plrnj
disturbed Dlrb-
compensate kpNa
complimentary kplmre
top-selling lp=sl

2 sorry sre
forced fs-
partial prsl
receipt rse
initiate insa
remainder rMr
certified Slf-
collection clj

3 line ln
lawn ln
uncommon ukn
competitive kplv

garden grdn
grass seed grs sd
promotions P-ys
gratifying grtf-

4 data dta
force fs
relating rla-
conducted kdc-
warranty -rNe
demonstration dmSry
convention kvny
teleconference TlkfrN

5 loan ln
draw dra
forth ft
tomorrow Tro
directly drl
Sterling Srlq
extensions Xnjs
debt service dt Svs

1

Ms. Anne Temple, Wesley Department Store, 688 Harper Street, Mobile, AL 36603

drs Tpl b no usd v rsv- r nu sm v mdse n ri l vprs r apy fu psN + USN. mn i hrd la r orjnl sm kln- sv dy- drs, uz v Dtrb-. i nu la

Intro DC

und- lz drs l rplns u slf Sc + la ch grnle-. erl dle lu, edlc Tc. spsl ofr l hlp kpNa f ne nkv lau ma v vp-. fu nx PCs vr Pdcs, el d. kplmre cs vr lp= sl Pdc, r hN +

Intro P

Ap

Paren Paren

Intro DC

2

Mr. Timothy Jason, Sheldon Men's Wear Company, 9535 Willard Avenue, Rockford, IL 61103

Intro P

Series Series

3

Mr. David A. Chester, Red Banks Lumber Company, 4219 Canyon Boulevard, Boulder, CO 80301

4

Mr. Harold B. Turner, Director of Marketing, Wentworth Corporation, 508 Market Street, Halifax, NS B3J 3A5

qs rla l (kdjs
uv lS- f ⌣rNe
Plcy, d ub avlB
l Dcs lz dlls ⌣
r sls + ⌢r Sf.
if ucn vzl r ofss
Psnll, Ph ucd ar (Intro DC)
f . UkfrN cl, sC
. cl d alo a ples
l knca frel, p
ll ⌢e no ho usd
Psd, vlu

5

Add commas to show two introductory dependent clauses, two parenthetical expressions, and one appositive.

Miss Barbara J. Sterling, Independent Information Analysts, Inc., 301 Birchwood Avenue, Madison, WI 53217

dM Srlg lgfL 9
vpln u fnnsl Sks, 17
Alo edu n uzl 23
grN Anys o aks 29
efl la ls , . spsl 35
cs, lrf er grN . 43
adyl 90 ds v cr 48
ou ln, sN edu 54
n pln l ncrs (59
ra v NS f ls adyl 66
dl Svs / l n b 72
nes l dra p . 77
nu kc, hoE . 82
fl agrem , b 87
Ppr- l sl fl (92
lrns v Anys, ul 99
v l sn ls agrem 105
bf / c q nl efc, 111
i USN la (grl 117
vu co l dpN drl 124
po ag (nu fsl 130
laur w Pss v b, 138
(ol rgs ev , 144
lau Pvd s ⌣ . 149
cpe v la PCs 154
agrem, (Anys 159

pprs lb rde Lro 165

afnn Jn l, u 170

~a k n ne L 174

l sn L, uvl 181

LESSON 49

SHORTHAND VOCABULARY REVIEW

1. Write a capital D for the word beginning *dis*.
Write a capital M for the word beginning *mis*.

discussion Dq
displays Dplas
disposal Dpzl
disturbance DlrbN
misleading Mld
mistake Mlc
misinformed Mnf-
misunderstood MUSd

2. Word beginnings, word endings, and sound blends that can also be individual words may be used to express those words.

end N
all a
extra X
miss M
men m
ad, add a
per P
mind m

TRANSCRIPTION AID

Spelling. Learn to distinguish between words that end in *cial* and words that end in *tial*. When in doubt, consult your dictionary.

cial

special spal
crucial cral

tial

potential plnal
substantial sSnal

judicial	*jdsl*	partial	*prsl*
official	*ofsl*	sequential	*sqnsl*
financial	*fnnsl*	influential	*nflunsl*

YOUR BUSINESS VOCABULARY

remittance *rlm* Money or credit sent as a payment on a bill.

☐ Please mail us your remittance of $15.33.

collectively *clcvl* Assembled or accumulated into a whole; a number of individuals acting as a group.

☐ The money for this donation was raised collectively by our employees.

READING AND WRITING EXERCISES

PREVIEW WORDS

1. sturdy *Srde* competitive *kplv*
 predict *Pdc* constructed *kSrc-*
 indoor *ndr* moneymakers *mevcrs*
 reorder *rod* folding chairs *fld Crs*

2. improvements *pvms* small *sl*
 options *opjs* health care *hll cr*
 directly *drl* modifications *dfjs*
 previously *Pvesl* oral surgery *orl Syre*

3. period *pred* meantime *ml*
 notation *nly* letterhead *Lhd*

unpaid upd
latter ltr
remittance rmtN
installment nSlm

4 ago aq
surpassed Sps-
expectations xpcys
substantial sSnsl
incentive nsnv
year-end yr=N
collectively clcvl
profit sharing Pfl Sr

5 depart dpl
image ⌢j
young yq
audience adeN
direction drj
traditional lrdjl
emphasize ⌢fsz
workmanship ⌢oms

Form letter to prospective customers from Arthur Benson

d K r enc- bclt l Nds u l r nu ln v fld Crs. p nl la lz r n ord Crs. ly dfr f me kplv brNs n la ly r kSrc- f r fnS ⌢trels. ly r dzn- f bo ndr + oldr us> u Ks l lc ~ f me rzns. lz Crs r apo f bs us, b ly l lc a~S z q n . rzdnsl st. ly dN rq X Plc; ly r z Srde z ly r alrcv> er ac lrul ods f .

mm v 12 Crs
⌣ pam du ⌣n 90
ds. er kfdN laul
sr r vm oN uv
sn r Pdc. rel (
Crs ⌣n 30 ds cf
ly du n pv lb
me⌣crs. l lSra
⌣u kfdN n ls
Intro P
Pdc, i Pdc la
ulb rde l rod
⌣n 30 ds, u ⌣a
pls u od ne b
bln 8a⌣ + 4 30p⌣.
el lc fw lu cl.
su

2

Memo to All Employees from Claudia Hardin, SUBJECT: Improvements in Insurance Benefits

mo l A ⌣pes
lqs l (efts vr

Intro P
rSC k, ec no
anoN nu opjs
n u ins bnfts.
lz opjs rep ⌣pl
⌣dfjs n u lol
hll cr pln, bgn
Intro P
o Jl, dNl cvrj
lb A- f . s⌣l
⌣ol fe. (a⌣l
v fe l dpN po
(No v mbrs
Paren
n u f⌣l, n adj,
u plse l cvr sp
lps v orl Sjre
la vn Pvesl b
I-. p rd (alC-
bcll crfl ldl
⌣l vpNs lb cvr-.
Intro DC
cf uv sp qs, p
brq b drl l (
Paren
Psnl ofs, aq, e
⌣s l lq (rSC

k f hlp s aCv
lz pvms n r
ins Pq.

3

Mr. Clark Harrison, 1864 Victor, Richmond, VA 23222

dr hrsn lqf Cc
f 895[17] n pam
vr inv 8093. u
r ltN arv- 15 ds
af r N v Dk
pred. lrf (Paren), u pam
sd vb 913[44]. u
ma fw . Cc f
adjl 18[27] or l
la al u nx
mol pam. if u
Cz r llr ld
v pam (Intro DC), p Pvd .
nly la r adjl
al , lb cr- lu
upd blN f Ap.
w mlh (Paren), er cr
u ak f . lol v
895[17]. u nx nSlm
sdb rsv- b Ma 6
n od l glf u f
Dk f la o. if
u rg frlr asSN (Intro DC),
p cl s f No ls-
abv n r Lhd.
vlu

4

Memo to All Employees from Alan H. Crenshaw, SUBJECT: Incentive Plan Update

mo l A pes 6
cs aq e anoN-
. nu nsnv pln
bs- 6 kspl v Pfl
sr. er dli- l rpl
la r suc v ls
pln hs Sps- A
pcys. bcz v kbn-

Intro P
efls v E1, Pdc
hs ncrs- b 18%.
kgjs o . jb l dn,
n adj l ncrs-
Intro P
Pdc, . fss o pv-
Psjrs hs rds- (
ra v errs b .
sSnfl ryn. if
Intro DC
e ku / ls ra, r
yr=N fnnsl rpl
l hld . spsl
Sprz f E pe,
ls cN v pln
hlps eC v s l
relz r kbjs l (
Paren
co. Nvl + clcvl,
er v . dr efc o
suc v ls corp.

5

Add commas to show two introductory dependent clauses, one direct address, and two conjunctions.

Mrs. Carolyn Hastings, H & H Advertising Agency, 4304 Durbin Avenue, Memphis, TN 38118

drs hS r nu ln 7
v dse l sn b 12
rde f r b , (19
r rde f sx, z 24
uno / hsb crc vr 32
co l fsz vprl 38
oms + lrdjl 44
Sl f a vr Pdcs. 50
n ev dzn- pS 56
av cpns ev 62
dr- r sj l . 67
lrdjl adeN, no 73
edlc l dpl f 78
la y. edlc lvu 86
Ppr . a cpn la 92
d apl esp l (yq 99
Pfjl r, ev a 107
b v sal- u 113
idas rs hS + 118

er kfdN la ulb 125

B l Pvd s ⌣ (130

ri drj oN aq, ⌢ 137

a avlB l Dcs 143

idas ⌣ u, p cl 148

⌢e / u kv, ul 156

LESSON 50

WORD DEVELOPMENT

Develop new words from the following brief forms:

every

everybody	*Ebde*
everyday	*Ed*
everyone	*E l*
everything	*E̱*
everywhere	*E̱r*

control

controls	*kls*
controllable	*klB*
uncontrollable	*uklB*
controllability	*klBˡ*
controller	*klr*

ship

leadership	*ldrs*
membership	*mbrs*
fellowship	*flos*
township	*lons*
scholarship	*sclrs*

friendship	*frNs*
hardship	*hrds*
salesmanship	*slsms*
sponsorship	*spNrs*
shipyard	*syd*

READING AND WRITING EXERCISES

PREVIEW WORDS

1 flowing *flo̱*
 assembly *as B*

 scheduling *scjl*
 adjustments *ajSms*

automated *at~a-*
procedures *Psyrs*

2 coats *cos*

c.o.d. *cod*

loading *ld_*

unusual *uuz*

3 phone *fn*

routine *rtn*

contacting *ktc_*

analysis *anlss*

4 sheet *se*

goods *gs*

leather *llr*

shortage *srly*

5 fallen *fln*

process *Pss*

spite *spi*

unusual *uuz*

maintenance *~ntnN*

administered *AmSr-*

transit *Tl*

freight *fra*

trucking *trc_*

minimum *mm*

qualifications *qlfss*

retail outlet *rtl otll*

Empire Roofing *~pz rf_*

distributorship *Drs*

higher *hur*

incurred *ncr-*

projected *Pjc-*

raw
materials *ra ~trels*

repeated *rpe-*

explanation *plny*

understanding *USN_*

bookkeeping *bccp_*

1

Memo to All Managers from Claude F. Singleton, SUBJECT: New Production Procedures

mo l a ~yrs .
od hsb pls- f nu

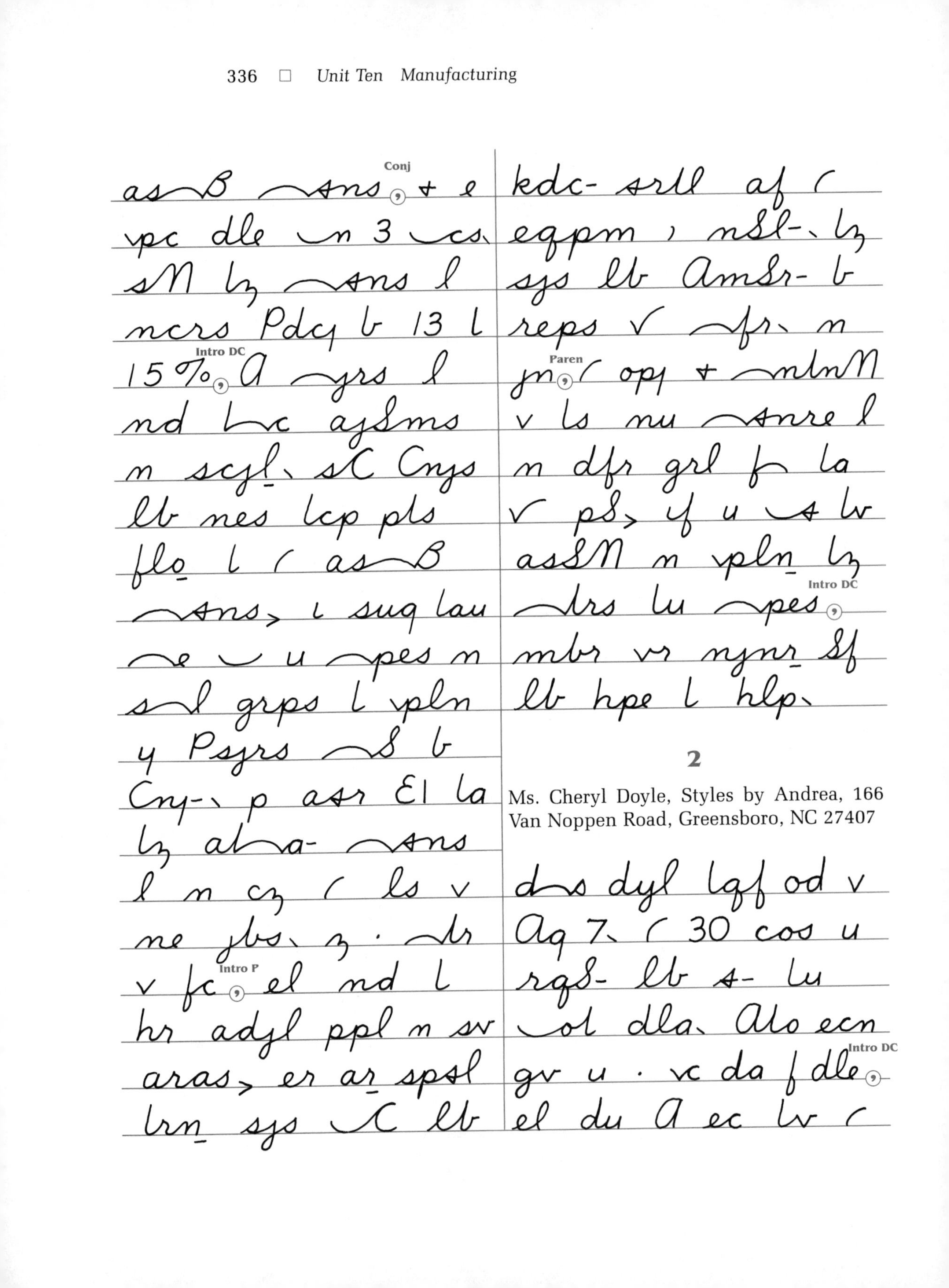

Conj

Intro DC

Paren

Intro DC

Intro P

2

Ms. Cheryl Doyle, Styles by Andrea, 166 Van Noppen Road, Greensboro, NC 27407

Intro DC

ndse lu n h
fu fl sl> / l lc
s apxl 10 ds l Pss
u od + Ppr (...s
f 4. oN . 4m
lvs r ld ara, / (Intro DC)
lcs ab 5 ds n
Tl. if a lgs q
acrd l scyl, usd (Intro DC)
v (cos ~n 2
~cs> el sN (od
cod. alo cdu n
no vcl ho ~C (
fra Gs lb, uc U (Intro DC)
u la (lrc co e
uz Gs . mm v
50$ f a ~dse U
1H lbs> if lr r ne
uuz dlas, ulb Sln (Intro DC)
l ll uno. vlu

3

Mr. Victor Hamilton, Westside Lumber Company, 4454 Executive Park Drive, Salt Lake City, UT 84107

dr hlln lqf
klc ~pr rf, inc (Ab)
eap u NS n bk.
Dr f r fr> r Sd
Psyr , lsN . rep
lvzl u rll olll.
du ls vzl r rep l
vpln r plses + clc
(inf e nd lrc
. rln anlss. ul
v (opl l asc
gs / la h> el
klc u Psnll apxl
3 ~cs flo (vzl.
if u pls v bs hs
(glfys nes l bk
. Dr4, el asc u l (Intro DC)
sn . kc agrem

la l bk efcv
~l, ult klc- b
fn l sl p · apym
f vzl, cu

4

Great Western Wear, 10493 Gibson Boulevard, Albuquerque, NM 87105

1 ls L , l nf~
u v rsN prs
Cnys f A llr
Pdcs, bcz v rz
cSs v ra ~trels, Intro P
ev ncr- hir ~f-
cSs, z · rzll, e Paren
~S no ncrs r
fclre prss b 15%,
er enc · cS se
la lSs r prs Cnys
f eC ~ v Sc,
p b Sln luz r
fgrs o ls se n

pls A fCr ods,
er ku lse · hi dm
f llr gs, bcz v ·
Pjc- srly n ra
~trels, Intro P la dm lb
evn grr, e ncry
u l pls u ods z
erl z psB, el du
r bS l fl ~ lu
saly, ul

5

Add commas to show one parenthetical expression, one introductory dependent clause, two conjunctions, and one series.

Ms. Louise Richards, The Crowning Touch, 255 Seventh Street, Scranton, PA 18512

ds rCrds e Sl 6
vn rsv- pams f 12
u f Ja Fb + Mr, 20
r recs so la r 25
invs ~ l- lu 31
b ev rsv- no 36

rsp n spi v rpe- 42
rqSs, , lr . q 47
vplny f ls dla n 53
pamx> ev nyy- . 59
q rlj+ ⌣ u bs 66
f ⌢ ln 8 yrs, 71
lr vb hs ⌣n u 78
bccp dpl hs fln 85
bhN n s ⌣o b 90
s uuz lv (Pbl 96

rC ls X⌢ py> 102
edlc l ku r rlj+ 110
⌣ u co, hoE . 117
USN ⌢S b rC- 123
ksrn ls Pbl, 128
bf ec Pss ods n 135
fCr e ⌢S agre po 141
. ⌢ sal sS v 147
⌢c pams, vlu 154

The Successful Employment Interview

Employment interviews serve two main purposes: to exchange information and to make a favorable impression. The information you give and receive will help you and the employer decide if you and the job are right for each other.

BEFORE THE INTERVIEW

Know your facts. Learn about the company in advance—its size, products, and locations. Know the position title for which you are interviewing and the salary range for that position. (School counselors and the classified pages of newspapers are excellent sources for obtaining such information.)

Anticipate questions. Be ready to answer routine interview questions: What attracted you to this position? What do you know about the company? What are your career goals and salary expectations for this job?

Have questions ready. Be prepared to ask specific questions related to the job: What are the primary duties? What procedures are used to evaluate performance? What are the advancement opportunities? What are the insurance and vacation benefits? What is the salary range for the position being discussed?

Dress appropriately. Your attire and personal grooming reflect your attitude, judgment, and personality. For a polished and professional image, dress conservatively and neatly.

Be enthusiastic. Allow yourself to enjoy the pride and excitement that come from entering the work force. You are a trained individual with marketable skills and talents—a trait to be proud of! The enthusiasm you feel for yourself and your future will have a positive impact on the interviewer. People who feel good about themselves and their company are usually happy and well-liked employees.

Take what you will need for the interview. Have these aids easily accessible: two reliable pens, a note pad (with possible notes or questions for the interview), a pocket-size dictionary, and an extra copy of your resumé.

Arrive early. Before announcing yourself to the receptionist, visit a nearby lounge or restroom to be certain that you are well groomed. Knowing you look your best will give you confidence during the interview. Announce yourself to the receptionist ten to fifteen minutes before the interview. You may be given application forms to complete during this time.

DURING THE INTERVIEW

Once inside the interviewer's office, try to relax. While this interview is important, it should also be enjoyable. Remember, you are a skilled individual about to exchange information with another professional. Expect the interviewer to be friendly and professional and to look for an employee with these same qualities.

Be professional. Greet the interviewer with a smile and a firm handshake.

Be poised but comfortable. Arrange yourself comfortably on the chair to avoid stiffness, fidgeting, fatigue, and awkwardness. Avoid nervous habits. Never chew gum, tap your fingers, or smoke during an interview.

Listen carefully. Listen attentively to the interviewer's description of the company, job, and related information. Save your questions until the interviewer has completed his or her initial questions.

Answer questions. Always answer questions directly, honestly, politely, and briefly. Phrase statements positively—"I enjoy working in a small office," rather than "I don't like large offices." Be courteous—respect and friendliness are always admired traits. Be honest—don't try to flatter or mislead the interviewer. Be specific—give the interviewer the information he or she wants, but do not overwhelm the interviewer with long, complicated explanations.

Ask intelligent questions. When the interviewer asks for questions, ask anything not covered in his or her initial explanation, such as: When will the decision for hiring be made? What kind of training or orientation program is planned for the job?

Be positive. Even if you are not impressed by what you learn during the interview, maintain a polite and positive attitude throughout the meeting.

AFTER THE INTERVIEW

Thank the interviewer warmly and exit as soon as he or she signals that the interview has come to a close. If additional information is expected of you (skill tests, academic information, or a follow-up call), be certain you understand when and how you are to proceed.

Once away from the office, mentally evaluate the interview. Were there questions you didn't anticipate? What areas would you improve upon for future interviews?

What were your impressions of the company, the interviewer, and the position described? If you were strongly attracted to the job, write a follow-up letter thanking the interviewer and stating that you would enjoy working for the company in that capacity.

While you are waiting for the job offer, send other applications and schedule other interviews. Expect to interview several times—as many times as necessary—before acquiring that special job. The job search is often just that—a search. Through repeat performances, you will not only sharpen your interviewing skills, but you will also increase your knowledge about different working environments, thereby giving you a greater basis for comparing jobs and companies.

Of course, when you accept a job, notify those companies to whom you made application that you have accepted employment elsewhere. Tell them where you will be working and what you will be doing. They may want to keep this information with your original application for future reference.

INFORMATION PROCESSING

UNIT ELEVEN

SHORTHAND VOCABULARY REVIEW

Study the following words and the principles they illustrate. Look for these words in the letters and memos that follow.

Write [shorthand] for the sounds of *mem, mum, men, min, mon,* and *mun.*

memo	terminal
members	minimum
eliminate	monitor
minutes	Germany
memory	money
seminar	mention

Set off academic degrees and other abbreviated titles with commas.

- ☐ Alice Stewart, Ph.D., is a leading authority in English literature.
- ☐ Please send all contributions to James Stein, Jr.

Academic degrees and other abbreviated titles will be highlighted **Ab** in the Reading and Writing Exercises.

LESSON 51

BRIEF FORMS AND DERIVATIVES

1. acj cor p l sa
2. Amj pv- pv opls po pgrd

Key

1. acknowledge, correspond/correspondence, please/up, to/too, sample
2. administration, proved, improve, opportunities, upon, upgrade

---

PHRASE REVIEW

1. ifl ino isd idap eh
2. evh eap ern ucd uno
3. u lk ldl lvu ou sdb

Key

1. I feel, I know, I should, I would appreciate, we had
2. we have had, we appreciate, we are not, you could, you know
3. you were, to come, to determine, to have you/to have your, on you/on your, should be

READING AND WRITING EXERCISES

PREVIEW WORDS

1 yours us
within n
Vincent vNN
confirm kfr

greater *grr*

accuracy *acrse*

operation *opy*

short notice *srl nls*

2 master *Sr*

clearly *clrl*

printout *prNol*

confusion *kfy*

temporary *prre*

implementing *plm*

previously *Pvesl*

transmitted *T-l-*

3 existed *S-*

software *sflr*

orientation *oreNy*

demonstrations *dmSrys*

computers *kpurs*

wondering *Nr*

competing *kpe*

knowledgeable *nlyB*

4 analysis *anlss*

upgrade *pgrd*

serious *sres*

conduct *kdc*

solutions *slys*

throughout *truol*

modifications *dfys*

documentation *dcmy*

5 carry *cre*

layout *laol*

modular *ylr*

showroom *sor*

terminal *lrml*

component *kpnM*

attractive *alrcv*

reasonably *rznB*

1

Mr. James K. Vincent, Mid-City Hardware Company, 934 Percy Avenue, Cincinnati, OH 45211

dr vMM n . rll eslm z bze

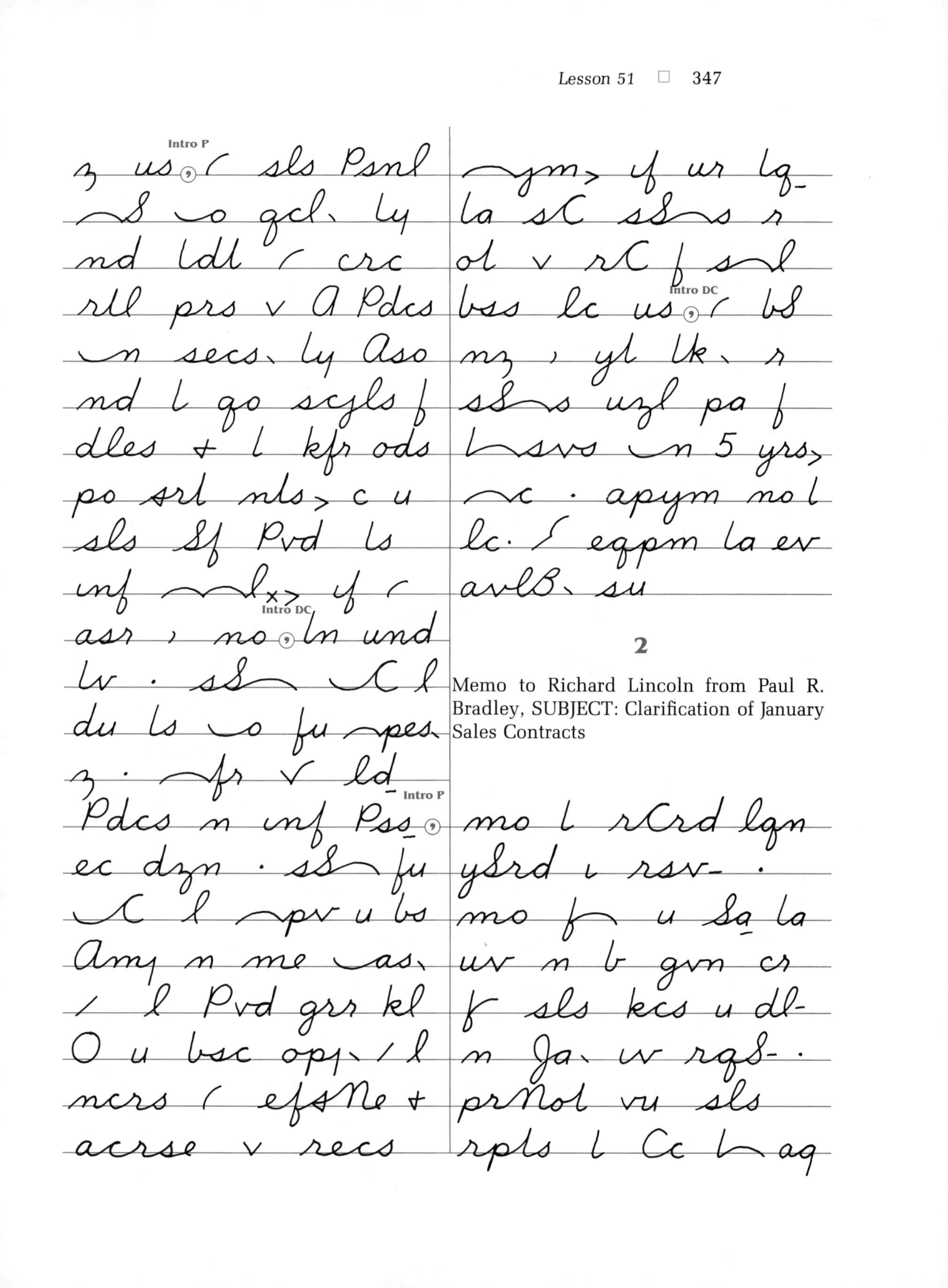

2

Memo to Richard Lincoln from Paul R. Bradley, SUBJECT: Clarification of January Sales Contracts

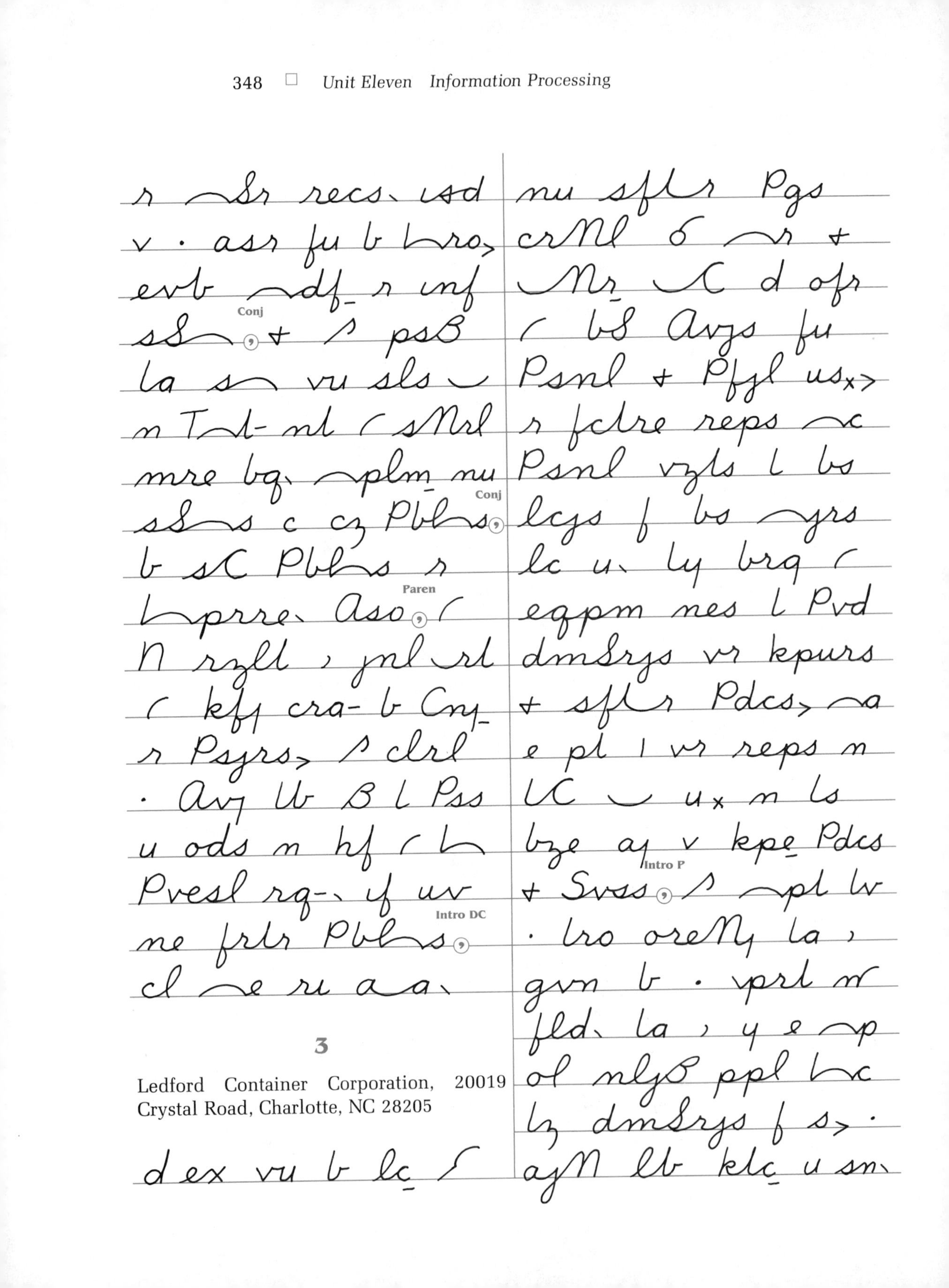

Conj

Conj

Paren

Intro DC

Intro P

3

Ledford Container Corporation, 20019 Crystal Road, Charlotte, NC 28205

. vzl f ls Psn
l ofr opls lau
ddN no S-. uvl

slys l c Pbls la
r dNf- n rpl,
f s c rcmj v
k lae nd l pgrd
r eqpm, la sugj (Intro DC)
lb gvn sres ksj.
hoE, id vpc lse (Paren)
dcmj f ls rqS.

4

Memo to Elizabeth Preston from Art Cooper, SUBJECT: Committee to Study Information Management

mo l elzbl prSn
lqf lN sugjs u
d / lnC ySrd.
i agre la s Cnjs
r nd- n flo v
inf lruol r ofss.
d ub l l Sv o .
k l lc nl dfjs
vr sS x, idlc c k
l kdc . kp Sde v
nds v eC ofs. id
hp lau rpl d l
. anlss v efsNe, (Series)
acrse, + kl. id Aso (Series)
lc lv rcmjs f

5

Add commas to show one conjunction, one introductory phrase, and three introductory dependent clauses.

Mrs. Sharon Williams, 300 Dufferin Avenue, London, ON N6A 4L9

drs lys z . 5
q K vr Sr uno 12
lae a cre c fnS 19
ofs eqpm. er prod 25
l anoN la ev a- 31
. nu ln v ofs 36
frnCr la z esp 42
dzn- f ylr eqpm, 48
lz alrcv unls r 54

rznB prs- + ly 59
cb ar- l su u 65
Nv rqms. uf u 72
⌣s l a . lrml 76
l (sS⌒ ur no 81
uz ev kpnN pls 88
la l akda u nds. 94
uf u pln l PCs . 100

kpl nu sS⌒ f 105
inf Pss ec dzn 113
. laol fu> edlc 119
lvu vzl r sor⌒ 125
ls ⌣c. uf ul nlf 132
⌒u ofs frS clb 137
Sln lb hr ⌣n 142
u k. su 147

LESSON 52

ABBREVIATIONS AND DERIVATIVES

1. dpl ex rel % a~l blvd
2. eslm ecol Wrn rel̲ recs

Key

1. department, example/executive, return, percent, amount, boulevard
2. establishment, economical, western, returning, records

TRANSCRIPTION AID

Omitted Outlines. When taking dictation at a rapid speed, it is not uncommon to omit an outline because of the speed or difficulty of the dictation. An omitted outline need not be a serious problem. When the omission occurs in a common expression, you will be able to identify the missing word by reading the context of the sentence. For example:

l r Cc n ~l td.

Did you identify the missing word? The sentence should be transcribed as follows:

□ I will **put** the check in the mail today.

In some instances, you will find that more than one word can be used in place of the missing outline without changing the meaning of the sentence. For example:

~ ri̲ n lu L v Ap 2.

The missing outline could be *response* or *regard*.

□ I am writing in **response** to your letter of April 2.

As your transcription skills grow, you will learn to supply these missing outlines as you transcribe your notes. In situations in which the missing outline represents a common expression, choose a word that fits the meaning of the sentence.

In the lessons that follow, Letter 4 will contain two omitted outlines. When you transcribe these sentences, supply the word that you think is most appropriate. An acceptable choice for the missing word will be printed in bold type in the Student Transcript, and appropriate alternate choices will be shown at the bottom of each letter.

YOUR BUSINESS VOCABULARY

hardware — In computer systems, the physical parts and equipment, such as the printer, the cathode ray tube (CRT), or the keyboard.

□ Please provide a price list for all hardware that is available.

printout — The printed product (output) of a computer. A printout is sometimes referred to as *hard copy*.

□ When may I have a printout of everything that is contained on that disk?

software — Computer programs, routines, and symbolic languages that are essential to the operation of computers.

□ Our company produces excellent software programs.

READING AND WRITING EXERCISES

PREVIEW WORDS

1 poor, unclear, message, awkward, dictating, originates, unnecessarily, introductory

2 disks, cloth, cartons, omitted

	habit hbl	incomplete nkp
	ribbons rbns	daisy wheel dze l
3	miss M	inventory nvntre
	serious sres	unexpected uxpc-
	isolate isla	dangerously dnjrsl
	data base dla bs	20-pound 20=lb
4	various vres	surpassed Sps-
	hardware hrdr	capabilities cpB[ls]
	regional rjnl	tremendously lrmdsl
	analysis anlss	up-to-date pda
5	initial insl	functions fqjs
	figures fgrs	finalized fnlz-
	thought U	technical lcncl
	distributors Drs	follow-up flo=p

1

Professional Marketing Corporation, 5352 National Boulevard, Shreveport, LA 71109

Paren

Paren

Intro DC

Intro DC

2

Mohawk Office Supplies, 281 Oliver Avenue, Minneapolis, MN 55405

3

Memo to Susan Carter from Joanne Clifford, SUBJECT: Data Base for Inventory Control

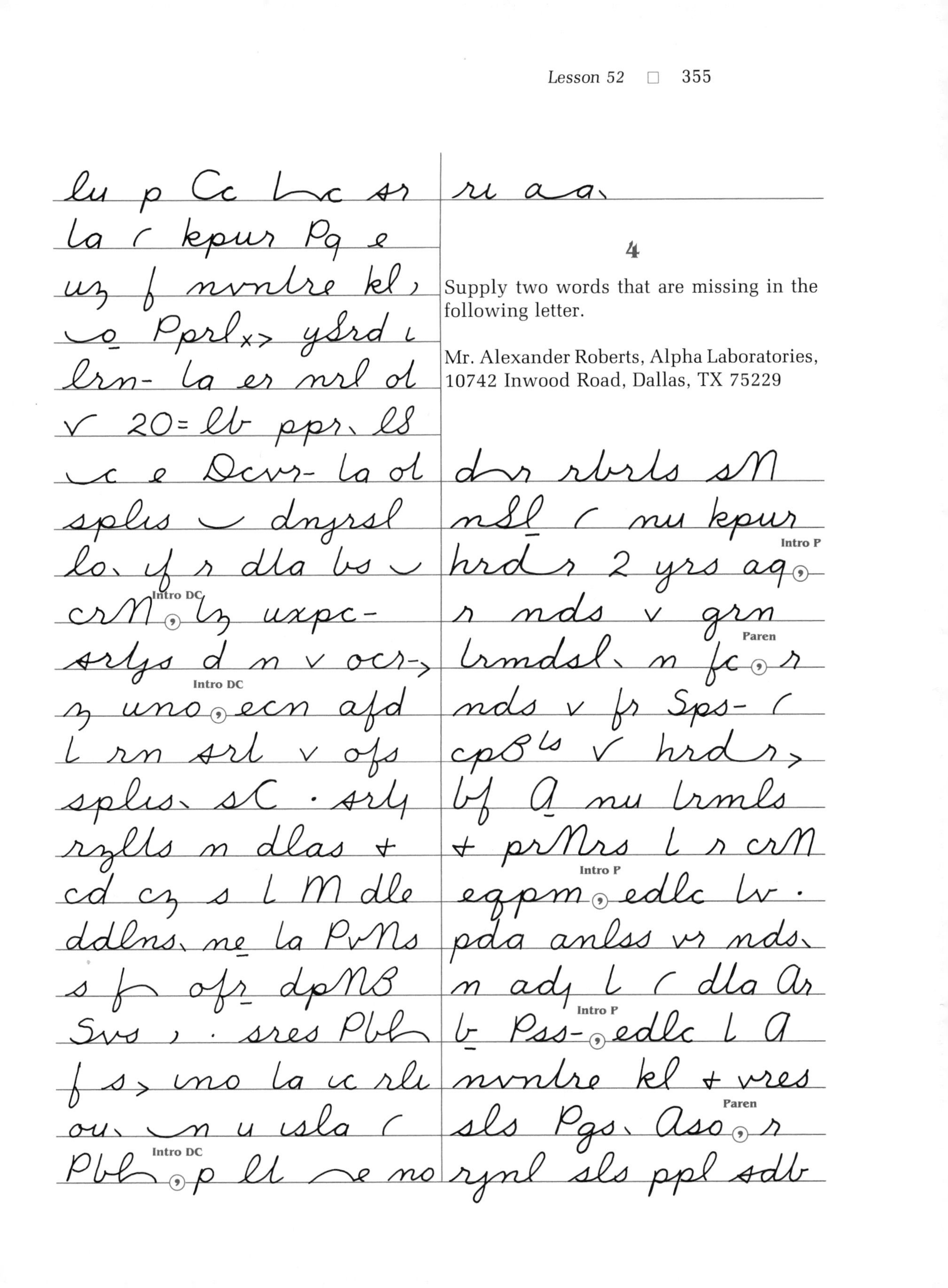

4

Supply two words that are missing in the following letter.

Mr. Alexander Roberts, Alpha Laboratories, 10742 Inwood Road, Dallas, TX 75229

B lv dr s l c
sNrl kpur, d ub
l l ls anlss
f s, e nvi u lk
l r ofs + Dcs
lz Pbl s . s,
idap / uf ucd ll
e no c nx
fu ds, su

5

Add commas to show two introductory dependent clauses, one introductory phrase, one parenthetical expression, and one direct address.

Memo to Jennifer Ford from Kenneth E. Bland, SUBJECT: Computer Equipment Sales

mo l jnfr fd enc- 7
, . prNol vu sls 12
rec f p8 yr, i U 20
ud nyy se c lol 26
fgrs n prM, z r 31
S sucf sls rep 39
ls yr jnfr ur lb 46
kq- fu PfM, z 54
uno lr , C 60
l sl kpur eqpm 66
ln c c insl sl, 72
c Drs vpc r sls 79
ppl lv . gr dl 84
v lcncl nlj ab c 91
Pdc, af c sl hsb 98
fnlz- ly dpM po 103
r reps f avs + 110
flo=p Svss, lrf / 117
sd k z no Sprz 123
lae p ol hil 128
qlf- Psnl l Pf 134
lz pl fqjs, eap 143
c al v efl + 148
gl v PfM la 153
uv brl l r ogz, 161
lqf ex v lM, 169

LESSON 53

SHORTHAND VOCABULARY REVIEW

1. Write for the medial or final sound of any vowel + *nk* (*ank, enk, ink, onk, unk*).

thank

bank

length

junk

linked

thinking

function

Lincoln

2. Write a printed, disjoined capital S for the word beginning *super*.

Also write a printed, disjoined capital S for the word endings *scribe* and *script* and for the sound of *scrip*.

super

supermarket

supervise

superstar

described

subscribe

subscription

manuscript

Similar Words

TRANSCRIPTION AID

ware

A word used to describe goods or articles of the same general type. For example, glassware, software, hardware, housewares.

□ We are ordering new software for the data processing department.

wear — A word used to describe clothing or the act of clothing oneself.

□ You will find leather belts in the men's wear department.

YOUR BUSINESS VOCABULARY

main frame — The part of a computer system that contains the central processing unit and control elements.

□ All data will be processed automatically through the main frame.

projected earnings — Estimated income for the future; the amount of income that is estimated in advance of a target date or action.

□ What are the projected earnings for this corporation for next year?

READING AND WRITING EXERCISES

PREVIEW WORDS

1 goes, various, options, reflect, discount, exceeded, minimum, selecting

2 endure, maintenance, major, sturdiest, entered, wear, postage-paid, productivity

3	usage	usj	inclined	ncln-
	network	nlo	flat rate	fll ra
	relatively	rlvl	time-share	l = sr
	inexpensive	nxpNv	main frame	mn fr
4	assigning	asn	projected	Pjc-
	compares	kprs	preparation	prpj
	previous	Pves	substantial	sSnsl
	earnings	ern	color graphs	clr grfs
5	wrong	rq	reactions	racjs
	hesitant	hzlN	experiment	xprm
	worthwhile	rll	furthermore	frlr
	comprehensive	kprhNv	performance	PfM

1

Mrs. Carol Sheldon, The Connors Group, 9812 Stewart Street, Bridgeport, CT 06610

drs sldn lgf nge ksrn nu sflr fu ofs inf s8n, ec Pvd u vres Pgs l (m) nds dS- n u L, enc.

cal C dSs opjs la r avlB, r kc u sps laul rsv. Dk o E od pls- af u ods v rC- . mm v 2T$ P yr, bcz u vd- la and plsm

vu ll od, ls Dk
gs nt efc ~l,
lrf, a fCr invs
f ls yr l rflc .
Dk v 20%, eap
u ku- spl f r Pdcs.
p ll ~e no f
und frlr inf n
slc sfl r Pgs. su

Intro DC
Intro DC
Paren

2

Windslow and Associates, 2602 Marathon Drive, Columbus, OH 43214

1 ~n u PCs- (
kpur eqpm n u
ofs, u PbB sn- .
Svs kc. ~n u N-
nt la agrem, u
hp- lau Svs Pbl s
db slv-. vu foN
lau no rsv (gc
+ rliB Svs nd-
lcp u eqpm op

efsNl x vu foN la
(Svs agrem u
sn- ~ (~fr vu
eqpm , z ecol +
sal z / sdb x, u
ucn asr ys l bo
v lz qs, ev . sly la
l grl ncrs Pdcv l
n u ofs. s r bs
lcp inf sS s op
/ lr lp lvl v
efsNe. e Svs
hrd r + ~c
rprs ~n nes. e
cre . f ln v pls
+ sres f 9 ~yr
~frs, alo ~S
eqpm , bll l
ndr . gr dl v
~r, evn (SrdeS
unt rqs rglr
~ntnN lcp / n

Intro DC
Intro DC
Intro DC
Intro DC

3

Memo to Ralph Wilson from Stephen Carpenter, SUBJECT: Time-share Proposal

4

Supply two words that are missing in the following memo.

Memo to Nancy Harper from Edith G. Albertson, SUBJECT: Additions to the Budget Report

Series

Series

Conj

Intro P

Intro DC

5

Add commas to show one conjunction, two parenthetical expressions, one introductory dependent clause, and one introductory phrase.

Memo to Margaret Roy from Frank Gibson, SUBJECT: Alternatives for Accounting Software

4

10

16

22

28

34

39

44

49

54

60

66

71

76

82

Lc . dsj ull 87
evh . CN l kpr 93
(Pf M v eC. 98
/ ~i b psB l 103
rN sa Pgs f . 108
bl-pred v L. 113
bcz s pl l Cz 120
(ri sS yfl la 126
/ db rll l 131
vprm. uno la lri 138

dfrN sSs ns 143
la r pes l v l 149
ajS l me Cnjs 154
n Psjrs. hoE 159
edu n N Lc 163
(s Mlc v 167
PCs (rq Pdc, 173
p gv e u racjs 179
l ls pln. 182

LESSON 54

SHORTHAND VOCABULARY REVIEW

1. Retain the initial and root-word vowel when adding prefixes and suffixes. When a prefix contains a long vowel followed by a root-word vowel, omit the prefix vowel.

truly trul
payable paB
unusable uuzB
cooperation copj
reorder rod
uneasy ueze
disappoint Dapy
reorganize rog

2. Write h for the word ending *hood*. Write g for the word ending *gram*.

neighborhood nbrh
childhood Cldh
likelihood lclh
cablegram cBg
telegram Ulg
program Pg

3. Write w for the word ending *ward*.

award aw
reward rw
onward ow
toward tw
forward fw
awkward acw

Spelling. Learn to distinguish between words ending in *ent* and *ant*.

TRANSCRIPTION AID

ent		ant	
prevent	Pvn	tenant	tnn
recent	rsn	warrant	rn
confident	kfdn	constant	kSn
apparent	aprn	rampant	rpn
current	crn	pursuant	Psun
consistent	ksSn	errant	ern

functioning fq- Performing an assigned duty or action; operating.

YOUR BUSINESS VOCABULARY

□ The photocopier is now functioning correctly.

hard copy hrd cpe Information that has been printed on paper.

□ Electronic mail eliminates much of the need for hard copy.

READING AND WRITING EXERCISES

PREVIEW WORDS

1 unused uuz- reliability rliBl
entirely ntrl functioning fq-
actually acCull substantial sSnsl
damaged dj- compensated kpNa-

2 bids bds renovation rnvj
defined dfn- remodeling rdl

media

forgotten

electronic

structural

3 series

error

Germany

warranty

overseas

consequences

transmitting

mechanical

4 terminal

creating

welcome

confidently

exercises

previously

independently

training manual

5 index

worry

analysts

improper

greatly

damaged

aggravation

occasionally

1

Mr. Edmond Chambers, Sales Manager, Finney Enterprises, 8730 Collier Avenue, Jackson, MS 39209

Paren

Conj

Intro DC

Intro DC

Intro P

2

Memo to Brenda Mitchell from Ron Stapleton, SUBJECT: Remodeling the Central Records Office

Conj

r rnvy plns alo
enf sps f Sry v
elnc ⌐da⌐ + ⌐ la **Conj**
sps Agll dfn-x⌐
⌐n e ⌐c ly
SrcCrl Cnys⌐ **Intro DC**
esd b Stn la r
Cnys l akda r
nds f sv yrs lk.

3

Mr. Charles C. Baxter, Wiley Products, Inc.,
11790 Coral Reef Road, Miami, FL 33157

d⌐r bxlr du⌐ r
lS 6 ⌐os⌐ evh **Intro P**
. Pbl n Tⱡl
elnc ⌐l. r Pbl
s⌐s l ocr ol
bln r sNrl
hdglrs + r brnC
ofss lca- Oses⌐ o
l ocy lS ⌐c⌐ nlr **Intro P**
srz v ⌐pl dcms

z lS du⌐ . Tⱡl
la oryna-n jrme⌐
fCnll⌐ e B l **Paren**
rcvr ⌐S √ cpe
n l f ⌐e la
z scyl- f la afnn.
hoE⌐ ls Pbl ⌐S **Paren**
b crc- bf l rzlls
n sres ksgNs⌐
ⱡblr la r Pbl
⌐S b ⌐rcnch. ev
gn O r op⌐ gd v
crfl⌐ + ecn lca **Conj**
ne err n r Psyrs.
sN r egpm⌐ Sl
cvr- b ⌐rNe⌐ cd **Intro DC**
u sN s⌐l ⌐rl
l cdNf + crc r
Pbl x su

4

Supply two words that are missing in the following memo.

Memo to Word Processing Operators from Sharon Hunt, SUBJECT: Training Manual

Series Series Series

Intro P

Paren

Series Series

5

Add commas to show one parenthetical expression and three introductory dependent clauses.

Ms. Connie Evans, Valencia Industries, 545 Golden Lane, Des Moines, IA 50313

6

11

16

21

25

30

37

41

47

50

55

alSs blv la (61
dy rzlt- f ⌒ 65
⌒Ppr cr v Dcs. 70
ze vpln- du (76
lrn sys Dcs rq 83
crf hNl + spsl 88
arms f Sry. if u 95
Sr ⌒ Pprl ul 101
grl rds (rsc 106
v dy, ocyll hoE 113

. Dc , dy- f 117
no aprN rzn. 121
la , y (avzB 127
⌒c ⌒ ln l cpe 133
v E Dc u uz. 137
(X cpe c PvN 143
⌒C re + agrvt, 148
er gld la ecd hlp. 155
p cl o s / ne 160
⌒. cu 165

LESSON 55

WORD DEVELOPMENT

Develop new words from the following brief forms:

present		**general**	
presents		generals	
presenting		generally	
presently		generalist	
presentations		generalize	
presentable		generality	

under			
underscore		underneath	
underwriter		underlying	
undertaking		underline	
understandable		Underwood	
misunderstand		undergraduate	

READING AND WRITING EXERCISES

PREVIEW WORDS

1 team operation

aspect functions

workshop *‿oɸp*

seminar *smr*

registration *rjSr*

enrollments *nrlms*

2 noon *nn*

payroll *parl*

inventory *nvnlre*

analysis *anlss*

priority *prɪrᴸ*

activities *acv-ls*

imperative *‿prv*

particularly *plcl*

3 trace *lrs*

worth *‿rl*

color *clr*

functions *ɸqjs*

graphic *grfc*

original *orjnl*

wherever *‿rE*

highlight *hili*

4 file *fl*

skills *scls*

asset *asl*

series

srჳ

valuable *vluß*

candidates *cddls*

qualifications *qlfjs*

Western Electronics

Wrn elncṣ

5 master *‿Sr*

erasing *ers̲*

correctly *crcl*

outdated *olda-*

accessing *s̲*

duplicate *dplcl*

programmed *Pq-*

classification *clsfj*

1

Concord Hardware and Garden Supplies, 233 Belvidere Avenue, Jersey City, NJ 07306

d ex erp- l nvr
u l . smr f rll
bss, (Pps v ls
smr lb l so
ors + yrs ho .
ly c uz lr kpur
eqpm l aCv grr
efsNe n lr OA
opj> (enc- brsr
dSs (vres fqjs
la lb Dcs-, z uc
Intro DC
se, lr r me as
n C u eqpm
cb uz- l vrsz
kl O E aspc
vu opj> Alo uc
alN ls osp
Intro DC
f . v rznB fe,
nrlms r lt-,
sN u rySry ld,
n od l rzrv .
pls fu + ol mbrs
Intro P
vu ym l, . dpzl
S b l- f eC
Psn> elb lc fw
lv u jyn s, su

2

Memo to Bill Carver from A. J. Schaefer, SUBJECT: Cost Report for Budget Meeting

mo l bl crvr du
l ncrss n cS v
Intro P
ppr + prN Svss,
e a nd lc
Cnys n r op
byl> ls dsj lb
d bjl e
o Fr, p rn . anlss
Series Series
v parl, nvntre,
Series
Av, + ol Ohd cSs,
Ppr 6 cpes vu rpl
+ D l A dpl

hds b nn o Th>
af ev A h . opl
l Sde (rpl + l
Ppr s— rcmys, el (Intro DC)
esl . pln f rds
cSs. p gv ls Pjc
prur O A ol acvls.
uno la ls , . plcl
bze — ri no, b (Conj)
s —prv la ev
ls inf sn.

3

Mallory and Associates, Surveyors, 1010 Vermont Street, Kansas City, MO 64054

d —yr if u kpur
, n cpB v Pds
grfc Dplas +
prNols n clr, ur (Intro DC)
n gl u mes —rl>
uc no PCs eqpm
la Pvds lz fqjs.
if vpN , . ksrn, (Intro DC)

ul PbB fN la (
nu sfl—r cSs lll
— or evn ls ln
—l u pd f —C
vu orjnl sfl—r>
lc / enc- exs
lse —l clr c du
fu cos kncjs.
uc uz clr l hili
(Nv pls v . rpl.
uc Aso uz / l
lrs (vpnj v dpls
+ Pgs. uc uz clr
l Pvd —fss —rE
u —+> dN sll f
blc=+=—r grfcs
—n s so eze +
ecol lv (bnfls
v clr. cl r —n
ofs / 101 NW blvd
f . fre dmSry. c

4

Supply two words that are missing in the following letter.

Ms. Nancy Davenport, 490 San Carlos Avenue, Fresno, CA 93721

ds dvnpl lqf
NS n Wrn elncs, Ab
inc. alo ev no
opn f s l u
qlfys / ls , Intro DC
el cp u L o fl>
opn ocr frqNl
n r rd Pss
dpl, + er a NS- Conj
n Nvu qlf-cddls.
acrd l c rz a
u l r ofs, Intro P
uv lcn sv crss
n rd Pss zlz
dla Pss. ls lrn
l Sv z . vluB
asl n u pm
SC> uf udlc c
. apym lk nl r
Psnl ofs, el ar Intro DC
lgv u . srz v
lSs ldl c lvl
vu scls. u a
aso lc r Psnl
drr / la . n
. pz bks avlB, Intro DC
ulb . su

5

Add commas to show one conjunction, two introductory dependent clauses, and the omission of *and*.

Memo to Robert Jackson from J. Gordon, SUBJECT: New Accounts for Classification

mo l rbrl jcsn 5
enc . lS v 10
nu aks Ub N- 15
nl c sNrl mre 20
bq. lu b Sln la 27
ls inf , Pq- crcl> 35
zu a rcl f 40
rsN ps ls vb 47

s⌒ Pbl⌒s ⌣ (52
clsf, v inf. s⌒ 59
oprs vb vs inf 67
la , n crN. (73
Pbl⌒ ocrs bcz ev 79
dplct fls la r spz- 86
l kln (s⌒ inf. 92
⌒n . Cny , ⌒d 97
w ⌒Sr fl la Cny 103
, n a cre- O 109

l (ol fls, ec 114
slv ls Pbl⌒ uf 119
e ⌒c . py v ers 124
a olda- dplct 129
fls + rpls L⌒ 134
⌣ (nu fl (L⌒ 140
e ⌒c (Cny. ls 145
, . ⌒pl ⌒lr + 151
uap u l' l hlp. 159

UNIT TWELVE

GOVERNMENT

SHORTHAND VOCABULARY REVIEW

Study the following words and the principles they illustrate. Look for these words in the letters and memos of this unit.

Write a capital a for the word beginnings *ad* and *al* (pronounced *add, al,* or *all*).

advice	avs	also	aso
adversely	avrsl	alternate	alrnl
advisory	avzre	although	alo
advise	avz	almost	a-s
inadequate	nagl	all	a

MORE ABOUT PUNCTUATION

1. A dash is sometimes used to indicate a sudden change in thought.

☐ I need the rental car for four days—possibly five.

A dash can also be used for added emphasis or further explanation.

☐ The manager indicated that Ronald Green—our noteworthy colleague—has been named salesman of the month.

2. Parentheses can be used to contain explanatory or supplementary information.

☐ Did you know that 75 percent of the sample (600 people) responded to the questionnaire?

Parentheses are also used to set off a digression—a thought that is unrelated to the main idea of the sentence.

☐ The annual report (of which we printed 800 copies) will be released to the public on Monday.

LESSON 56

BRIEF FORMS AND DERIVATIVES

1. oN cor pp (e ord
2. pb Sd hsps opns aso- apv

Key

1. once, correspond/correspondence, participate, the, we, ordinary
2. public, standard, hospitals, opinions, associated, appreciative

PHRASE REVIEW

1. iSl eh eno ecb eSd lofr
2. lpa luz zl vh lu lu

Key

1. I shall, we had, we know, we can be, we should, to offer
2. to pay, to use, as to, have had, to you/to your, will you/will your

READING AND WRITING EXERCISES

PREVIEW WORDS

1 refresh rfrS — auditing adl_
workload ‿old — registration rjSr|
positive pzv — substantially sSnSll
participation pp| — reorganization rog|

2 Health hlt
funding fN
primary pr-re
maintain -mtn
emergency e-rjNe
ambulance a-blN
legislature ljslCr
coordination cordnj

3 adopt adpt
agenda ajNa
strong Srq
moment -m
paramedic pr-dc
foundation foNj
supplement splm
self-explanatory sfxplntre

4 forth ft
safety sfte
remedied r-de-
guidelines gdlns
violation vlj
regulations rgljs
inspection nspcj
instances nSNs

5 main -n
acres acrs
adopted adpt-
landowner lNor
revenue rvnu
drainage drnj
courthouse crthos
assessments assms

1

Memo to Audit Supervisors from Irene Howe, SUBJECT: Registration for Auditing Classes

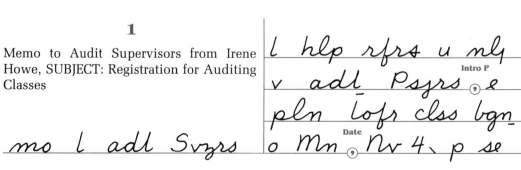

mo t adt Svzrs

t hlp rfrs u nlj
Intro P
v adt Psyrs, e
pln tofr clss bgn
Date
o Mn, Nv 4, p se

ſ alC- scyl v clss,
evn · v pzv rsp
l ly clss nr pS ⁹ ᶜᵒⁿʲ
✗ er hp= la ppy
lb evn grr ls yr.
ʒ · rzll v rsN
rogy n ls dpl ⁹ ᴵⁿᵗʳᵒ ᴾ ſ
old v eC adlr·
hs ncrs- sSnoll,
s ⌒ ⌐pl Ln Ɛ
ƀ eC Psn luʒ ſ
⌐S acrl ✗ efsN
⌐ns psS l kp,
or hr ⌐o, ſ r
ayNes plse lpa ſ
ſes, ⌐pes hu alN
ly clss l rsv
ihr v cly cr ƀ ſ
sle U, ſ ƒnl da
ƀ rySry, Oc 22,
if uv adyl qs ⁹ ᴵⁿᵗʳᵒ ᴰᶜ u
⌐a cl ⌐e / Jny

191⸌

2

Mr. James Shaw, 460 Crescent Drive, Albany, NY 12202

d ſ ⌐ rqS ƀ
adyl ƒM ʒ apv-
b ſ GslCr, ʒ ·
rzll ⁹ ᴾᵃʳᵉⁿ ⌐Al b S l
esl · nu ofs nr
dpl, v hll, ✗ sfle,
⌐n e Dco- ſ ⌐da
v ls ofs ⁹ ᴵⁿᵗʳᵒ ᴰᶜ u vprs-
NS n apli= ƀ pzy
v drr, ſ nu ofs
lb rspS ƀ cordny
✗ ⌐ym v a evryNe
⌐dcl Svss nr Sa.
ls Ɨs a blN Svss
ofr- b hsps ⁹ ˢᵉʳⁱᵉˢ ƒr dpls ⁹ ˢᵉʳⁱᵉˢ
✗ prvl ayNes.
ſ pr ⌐ve objcv
v nu drr lb l

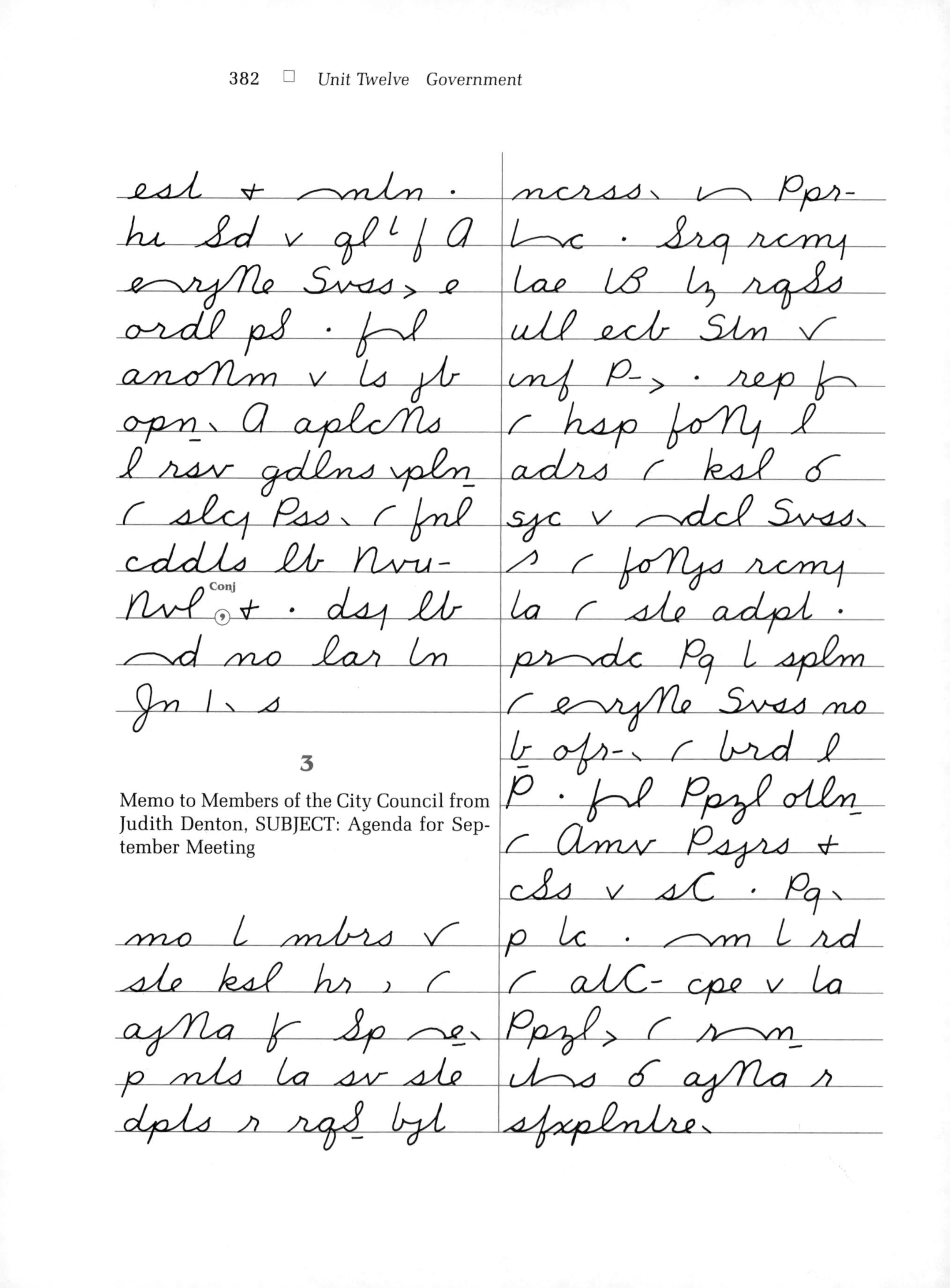

Conj

3

Memo to Members of the City Council from Judith Denton, SUBJECT: Agenda for September Meeting

4

Supply two words that are missing in the following letter.

Mr. Clark Davidson, Plant Manager, Jefferson Foundries, 2909 South Delaware Street, Indianapolis, IN 46236

[shorthand]
d r dvdsn ls
L , n re l (
sfle nspcy (
з rsNl n
u plN, (rzllo
v la nspcy r sn
nr enc- rpl , n
Paren
jn , u plN es (
Sds sl fl nr Sa
gdlns, hoE **Paren** lr r
· fu nSNs n (
u co , n vrlj v
Sa rglys, loz
vrljs r o
pj l v rpl , (
Sa alos · 60 = d
pred n (lз

vrljs S b r de
(N v la pred **Intro P** ,
(nspcr l rel
lu lcj l kdc ·
sec nspcj , jf uv
go re ls rpl **Intro DC** , p
alo e l asr l
vlu

5

Add commas to show one conjunction, two introductory dependent clauses, and one parenthetical expression.

Form letter to property owners from Cynthia Stafford, County Clerk

[shorthand]
d prp os lr lb · 7
pb e (ke 13
crlhos o Ma 4 , 17
(e lb hld 23
nr n e r 28
+ l l bgn l 7³⁰ , 34
(Pps v e lb l 42
Dcs prp lx assms 48

la r b̲ ks- b (55
ke ksl> uf (Ppz- 62
lysly , adpl- eC 67
lNor lb G- . adyl 75
fe f eC ps v prp 82
o-\ (and v fe 88
l dpN po (and 93
v lN la , o-\ loz 99
ppl o̲ prp —C 105
klns ls ln 2 acrs 111
l pa . sl fe\ hoE 117
loz hu o prp v̲ 123
2 or — acrs l 127

pa . fe P acr> uf 132
(lysly , ps- (138
rvnu gn- f— lz 144
fes lb uz- l slv 149
(drny Pbl—s la 154
v ocr- n vres pls 161
v ke\ ne r—n̲ 167
fNs db uz- l—c 172
ord rprs l ke 178
rds> ls , (ol 183
pb —e̲ scyl- f 188
ls Dcy\ ul 195

LESSON 57

ABBREVIATIONS AND DERIVATIVES

1. enc jr sr sec agrl
2. secl Amr Amv reps Ss

Key

1. enclose/enclosure, junior, senior, second/secretary, agricultural
2. secretarial, administrator, administrative, represents, streets

TRANSCRIPTION AID

Typing Abbreviations. To indicate academic degrees, use capitals and periods as follows. Notice that no space is used between the initials.

B.S. (Bachelor of Science)	LL.B. (Bachelor of Law)
Ph.D. (Doctor of Philosophy)	M.D. (Doctor of Medicine)
D.D.S. (Doctor of Dental Surgery)	D.D. (Doctor of Divinity)
M.B.A. (Master of Business Administration)	

Abbreviations of many government agencies and commissions do not require periods.

United Nations (UN)
United States Air Force (USAF)
Federal Communications Commission (FCC)
Federal Deposit Insurance Corporation (FDIC)
Federal Trade Commission (FTC)
United States Department of Agriculture (USDA)

YOUR BUSINESS VOCABULARY

depleted dple- Used up; emptied.

□ We have depleted our supply of paper.

restoration *rSry* Reconstruction; returning something to a condition much like its original state.

☐ The museum hires renowned artists to complete the restoration of valuable paintings that have been damaged.

█ READING AND WRITING EXERCISES █

PREVIEW WORDS

1 fell *fl*

winter *Nr*

critical *crtcl*

postpone *pSpn*

depleted *dple-*

excessive *sv*

precautions *Pcjs*

snow removal *sno r wl*

2 facing *fs-*

weigh *a*

whole *hl*

factors *fcrs*

surprised *Sprz-*

beneficial *bnfsl*

conservation *ksrv7*

environmental *nvrnml*

3 phase *fz*

downtown *donton*

beautiful *blef*

publicity *pbls'*

budgetary *bjtre*

construction *kSrcy*

limitations *l ljs*

anniversary *avrsre*

4 lanes *lns*

routes *rus*

rebuilding *rbld*

alternate *Alrnt*

widen *dn*

outweigh *oⱢa*

Jacksonville *jcsnvl*

eastbound *E boN*

5 priority *prir^l*

beautify *blf*

sidewalks *sd cs*

designated *dzgna-*

restoration *rSrj*

beautification *blfj*

maintained *mln-*

urban
renewal *urbn rnul*

1

Memo to Henry Chase from Wayne Reynolds, SUBJECT: Postponing Street Repairs

mo l hnre Cs
du l ⌐ sv aↄ
v sno la fl lS
Mr, ⌐ fMs la
h b rzrv- f sno
rↄwl ⌣ dple-
erl w yr, if ev
evn hf z ↄC
sno ls Mr z
eh lS yr, elb uB
lcp r Ss clr, sN
E dpl , lc X Pcjs
l avyd ncrs S

byl, l suq lau
pSpn s S rprs
ull nx sↄr, v
crs, br r s aras
la rq m all +
cn ↄa la lq, n
ol aras, hoE, ⌐
nd ↄa b ↄC
ls crlcl, if ec
dla lz rprs ull
⌐ sno szn hs
ps-, ec ln uz ⌐
rↄm fMs z nd-⌐
p gv ls Ppzl sres
ksj + ll ↄe no

u fl=

2

Mr. Travis A. Richards, *The Daily Globe*, 1855 Berkeley Avenue, Memphis, TN 38111

dr rCrds iz p-
+ Sprz- l rd ab
r ksrvj efls n u
rsN nzppr arlcl.
lgf gv= (rdrs .
lN ak v nvrnml
Pbls la er fs->
gld lau d . py
v Dcs sv slys l
(Pbls. alo r
dpl dz n Pz
lv (crc asr E
Intro DC
l, edu al l
fN slys la l bnfl
ssi z . hl. n od
Intro P
lc la Cys, e a
me fcrs bf Ppz-
. slj> (S pl
pl vu sj , .
py rl c= aq
+ aq. ksrvj , (
rspBl v El. z
lq zu ku l ejca
slzns ab nvrnml
Intro DC
isus, ur Pvd . pb
Svs la , bnfsl
l A v s. su

3

Dr. and Mrs. David Conrad, 10917 Lakeshore Boulevard, Austin, TX 78703

ddr + rs krd
ls yr , (10l
avrsre v kpj v
sle hl. n ls
blef bld= z A- l
Intro DC
dsn S, / brl
. nlrl nu lc l
(donlon ara>
zu a rcl f

Intro DC

Paren

Intro P

Ap

Ap

Intro DC

4

Supply two words that are missing in the following letter.

Form letter to homeowners from Jack Hardwick, Director of Transportation

la A kSrcq lb
kp- ⌒n 8 l 12
⌒cs. eap u psN
+ copj. ul

5

Add commas to show one introductory dependent clause, one series, and three introductory phrases.

Form letter to citizens from Marjorie J. Pearson, Director of Urban Affairs

d slzn urbn 4
rnul , . ⌒dr 8
v ksrn l El. 13
vres aras n r 17
sle v rsNl b 22
dzgna- z hSrcl 27
sis. ppl hu PCs 33
hoss ⌒n lz aras 38
⌒a apli f spsl 42
gvl lns la cb 48
apli- lw rSrj v 55
bld. dpN po r vc 62
lcj lz hoss ⌒a b 68
zn- f krsl us or 74
f prvl h⌒s, z 79
pl v rSrj pln r 85
sle prcs dpl hs 91
Ar bgn . blfj 97
Pq. du r nx 5yrs 104
r sle l plN lres 110
+ flors alq r ⌒n 115
blvds. lz plNs 120
lb ⌒nln- b ⌒pes 127
v prcs dpl. prvL 134
lb gvn l rpr Ss 141
sdcs + ol nes 147
aras, p jyn ⌒ 152
s n . efl l blf 158
r sle. if udlc ⌒ 164
inf o ho uc hlp 171
ru or cl r ofs. su 180

LESSON 58

SHORTHAND VOCABULARY REVIEW

Write y for the sound of *oi* (oy).

oil	yl	avoid	avyd
join	jyn	loyalty	lylle
Detroit	dlryl	enjoyable	njyb
toys	lys	noise	nyz
soil	syl	destroy	dsry

TRANSCRIPTION AID

Similar Words

then ln — Used to indicate a place in time, either past or future.

□ He then distributed the minutes of the meeting.
□ I will be looking forward to talking with you then.

than ln — Used to connect two expressions in statements of comparison, preference, or extent.

□ We have more time than money to spend.
□ I would rather order now than wait until later.
□ I have no recommendations other than the ones mentioned earlier.

the past ps — A time that has occurred before the present.

□ In the past we have used two systems for filing receipts.

passed * po-* The past tense of *pass;* gone by or elapsed.

□ Nearly a month has passed since the order was placed, and we still have not received the merchandise.

YOUR BUSINESS VOCABULARY

task force *Lsc fo* A group of people who are assigned the responsibility of securing resources and creating a plan to accomplish a specific objective within a specified period of time.

□ The mayor will appoint a task force to make recommendations regarding future construction projects.

resolution *rzly* In reference to legal action, a formal statement of a decision or expression of opinion made by an assembly.

□ The legislature adopted a resolution to honor top-ranked students for their excellence in education.

▰▰ READING AND WRITING EXERCISES ▰▰

PREVIEW WORDS

1

quiet *qul*	guiding *gd*
force *fo*	advisory *avzre*
freedom *fred*	prospered *Pspr-*
outstanding *olsn*	excellence *en*

2

data *dla*	extend *en*
gather *glr*	auditors *adlro*
tight *li*	courtesy *crlse*
yourself *usf*	extremely *x-l*

3	pending	pN	carefully	crfl
	Congress	kgrs	communicate	knca
	grateful	grf	legislation	lysl
	comforting	kfl	appreciative	apv
4	growth	grl	newcomer	nukr
	ensure	nsr	commitment	klm
	creation	crey	administrator	Amr
	resided	rzd-	coordinate	cordna
5	whose	hz	expertise	vprls
	master	-Sr	architect	arclc
	mission	-y	resolution	rzly
	primary	pr-re	task force	lsc fs

1

Mr. Walter Belmont, 601 Spadina Crescent East, Saskatoon, SK S7K 3G8

d -Mr s . plzr
l kq u ou olSN
Svs l ls ajNe du
r ps 30 yrs, uv (Intro P)
sl . ex v lN
n u PfMN uv
Sv- n 3 dfrN
dpls, + eC v lo (Conj)
dpls hs Pspr-U
u ldrs e a -N
l lN r bS -ss
f . nyyS + sal
rlrm no u z
idu, idu n vpc (Intro P)
u rlrm lb . gul
1 uv no dol laul

And O

Intro P

Intro DC

Intro DC

Conj

Intro DC

2

Memo to All Department Heads from Joseph King, SUBJECT: Hosting State Auditors

Intro P

3

Mr. and Mrs. Stephen Gray, 333 Marconi Drive, Madison, WI 53705

Intro P

Intro P

4

Supply two words that are missing in the following memo.

Memo to All Directors from Morgan C. Douglas, SUBJECT: Appointment of Judy Marshall to the Office of Development and Planning

la · nu dpl hsb
cra- = (ofs v
dvm + pln. w
apy- jde rsl, Ap
· vp- + cpB Amr, Ap
z drr. se l
hr nu dles o Fb l>
(n rspB^l v
nu dpl lb l
cordna a bld
+ zn rqSs. (
crej v ls l
hlp l nsr la r
sle , Ppr- l e
(Cnys la r aso-
Sde grl> jde
, n · nukr
l r sle Amj. se
hs Sv- z byl
cordnar + aso
z asSN drr v
prcs. hr pS vp
z · vlntr n ls
sle + + n ol sles
n C se hs ryd-
, frlr prf v hr
klm l kn^l pvms>
p jyn e n hlp
jde fl lk n hr
nu cps^l.

5

Add commas to show two introductory dependent clauses, one conjunction, one direct address, and one series.

Mr. Curtis B. Davidson, 7898 Grange Road, Allentown, PA 18106

drr dvdsn (5
sle ksl hs ps- 9
· ryl l Pvd · 15
pln f rnva r 19
donlon ara. er 24
asc ol (S vp- 31
+ ddca- Nvs l 36
Sv o ls lsc fs. 42
bcz ur · arclc 48

hz ‿o , ‿dl 52
rcgnz- f s lN 58
ud brq vluB 63
gdN l ls k, d 70
u agre l pp×> 75
(objcv v ls k 82
lb l kdc rSC 88
Ppr . ‿Sr pln 93
+ rpl s rcmys 98
l (sle Amy n 104
apxl 1 yr, er asc 112
(k l ‿e + est 119
s pr‿re gls erl 124
nx ‿o> (‿o 129

v ls lsc fs lb 134
fN- b . grN f 139
lcl corps + byl 146
inf lb ‿d avlB 153
n AvN vu frS 158
‿e, (‿y v ls 164
k , vll l (fCr 170
vr sle ‿r dvdsn 176
uf ev (bnfl vu 182
nly + yym efl 188
Sln la el v (194
vprls nd- l aCv 200
r gls, su 206

LESSON

59

SHORTHAND VOCABULARY REVIEW

1. Write a disjoined, capital P for the word beginnings per, pur, pre, pro, and pro (prah).

person *Psn*

personnel *Psnl*

purpose *Pps*

purchase *PCs*

presume *Pz*

prevented *PvM-*

preserved *Pzrv-*

previous *Pves*

protest *PLS*

program *Pq*

proposal *Ppzl*

procedures *Psyrs*

profit *Pfl*

projects *Pjcs*

problems *Pbls*

prospered *Pspr-*

2. Write ⌒ for the initial sound of em or im.

emphasize *fsz*

emphasis *fss*

emphatic *flc*

embarrass *brs*

impression *pry*

impact *pc*

improve *pv*

impossible *psB*

TRANSCRIPTION AID

Spelling. The following words are often misspelled because one of the double consonants is omitted by accident. Until you have learned to spell these words correctly, always consult a dictionary.

committee	recommend
omitted	remitting
accept	excellent
apparent	planning
occurred	beginning
shipping	personnel
assistance	accommodation
unnecessary	cancellation
equipped	possession
accident	questionnaire

YOUR BUSINESS VOCABULARY

doctoral dissertation — A formal research study written as a requirement for a doctoral degree.

□ I am compiling research data to be used in my doctoral dissertation.

counselor — A person who gives advice or provides guidance in a specialized area.

□ Charlotte Steinway is the guidance counselor at the new high school.

READING AND WRITING EXERCISES

PREVIEW WORDS

1 greet welcome

timely redevelopment

expand
subject
2 basic
submit
completion
Resources
3 lanes
widen
welfare
traffic
4 commend
district
trade
elements
5 deemed
sanitary
mandatory
evaluation

urban affairs
dissertation
counselor
evaluate
sufficiently
application
reversed
expedite
populated
expressway
weigh
affecting
international
communicate
essential
intervals
cooperation
restaurant

1

Mrs. Claudia Hamilton, 761 Wesley Oaks Drive, Atlanta, GA 30327

~c u h~ hr. l
er a egr l gre
nu slzns n ls
knt, s esp ns l (Intro DC)
lk ppl hu v .
bcgroN n urbn
afrs, ~ plcl
NS- n u ~S rsN
Pjc, u drl Drly. ((Ap)
sjc v urbn rdvm
, hl, + er a (Conj)
n nd v nu dla.
if udb so cN zl
~l . cpe l ~e, (Intro DC)
il se la / rCs
(apo dpl, edb
hpe l ~e ~ u
l Dcs fCr ~pm.
alo edu n v .
opn no la rqs
u qlfjs, er vpc (Intro DC)
l vpN r dpl v
urbn afrs. Ph
lr lb . pzj fu
~n 6 ~os, p fl
fre lvzl s (nx
h~ ur n lon. su

2

Miss Donna Edwards, 202 Staton Drive, Charleston, WV 25306

d M edws lqf
aplc f . secl
pzj n dpl v
nCrl rsrss. alo
ev no pzjs avlB
(P h~, lr ~a (Intro DC)
b ol opls f ~pm
n Sa ofs bld. e
sug lau fl . aplc
~ (Psnl dvj, l
s~l . aplcj, u (Intro P)
~a k l (Psnl
ofs bln (hrs v
8a~ + 5p~ dl.

Intro DC

Intro P

Intro DC

Intro DC

Paren

Intro P

3

Board of Public Works, City Hall, 120 Wabash Avenue, Terre Haute, IN 47803

sle du_ (mrn +
ol v sle du_ (
afnn, p du n
mc . dsj o ls
mlr -ol ks_ (
lfr v rzdnsl
kn^l, e rq8 . hr_ l
alo r vus lb hrd,
ul

+ sr u ksrns, l
m8 -a lz ksrns
f agrl dvm aq
loz afc_ ol elms
vr eco, chp laul
ku l u
rSC + avs l
me, uc A bnfl
f (opns v
nf- slzns lc
u, cu

4

Supply two words that are missing in the following letter.

Miss Diana Arnold, 915 Crown Drive, Boise, ID 83706

dM arnld lqf ru_
l knca u ksrns
ab (fed plses
afc_ Nnyl lrd, w
ks- (mrels u
Conj
sM, + l
l kM u 6 kvM_
cs u P-, z (rep
Intro P
vu Dlrc, l USM

5

Add commas to show one parenthetical expression, one conjunction, one introductory dependent clause, and one appositive.

Ms. Deborah Brown, Home and Hearth Restaurant, 2005 Coggins Avenue, Flint, MI 48507

d-s bron lqf 7
copj du_ r rsM 13
nspcj vu rSrM, 19
l- - (encs n 26
ls L , . rpl la 32
gvs (rzlts vr 37

evluy. Aso lr , . 43
Slfcl v apvl C 49
Sas lau eslm hs 56
ps- r nspcy + hs 62
aCv- (hs rq f 68
snlre kdys, z r 74
ajN j hrsn a 79
v pln- lu . la z 86
ps- du (l8 sy 92
v Sa lysl Cr c 98
/ Mlre lae kdc 104

. nspcy v E pb el 111
eslm / rgls Nvls. 119
ls acy , d- lb 124
esnsl l Pzrv (130
hll + sfle Sds 135
sl fl b (Sa cd, 141
e ∪ u ku- suc 147
n u bs + e lc 153
fu lvzl u aq. 160
ul 163

LESSON

60

WORD
DEVELOPMENT

Develop new words from the following brief forms:

ever

evergreen *Egrn*

whatever *ৰE*

whenever *nE*

wherever *rE*

whoever *huE*

complete

completes *kps*

completed *kp-*

completely *kpl*

completion *kpy*

incomplete *nkp*

point

disappointed *Dapy-*

reappoint *rapy*

viewpoint *vupy*

standpoint *SNpy*

appointment *apym*

for

reformed *rf_-*

transform *Tf_*

reinforcing *rnfs_*

performance *Pf_M*

informative *nf_v*

READING AND WRITING EXERCISES

**PREVIEW
WORDS**

1 site *sl*

operation *opy*

rezoning *rzn_*

recognized *rcgnz-*

commission *ky*

intersection *nscy*

2 FCC *FCC*

secure *scr*

various *vres*

materials *trels*

3 hence *hn*

solicit *slsl*

farmers *fr—rs*

participants *ppns*

4 ensure *nsr*

dollar *$*

method *td*

apologize *aplyz*

5 refund *rfn*

bylaws *blas*

ordinarily *ordl*

accordance *acrdn*

industrial *nl*

Interstate *nsa*

publications *pbys*

electronics *elncs*

broadcasting *brdc8*

communications *kncys*

enlisted *nl8-*

effective *efcv*

cooperation *copy*

conservation *ksrvy*

confusion *kfy*

difficulties *dfces*

direct-deposit *dr = dpzl*

social security *ssl scrl*

duplicate *dplcl*

certificate *Slfcl*

incorporation *incy*

not-for-profit *n = f = Pfl*

1

Form letter to residents from Dan Long, Chairman

l —e / 73⁰p— o

Wd ₍₉₎ Jn 8, (Pps

dS— (yn ky v ls —e llb l ks

. rqS f rzn 13
acrs v lN nr (
Nscj v Sa rd 231
+ NSa 40. (or
v prp hs rqS-
la (lN, C,
crNl zn- f agrl
us, b rzn- f Nl
us, reps v . Nl
fr v vprs- NS n
PCs pl v lN y
(zn Cnj, grN-.
reps v ls fr lb
P E e l dS
(Nl opj la,
b pln- f ls si,
if u l P
u vus ab ls zn
rqS, lu p nlf
r ofs b Tu lau
Ub rcgnz-x
af a vus vb P-

b (pb, (brd
l kdc . jn Dcj.
bcz e vpc lgv
ls isu . gr dl
v ksj bf c .
dsj, ro l n lc
pls bf (Jl e
ul

2

Mr. Anthony T. Preston, 8232 Spring Valley Drive, Little Rock, AR 72201

dr prSn ls L
, l acj lae rsv-
u rqS f prN-
trels. (fed
kncjs kj dz c
vres brsrs avlB
fre v G l (pb.
s exs v sjc
ls cvr- r z
flos: . dSj v
FCC, inf ab (

brdcS N, hSre v elncs, hSre v kncys, elc. el gldl sN u sv cpes vr pbys f us n u yr + sr clss. ly lb -l- lu scl -l, if udlc lv . kp cpe v rls + rglys v FCC, u -a scr / f- (gvl prN ofs f . s-l fe. er dli- l asS n ejcyl Pjcs -nE psB. p klc s aq -n r Svss r nd-. su

(Series) (Series) (Series) (Intro DC)

3

Memo to County Extension Agents from Franklin G. Osgood, Chairman, SUBJECT: Conservation Studies

mo l ke lny ajNs (dpl v agr , pln l kdc Sdes n 4 -yr aras v ksrvj. p se (encs f dll- dSys v eC Sde, n od -c r rSC efcv, el nd lv . lry No v fr-rs pp n lz Sdes; hN, er asc A ke ajNs l slsl (copj v fr-rs n lr aras. e rcm la (ajNs bgn b ar grp -e + vpln (Psyrs l (fr-rs. bcz v nCr v lz Sdes, er alspa . q rsp

(Intro P) (Semi) (Paren) (Intro P)

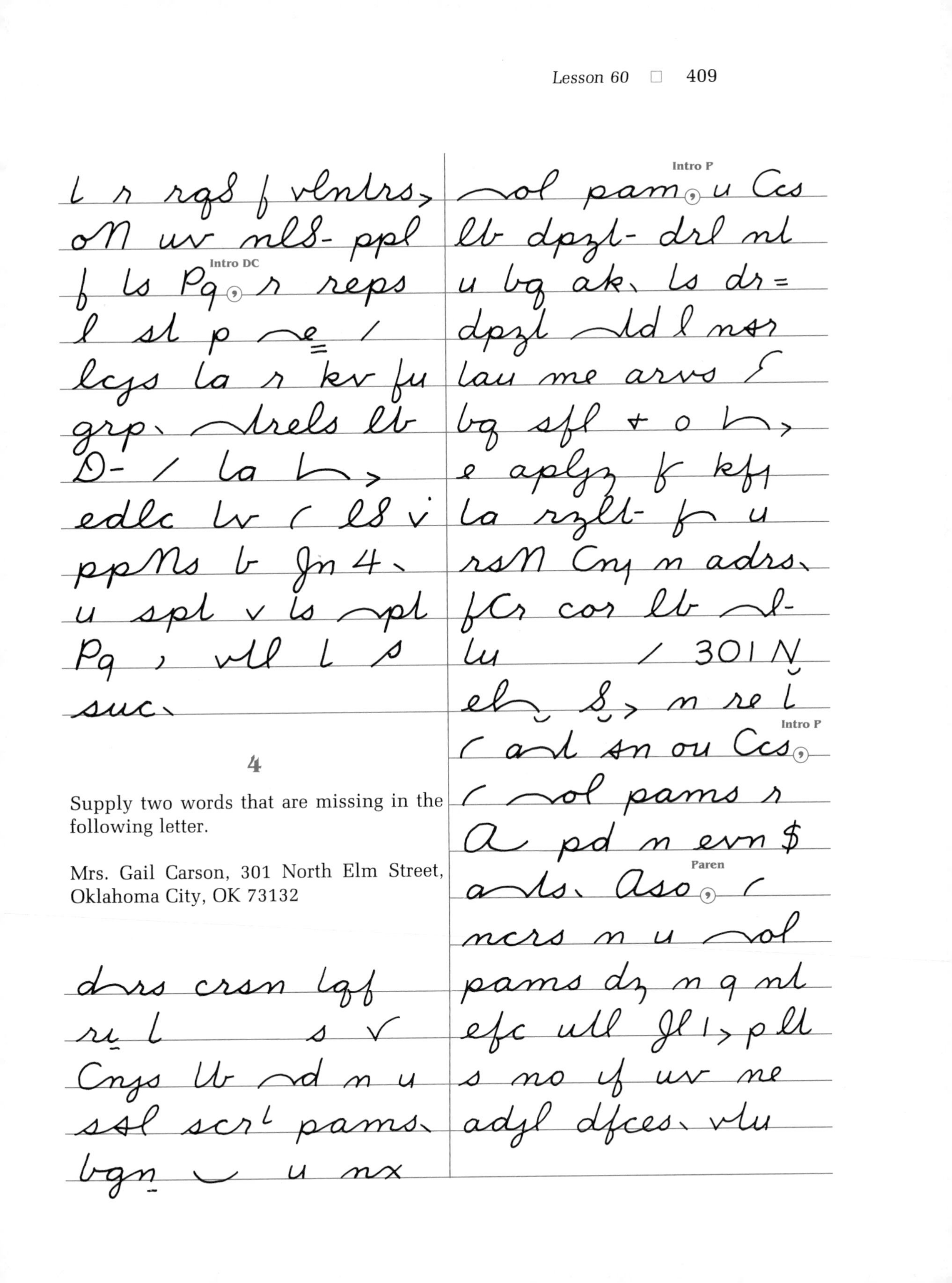

Intro DC

Intro P

Intro P

Paren

4

Supply two words that are missing in the following letter.

Mrs. Gail Carson, 301 North Elm Street, Oklahoma City, OK 73132

5

Add commas to show two introductory phrases, one direct address, and one parenthetical expression.

Ms. Lynn Hamilton, 7995 Chipman Road, Phoenix, AZ 85023

5 d-s hmltn u
12 rqs f incl hsb
17 grN-, enc-) .
22 Stfcl C hsb
27 sn- b r sec v
33 Sa, n ady l r
38 artcls v incl
44 er Aso enc cpes
51 v blas vu og,
57 dplcl cpes v lz
62 dcms vb fl- n
68 r ofs, p nl la
74 r enc- Stfcl z
79 grN- U r nu la
84 gvrn n=f=Pft
90 ogys, n acrdN
96 — r nu lgsly
101 r fe f isu u
107 Stfcl, ls ln la
112 C, ordl rq-
120 f Pft ogys, lrf
126 ev d- . rfN —
135 ls L, eap u psN
141 n a f ls Stfcl
148 -s hmltn, su

BRIEF FORMS BY ALPHABETICAL ORDER

To use the table as a reference for brief forms in alphabetical order, read from left to right across each numbered row.

	A	B	C	D	E	F	G	H
1	.	B	ab	ac	ak	acq	am	Avy
2	af	aq	ar	a	⌒	ap	apo	apx
3	r	ar	z	aso	b	bln	bo	bs
4	c	crc	G	Sk	k	kp	kq	ks
5	ku	kc	kb	kl	kv	cor	K	dl
6	dl	dv	dfc	D	dr	du	⌒p	E
7	vp	fr	f	f⌒	jn	g	gr	hs
8	h	hsp	⌒⌒	⌒pl	m	⌣l	Nv	N
9	,	/	L	⌒y	⌒f	⌒r	nes	nx
10	nl	v	o	oN	op	opn	opl	od
11	ord	oq	ol	O	pl	pp	plc	Ph
12	p	py	P	prp	pv	pb	rf	rsp
13	sa	sal	sv	s	siq	sil	sp	Sd
14	suc	suq	la	´	ly	loz	l	U
15	s	uz	e	⌣	y	l	⌣o	d
16	u							

ABBREVIATIONS BY ALPHABETICAL ORDER

To use the table as a reference for abbreviations in alphabetical order, read from left to right across each numbered row.

	A	B	C	D	E	F	G	H
1	av	agr	a⁀	a–d	+	all	ave	B
2	blvd	cal	¢	X–s	co	corp	cr	d
3	dpl	$	E	eco	enc	env	esp	est
4	etc	ex	fed	fl	gvt	hr	H	in
5	inc	inf	ins	inv	jr	ltl	–dse	M
6	m	–o	–r	–rs	–s	N	No	ok
7	oz	%	lb	p	qt	q	rec	re
8	rep	rel	sec	sr	S	sq	&	S
9	T	tot	U	VP	vol	W	yd	

PHRASES BY ORDER OF CATEGORY

To use the table as a reference for phrases in alphabetical segments, read from left to right across each numbered row.

	A	B	C	D	E	F	G	H
1	[illegible]	cap	cblv	cc	ccb	ccn	ccd	cdu
2	cfl	ch	cv	cvb	cvh	chp	cno	clc
3	csl	csd	cz	cl	clb	cd	cdap	cdb
4	cdlc	eap	er	ern	erp-	eblv	ec	ecb
5	ecn	ecd	edu	efl	eh	ev	evb	evh
6	ehp	eno	esl	esd	e[illegible]	el	elb	ed
7	edap	edb	edlc	ur	uc	ucn	ucb	ucd
8	udu	uh	uv	uvb	uvh	uno	und	usd
9	u[illegible]	ul	ulb	ulfN	ud	udb	udlc	Lb
10	lcl	Lk	ldl	ldu	lgl	lgv	lq	lv
11	lvu	lvu	lhr	lcp	lno	[illegible]	lofr	lpa
12	lrsv	lsa	lse	lsN	luz	lvzl	Lo	[illegible]
13	zi	zl	ze	zlz	zu	zu	[illegible]	cb
14	cdb	fcla	f	fu	fu	hsb	vb	vh
15	vn	vu	vu	nr	s	vr	v	vu
16	vu	6	ou	ou	sdb	lqu	lai	lae
17	lau	laur	laul	lau	lu	lu	lb	lu
18	lu	db	dlc	zz	nvrls	nnls	lqf	lqf
19	lqfL	[illegible]	pda					

KEY TO BRIEF FORMS

	A	B	C	D	E	F	G	H
1	a an	able	about	accept	accomplish	acknowledge	administrate	advantage
2	after	again against	already	always	am more	appreciate	appropriate	approximate
3	are our	arrange	as was	associate	be, but been buy, by	between	both	business
4	can	character characteristic	charge	circumstance	come came committee	complete	congratulate	consider
5	continue	contract	contribute	control	convenient convenience	correspond correspon- dence	customer	deliver
6	determine	develop	difficult	distribute	doctor direct	during	employ	ever every
7	experience	firm	for full	from	general	go good	great grate	has
8	he had him	hospital	immediate	important importance	in not	include	individual	industry
9	is his	it at	letter	manage	manufacture	market	necessary	next
10	note	of have very	on own	once	operate	opinion	opportunity	order
11	ordinary	organize	other	over	part port	participate	particular	perhaps
12	please up	point	present	property	prove	public	refer	respond response
13	sample	satisfy satisfactory	several	ship	signature significant significance	situate	specific specify	standard
14	success	suggest	that	the	they	those	to too	under
15	us	usual	we	were with	why	will well	work world	would
16	your							

KEY TO ABBREVIATIONS

	A	B	C	D	E	F	G	H
1	advertise	agriculture	America American	amount	and	attention	avenue	billion
2	boulevard	catalog	cent cents	Christmas	company	corporation	credit	day
3	department	dollar dollars	east	economic economy	enclose enclosure	envelope	especially	establish
4	et cetera	example executive	federal	feet	government	hour	hundred	inch
5	incorporate incorporated	information	insurance	invoice	junior	literature	merchandise	million
6	Miss	month	Mr.	Mrs.	Ms.	north	number	okay
7	ounce	percent	pound	president	quart	question	record	regard
8	represent represen- tative	return	second secretary	senior	south	square	street	superin- tendent
9	thousand	total	university	vice president	volume	west	yard	

KEY TO PHRASES

	A	B	C	D	E	F	G	H
1	I am	I appreciate	I believe	I can	I can be	I cannot	I could	I do
2	I feel	I had	I have	I have been	I have had	I hope	I know	I look
3	I shall	I should	I was	I will	I will be	I would	I would appreciate	I would be
4	I would like	we appreciate	we are	we are not	we are pleased	we believe	we can	we can be
5	we cannot	we could	we do	we feel	we had	we have	we have been	we have had
6	we hope	we know	we shall	we should	we were	we will	we will be	we would
7	we would appreciate	we would be	we would like	you are	you can	you cannot	you can be	you could
8	you do	you had	you have	you have been	you have had	you know	you need	you should
9	you were	you will	you will be	you will find	you would	you would be	you would like	to be
10	to call	to come	to determine	to do	to get	to give	to go	to have
11	to have you	to have your	to hear	to keep	to know	to make	to offer	to pay
12	to receive	to say	to see	to send	to use	to visit	to work	and the
13	as I	as to	as we	as well as	as you	as your	at the	can be
14	could be	fact that	for the	for you	for your	has been	have been	have had
15	have not	have you	have your	in the	it is	of our	of the	of you
16	of your	on the	on you	on your	should be	thank you	that I	that we
17	that you	that you are	that you will	that your	to you	to your	will be	will you
18	will your	would be	would like	as soon as	neverthe-less	nonethe-less	thank you for	thank you for your
19	thank you for your letter	time to time	up to date					

SPEEDWRITING SHORTHAND PRINCIPLES BY SYSTEM CATEGORY

Simple Sounds

Principle	Word	Outline
1. Write what you hear.	high	hi
2. Write c for the sound of *k*.	copy	cpe
3. Write [symbol] for the sound of *m*.	may	
4. Write [symbol] for the sound of *w*.	way	
5. Write s to form the plural of any outline, to show possession, or to add s to a verb.	books	bcs
	runs	rns
6. Omit *p* in the sound of *mpt*.	empty	
7. Write x for the medial and final sound of x.	boxes	bxs
	tax	tx
8. Omit the final *t* of a root word after the sound of *k*.	act	ac

Vowels

Principle	Word	Outline
1. Drop medial vowels.	build	bld
2. Write initial and final vowels.	office	ofs
	fee	fe
3. Retain beginning or ending vowels when building compound words.	payroll	parl
	headache	hdac
4. Retain root-word vowels when adding prefixes and suffixes.	disappear	Dapr
	payment	pam

5. For words ending in a long vowel + *t*, omit the *t* and write the vowel. — rate: ra; meet

6. When a word contains two medial, consecutively pronounced vowels, write the first vowel. — trial: tril

7. When a word ends in two consecutively pronounced vowels, write only the last vowel. — idea: ida

Vowel Blends

1. Write o for the sound of *ow*. — allow: alo

2. Write y for the sound of *oi*. — boy: by

3. Write a for the initial and final sound of *aw*. — law: la; audit: adl

Consonant Blends

1. Write a capital C for the sound of *ch*. — check: Cc

2. Write ‿ for the sound of *wh*. — when

3. Write a capital N for the sound of *nt*. — sent: sN

4. Write for the sound of *ish* or *sh*. — finish

5. Write l for the sound of *ith* or *th*. — them

6. Write q for the medial or final sound of any vowel + *nk*. — bank: bq; link: lq

Principle	Word	Outline
7. Write q for the sound of *kw*.	quick	qc
8. Write a capital N for the sound of *nd*.	friend	frN
9. Write S for the sound of *st*.	rest	rS
10. Write z for the sound of *zh*.	pleasure	plzr
11. Write g for the medial or final sound of any vowel + *ng*.	rang	rg
	single	sgl
12. Write M for the sound of *ance, ence, nce, nse*.	balance	blM

Compound Sounds

Principle	Word	Outline
1. Write m for the sounds of *mem* and *mum*.	memo	mo
2. Write m for the sounds of *men, min, mon, mun*.	menu	mu
	money	me
3. Write k for the sounds of *com, con, coun, count*.	common	kn
	convey	kva
	counsel	ksl
	account	ak

Word Beginnings

Principle	Word	Outline
1. Write a capital A for the word beginnings *ad, all,* and *al*.	admit	Ad
	also	Aso
2. Write n for the initial sound of *in* and *en*.	indent	ndN

Rule	Word	Outline
3. Write a printed capital S (joined) for the word beginnings *cer, cir, ser, sur.*	certain	Sln
	survey	Sva
4. Write a capital D for the word beginning *dis.*	discuss	Dcs
5. Write a capital M for the word beginning *mis.*	misplace	Mpls
6. Write a capital P (disjoined) for the word beginnings *per, pur, pre, pro, pro* (prah).	person	Psn
	prepare	Ppr
	provide	Pvd
	problem	Pbl
7. Write a for the word beginning *an.*	answer	asr
8. Write a capital S (disjoined) for the word beginning *super.*	supervise	S vz
9. Write el for the word beginning *electr.*	electronic	elnc
10. Write ⌒ for the initial sound of *em* or *im.*	emphasize	⌒fsz
	impress	⌒prs
11. Write \ for words beginning with the sound of any vowel + x.	explain	\pln
	accident	\dN
12. Write X for the word beginnings *extr* and *extra.*	extreme	X⌒
	extraordinary	Xord
13. Write u for the word beginning *un.*	until	ull
14. Write s for the word beginning *sub.*	submit	s⌒d

Principle	Word	Outline
15. Write a capital N for the word beginnings *enter, inter, intro.*	enterprise	Nprz
	interest	N8
	introduce	Nds
16. Write sf for the word beginning *self.*	self-made	sfmd
17. Write T for the word beginnings *tran* and *trans.*	transfer	Tfr

Word Endings

Principle	Word	Outline
1. Underscore the last letter of the outline to add *ing* or *thing* as a word ending.	billing	bl̲
	something	s–̲
2. To form the plural of any outline ending in a mark of punctuation, double the last mark of punctuation.	savings	sv̳
3. To form the past tense of a regular verb, write a hyphen after the outline.	used	uz-
4. Write m for the word endings *mand, mend, mind, ment.*	demand	dm
	amend	am
	remind	rm
	payment	pam
5. Write l for the word ending *ly* or *ily.*	family	fml
6. Write g for the word ending *gram.*	telegram	tlg
7. Write a capital S (disjoined) for the word endings *scribe* and *script.*	describe	dS
	manuscript	mnS

8. Write *w* for the word ending *ward*.	backward	*bcw*
9. Write *h* for the word ending *hood*.	boyhood	*byh*
10. Write *1* for the word ending *tion* or *sion*.	vacation	*v1*
11. Write *g* for the word ending *quire*.	require	*rg*
12. Write ′ for the word ending *ness*.	kindness	*cN*′
13. Write *B* for the word endings *bil, ble, bly*.	possible	*psB*
	probably	*PbB*
14. Write *ι* (slightly raised and disjoined) for the word ending *ity*.	quality	*gl*ι
15. Write *sl* for the sound of *shul* and the word ending *chul*.	financial	*fnnsl*
16. Write *v* for the medial and final sound of *tive*.	effective	*efcv*
17. Write *f* for the word endings *ful* and *ify*.	careful	*crf*
	justify	*jSf*
18. Write *fj* for the word ending *ification*.	qualifications	*glfjs*
19. Write *sf* for the word ending *self*.	myself	*msf*
20. Write *svs* for the word ending *selves*.	ourselves	*rsvs*

Marks of Punctuation

1. Underscore the last letter of the outline to add *ing* or *thing* as a word ending. — billing: bl; something: s
2. To form the plural of any outline ending in a mark of punctuation, double the last mark of punctuation. — savings: sv
3. To form the past tense of a regular verb, write a hyphen after the outline. — used: uz-
4. Write / for the word ending *ness*. — kindness: cN'
5. To show capitalization, draw a small curved line under the last letter of the outline. — Bill: bl
6. Write \ to indicate a period at the end of a sentence.
7. Write × to indicate a question mark.
8. Write > to indicate the end of a paragraph.
9. Write ! to indicate an exclamation mark.
10. Write = to indicate a dash.
11. Write = to indicate a hyphen.
12. To indicate solid capitalization, double the curved line underneath the last letter of the outline.
13. To indicate an underlined title, draw a solid line under the outline.
14. Write ≠ ≠ to indicate parentheses.